West Country Regiments on the Somme

West Country Regiments on the Somme

Tim Saunders

LEO COOPER

This book is dedicated to the West Country soldiers of
the Devonshire and Dorset Regiments,
past and present.

'Semper Fidelis'
'Who's Afeared?'

OTHER BOOKS BY TIM SAUNDERS:
Hill 112 – Normandy
Hell's Highway – Market Garden
Nijmegen – Market Garden
The Island – Market Garden
Gold Beach-Jig – Normandy
Juno Beach – Normandy
Operation Epsom – Normandy

First published in Great Britain in 2004 by
Pen & Sword Military
an imprint of
Pen & Sword Books Ltd
47 Church Street
Barnsley
South Yorkshire
S70 2AS

ISBN 1 84415 018 6

A CIP catalogue record for this book is
available from the British Library

Typeset in Sabon 10pt

Printed and bound in the United Kingdom by CPI

Pen & Sword Books Ltd incorporates the Imprints of Pen & Sword Aviation, Pen
& Sword Maritime, Pen & Sword Military, Wharncliffe Local History, Pen and
Sword Select, Pen and Sword Military Classics and Leo Cooper.
For a complete list of Pen & Sword titles, please contact
Pen & Sword Books Limited
47 Church Street, Barnsley, South Yorkshire, S70 2AS, England
E-mail: enquiries@pen-and-sword.co.uk
Website: www.pen-and-sword.co.uk

CONTENTS

INTRODUCTION and ACKNOWLEDGEMENTS....................................6

CHAPTER 1   The West Country Regiments in 1914 8

CHAPTER 2   The Somme: 1915 23

CHAPTER 3   1916: Preliminary Operations and Preparations 35

CHAPTER 4   Fourth Army Plan and the 57
             Preliminary Bombardment

CHAPTER 5   2/Devons' Attack on Ovillers....................................69

CHAPTER 6   1/Dorsets' Attack on Leipzig Redoubt 89

CHAPTER 7   6/Dorsets at Fricourt 105

CHAPTER 8   8/ and 9/Devons at Mametz 113

CHAPTER 9   Fricourt and Mametz Wood: The Second Phase ...137

CHAPTER 10   The Battle of Bazentin Ridge....................................151

CHAPTER 11   The High Wood Attack, and Veale VC 173

CHAPTER 12   Holding the Line....................................189

CHAPTER 13   Guillemont and Leuze Wood 203

CHAPTER 14   Ginchy....................................215

CHAPTER 15   Mouquet Farm....................................231

CHAPTER 16   Morval....................................252

CHAPTER 17   Le Transloy....................................259

CHAPTER 18   Battle of the Ancre....................................273

             Index....................................285

Introduction and Acknowledgements

In writing this book, I have fulfilled an ambition of ten years, standing. It started with my own visits to the Somme and was strengthened by taking my first groups of Devon and Dorset soldiers around the scenes of some of the engagements described in this book. From the beginning, we shared strong emotions during the telling of the powerful story of our predecessors' battles on the uplands of Picardy in 1916. Faltering voices, moist eyes, and men I know to be accomplished soldiers seeking moments of quiet reflection, convinced me that our two small West Country regiments had a tale to be told that was second to none. But this book is not just for the benefit of today's Devon and Dorset soldiers, or those who have regional connections; the deeds of West Country soldiers on the Somme are worthy of the widest audience.

In a battle that is often described as being fought by men from the urban parts of northern Britain, four battalions of the Devonshire Regiment and three battalions of the Dorsetshire Regiment fought in virtually all phases of the Somme. Through their experience, it is possible to chart the Somme's transformation, from a quiet sector in 1915, through the optimistic expectations before the battle, to the attack itself. The five West Country battalions in action on 1 July 1916 experienced disastrous failure, success and a lucky escape, reflecting the results of the first day of the battle as a whole. In the following days, the West Countrymen were engaged in some hard fighting in the early stages of the battle, culminating in the successful attack on the German's second position, which tragically ended with one of the great missed opportunities of the war. There followed a period of bitter stalemate, before the front started to inch forward again in September 1916. Thereafter, the Devons and the Dorsets were forced to endure unspeakable conditions, where, in the worst case, before le Transloy, the Germans ceased to be the main enemy, as rain reduced the battlefield to glutinous mud and cold became a killer.

I have drawn on several peerless accounts of the fighting on the Somme. One is the account of a well-educated wartime officer, Charles Douie, and another is by an admirable product of the Edwardian Army's education system, a Regular Army sergeant major, Ernest Shephard. The books written by these two men have, among half a dozen others, been my constant companions for many years, and should be read by all enthusiasts of the Great War and even by modern soldiers.

I have used many sources: published, privately printed, and from regimental or public records. There are often several quotations from the same source in a chapter, so to avoid a lengthy list of unhelpful and distracting endnotes, I have only referenced the first use of a source in each chapter. The photographs used in this book come from the Devon and Dorsets' unique collection of glass negatives. Clearly, not all are of soldiers of the regiment in action but a number are attributed by the collector in the 1920s to the Dorset Regiment. Where this is so, I have taken his word, and reflected this in the captions.

I would like to thank Colonel John Hughes-Wilson for his permission to quote from his book *Blindfold and Alone,* and the staff of Regimental Headquarters and the Museum, especially archivist Terry Bishop, for their help in locating pictures and documents. Finally, I would like to thank all those who have helped me with correcting the numerous drafts of this book who I hope will find this book worthy of their considerable dedication and enthusiasm. For the reader, my dearest wish is that this book may inspire a visit to the Somme and the places described in these pages, which are the last resting place of so many West Country soldiers.

T.J.J.S.
WARMINSTER, 2004

Chapter One

The West Country Regiments in 1914

As he died in 1913, Alfred von Schlieffen, the architect of Germany's war plan, uttered the words, 'It must come to a fight'. In the summer of 1914, Europe was poised for war.

In the final months of peace before the four cataclysmic years of 1914 to 1918, the constituent parts of the West Country regiments of Devonshire and Dorset were deployed in accordance with Imperial Foreign and Defence Policy. The regiments' Regular Army battalions in the United Kingdom were providing drafts of trained soldiers for their sister battalions serving overseas, while the volunteers of the Territorial Force attended their weekly drill nights and annual camps. The depots in Dorchester and Exeter continued to train a steady flow of young men for the service of the King and Empire.

Traditionally, British policy had aimed at avoiding a military commitment to continental Europe. This strategy was based on the belief that the Royal Navy would protect the British Isles from invasion. However, an almost twenty-year-long arms race between the Central Powers of Germany and Austria and the

July 1914. As political tension mounted the Devon and Cornwall Brigade were at Annual Camp at Bulford on Salisbury Plain. 4/Dorsets' machine-gun section pose around one of their two guns. The other lies in the grass in the foreground, while the section's cart can be seen in the background.

Day one of mobilization. Reservists from Weymouth and Portland are mustered at the station before going to the depot at Dorchester to be kitted out and joining the 1st Battalion.

other European nations had turned the continent into an armed camp. For Britain in her island fortress, the growth of the German Imperial Fleet was of the greatest significance. Realizing that the Germans could challenge the Royal Navy's command of the seas, and that another French defeat, like that of 1871, would place a German army of 5 million men within sight of Dover, Britain joined the *Entente Cordiale*. In joining the *Entente* led by France and Russia, Britain became committed to the fight in continental Europe.

'The spark that lit the tinderbox' was the murder of Archduke Franz Ferdinand of Austria on 28 June 1914 during a visit to Bosnia on 28 June 1914. His murder in Sarajevo by Serbian nationalists provoked an escalating Balkan crisis. On 23 July, the Austro-Hungarians sent an ultimatum to Serbia's sponsor, Russia, that challenged the status quo in the region. Unable to accede to the Austrian demands, Russia started to mobilize her forces on 29 July.

A network of alliances now propelled Europe to war. If Austria went to war with Russia, Germany, as an Austrian ally, would become involved, and this would precipitate French mobilization. Faced with the prospect of a war on two fronts, against both France and Russia, Germany mobilized on 31 July 1914. The Schlieffen Plan swung into operation, with Germany's railway system at its heart. Germany intended to concentrate her army in the west, and defeat France before Russia could fully mobilize. The intention to violate Belgian sovereignty, guaranteed by treaty since 1839, brought Britain into the war on 4 August 1914.

Mobilization

The West Country Regiments' home-based Regular battalions were expecting mobilization, having followed the mounting international crisis in the press.

In the officers' mess of 1st Battalion the Dorsetshire Regiment in Victoria Barracks Belfast, Captain Ransom recalled:

> The possibilities of a European war were being discussed during the last week of July, and, just when it was felt that the crisis might pass, orders suddenly arrived one evening that the instructions for what was officially termed the 'precautionary period', were to be put into practice.[1]

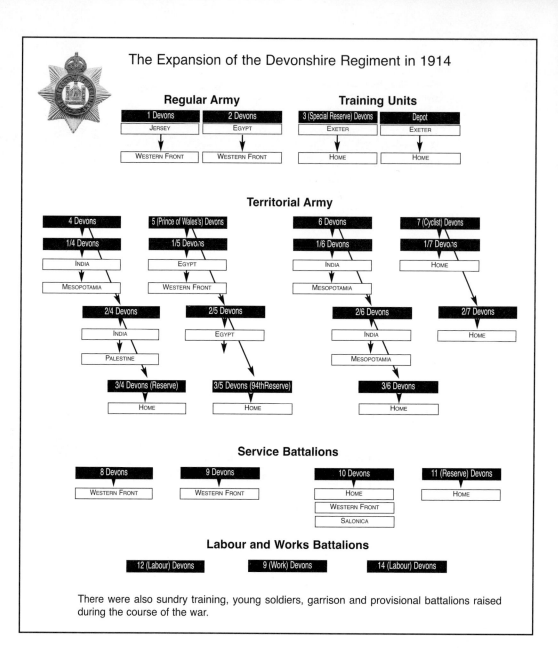

The Expansion of the Devonshire Regiment in 1914

Regular Army

1 Devons	2 Devons
JERSEY	EGYPT
WESTERN FRONT	WESTERN FRONT

Training Units

3 (Special Reserve) Devons	Depot
EXETER	EXETER
HOME	HOME

Territorial Army

4 Devons
1/4 Devons
INDIA
MESOPOTAMIA

5 (Prince of Wales's) Devons
1/5 Devons
EGYPT
WESTERN FRONT

6 Devons
1/6 Devons
INDIA
MESOPOTAMIA

7 (Cyclist) Devons
1/7 Devons
HOME

2/4 Devons
INDIA
PALESTINE

2/5 Devons
EGYPT

2/6 Devons
INDIA
MESOPOTAMIA

2/7 Devons
HOME

3/4 Devons (Reserve)
HOME

3/5 Devons (94thReserve)
HOME

3/6 Devons
HOME

Service Battalions

8 Devons	9 Devons	10 Devons	11 (Reserve) Devons
WESTERN FRONT	WESTERN FRONT	HOME	HOME
		WESTERN FRONT	
		SALONICA	

Labour and Works Battalions

12 (Labour) Devons	9 (Work) Devons	14 (Labour) Devons

There were also sundry training, young soldiers, garrison and provisional battalions raised during the course of the war.

1st Battalion the Devonshire Regiment, based in Jersey as a part of the Channel Islands garrison, was similarly placed on a higher state of readiness. For both 1st Battalions, the process of preparing for war was not unlike the deployment for annual manoeuvres, except that it was complicated by having to pack away all individual and battalion property for dispatch to regimental depots in Dorchester and Exeter. While packing and awaiting full mobilization and detailed deployment orders, troops were

> *provided for the protection of vulnerable points in the neighbourhood of Belfast – forts on the coast, waterworks, cable lines,*

etc. – and protective detachments were always in readiness for the purpose.

The fateful order was received at 5.39 a.m. on the 4 August, giving Wednesday 5th as the first day of mobilization. ... At 9.30 p.m. Lieut Pitt, 2/Lieut Chapman, and three NCOs left Belfast for Dorchester to conduct reservists, and took with them the colours...

The next day saw the mobilization scheme in full swing. All ranks were medically inspected, and the men under age [those below twenty years old] and medically unfit (there were very few of the latter) were handed over to the 'details'[2]

Captain Ransome, Lieutenant Pitt and Sergeant Boater lead a party of reservists into Victoria Barracks, Belfast.

The Expansion of the Dorset Regiment in 1914

Regular Army

1 Dorsets	2 Dorsets
BELFAST	INDIA
↓	↓
WESTERN FRONT	MESOPOTAMIA

Training Units

3 (Special Reserve) Dorsets	Depot
DORCHESTER	DORCHESTER
↓	↓
HOME	HOME

Territorial Army

4 Dorsets
1/4 Dorsets
INDIA
↓
MESOPOTAMIA

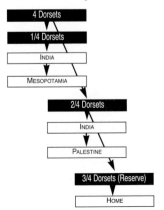

2/4 Dorsets
INDIA
↓
PALESTINE

3/4 Dorsets (Reserve)
HOME

Service Battalions

5 Dorsets	6 Dorsets	7 (Reserve) Dorsets
GALLIPOLI	WESTERN FRONT	HOME
WESTERN FRONT		

8 Dorsets
HOME

There were also sundry training, young soldiers, garrison and provisional battalions raised during the course of the war.

Just arrived: Dorset Regiment reservists being mustered into companies at Victoria Barracks, Belfast.

The officers of 1/Devons photographed in Jersey during mobilization.

Officers 1/Dorsets on the eve of embarkation, 13 August 1914 (Belfast). "from back row"
George, White, Willes
A. S. Fraser, Grant-Dalton, Woodhouse,
Butcher, Gregory, Shannon, Kitchen
Leishman, Clutterbuck, Clarke, Turner, Houlton-Barzett
Burnand, King, Roe, Gyngell, Partridge, Rathbone, Hyslop, Pitt, Hawkins, Priestley, Kelsall,
Williams, W.A.C. Fraser, Roper, Bols, Saunders, Davidson, Ransome

A key part of mobilization was the embodying of reservists to bring battalions up to war establishment. These ex-regulars or high-readiness volunteers from Special Reserve battalions reported to regimental depots for the issue of equipment and dispatch to the Regular battalions. The first group of ninety-six Dorset reservists arrived in Belfast on 6 August, and by the 9th, the Battalion was at war establishment, having received eleven officers and 595 reservists. This was a typical allocation to lower-establishment, home-service battalions. 1/Dorsets' history[3] records that one group of reservists were 'a very fine party, and the appearance of the men made a great impression as they marched through the main streets to Victoria Barracks'. The Dorsets' moblization had been remarkably smooth, but for 1/Devons, isolated in Jersey, matters were more complicated. They mobilized just 450 men (with 180 young soldiers being left in rear details) and their 500-odd reservists were retained in the overflowing Regimental Depot at Higher Barracks, Exeter, until ordered to France to join 1/Devons.

Having mobilized, there was a period of waiting for deployment orders. This afforded an opportunity for training, with route marches, weapon training and range practice being of particular importance in brushing up the reservists' skills.

1/Devons leaving Fort Requent in Jersey in August 1914.

A channel ferry pressed into service as a troop ship takes 1/Devons from Jersey to Le Havre in August 1914.

Overseas, 2/Devons, in Egypt, received mobilization orders on 6 August, and deployed to guard key points at Suez. However, with the scale of the war in Europe becoming obvious, 2/Devons embarked from Alexandria and arrived at Southampton on 1 October, where they joined the newly formed 8th Division. This Division consisted largley of regulars brought back from overseas stations, as far afield as Bermuda, South Africa and India. Meanwhile, 2/Dorsets stationed with 16 Poona Brigade in India, after many changes of plan, eventually fought in Mesopotamia.

At home in the West Country, the 3rd (Special Reserve) battalions and Territorial Force battalions also mobilized. However, the majority of Territorials were already embodied for training at their two-week annual camp. 4, 5 and 6/Devons were at camp with the Devon and Cornwall Brigade, while 4/Dorsets were on Salisbury Plain at Sling Camp, Bulford. These battalions were dispatched to Plymouth to relieve Regular units in the Devonport defences, namely Renney, Scrasden and Tregantle Forts. Meanwhile, the Devons' 7/(Cyclist) Battalion, who had just finished camp, mobilized at their drill halls and were deployed to patrol the West Country coast in a manner reminiscent of the Yeomanry cavalry during the Napoleonic Wars. The West Country Territorial Force 'volunteered' for overseas service, and was concentrated at Bulford before embarking with Wessex Division to take over the garrisoning of India from Regular Army battalions.

The West Country 'Pals'

Within days of the outbreak of war, Field Marshal Lord Kitchener, Secretary of State for War, was briefing Prime Minister Asquith and his Cabinet. Contrary to the popular opinion that the war would be over by Christmas, Kitchener believed the war could last three years, and that Britain would need to arm a million men. The politicians authorized him to call for 300,000 volunteers to form six new infantry divisions. As volunteers flocked to the depots, Regular battalions serving at home were each tasked to provide a cadre of three officers and fifteen NCOs, around which the 'Service Battalions' would be formed. In a similar move, the Territorial battalions were doubled, with, for example, 4th Battalions becoming 1st/4th and 2nd/4th Battalions. As the West Country Territorials did not fight in France and Flanders, we will concentrate on the formation of the Service Battalions and the difficulties of raising an army from small beginnings.

The order to form the 8th (Service) Battalion, the Devonshire Regiment at the Regimental Depot

Perhaps one of Britain's best-known images of the twentieth century; Kitchener's appeal brought hundreds of thousands of volunteers to the colours in a matter of months.

15

was signed on 7 August 1914. In the haste of the moment, a commanding officer was appointed from outside the Regiment: Lieutenant Colonel Grant of the West African Regiment. The second in command, Major Carden, who came out of retirement to take his post, was reputedly 'so determined to serve with his own Regiment that he refused the offer of the command of a battalion of another'. The Devons' regimental historian[4] recorded that:

> NCOs from the 1st Battalion or from the Depot filled most of the posts on the battalion and company staffs. Recruits came in quickly, including many who did not deserve that description, being old soldiers who had served their time with the Reserve and now rejoined. This element provided NCOs of experience whose assistance was of the utmost value and who served to imbue the new unit with the traditions of the Regiment. From the first, all ranks set to work with the utmost zeal and enthusiasm to make themselves efficient soldiers, and the discomforts and hardships inevitable in the unprepared and ill-provided state of the country, the overcrowding in barracks and billets, the lack of essential equipment, of uniform, of weapons for training, were born with patience and good humour.

With the regimental system strong in the West Country, and with, initially, only one service battalion to form, finding NCOs was not difficult. Providing officers

Men of the first wave of Kitchener volunteers, destined to serve with 5/Dorsets on the Somme, receive lesson one of the all-important drill syllabus.

Lieutenant Colonel Wheatley and the first Kitchener volunteers from Poole on parade with a handful of Regular Army NCOs.

was also a problem that could be resolved relatively quickly. Young gentlemen who volunteered to serve as officers needed a month's training at the Officer Training Corps camps, which sprang up across the country. The Devons' historian described the first batch that arrived to join the Battalion during the autumn.

> When the subalterns at last appeared they proved to be thoroughly characteristic young Englishmen selected out of many thousands of applicants to officer the First Hundred Thousand. Six came from Oxford, three from Cambridge, three from the Artists' Rifles, the rest straight from Public Schools. They included an author, a Rugby Union International forward, and a county squire. Most of them started with the slenderest knowledge of their work, but they were first-class officer material, and it was extraordinary how quickly they picked it up under the instruction of the handful of Regular officers and with the help of their platoon sergeants, and very soon they were confidently instructing their men, most of whom, after all, knew less than they did.

In Spetember, the 8th Battalion left Exeter for a tented camp at Rushmoor, near Aldershot. Training progressed apace, but such were the numbers volunteering, the six Divisions of the 1st Kitchener Army (K1) were soon fully established, and the Field Marshal raised his target to twelve divisions (K2) and finally twenty-four (K3). With this growth of the Army, 9/Devons was ordered to be formed, on 7 September 1914, alongside the 8th at Rushmoor. However, providing a hardcore around which to build this new battalion was now a problem. The 8/Devons could only send over four officers and six NCOs.

> *This staff had to deal with 500 recruits who arrived at Rushmoor that evening from Exeter. Only about 20 of these were Devonshire men, the majority being Welshmen, and a few from Birmingham.*

The niceties of the county-based regimental system had soon broken down under the pressure of numbers, with volunteers being issued railway warrants and instructions to join the nearest forming battalion, with scant regard to recruiting areas[5]. The draft for the 9th arrived 'unaccompanied by NCOs – they were without uniform, equipment, or even documents by which to be identified'. Two former Warrant Officers of the Regiment were persuaded to come out of retirement, and Sergeant Major Grubb took up the post of RSM despite being offered a commission, while Lieutenant Adams joined as quartermaster. A former Devon, Colonel Davies CB DSO, veteran of Burma (1889-92) and South Africa (1900), was also 'dugout' of retirement and appointed as Commanding Officer.

> *Towards the end of September, the 8th and 9th made their first real appearance on parade as battalions, when the King and Queen, accompanied by Lord Kitchener, inspected the "New Army" units at Aldershot upon the Queen's Parade. The spectacle was quite remarkable: most battalions were still without any uniform, to say nothing of equipment and rifles, and the sight of these hosts of men in civilian kit but already beginning to bear themselves like soldiers, was an indication at once of the country's unreadiness for war and of the resolution with which it was throwing itself into the struggle.*

At the end of September, 9/Devons were issued blue uniforms, and on 2 October 'a consignment of one hundred service rifles had been received, which were respectfully handed from platoon to platoon in turn'. 8 and 9/Devons eventually crossed the Channel to France in July 1915, eleven months after their formation. The Devons formed two further service battalions during the autumn of 1914 with increasing difficulty. However, they were destined not to fight on the Somme, and the junior unit became a reserve battalion, responsible for sending trained soldiers to battalions at the front.

The story of the formation of the Dorsets' 5th and 6th (Service) Battalions, who were both to fight on the Somme, followed a similar pattern to the raising of the Devons' service battalions. Having dispatched reservists to the 1st Battalion in Belfast, the Depot in Dorchester turned to the recruits who were queuing to join the 5th (Service) Battalion. Seventy-five per cent of the recruits came from Dorset, with most of the remainder having family connections with the Regiment. The proportion of former Regulars and Special Reserve volunteers amongst the recruits was high. The 5th was also unusually well off for Regular officers, as several who had been serving in the 3rd Battalion and three belonging to the 2nd Battalion, who happened to be at home on leave, supplemented the 1st Battalion's draft of three officers. 'On August 19th Major C.C. Hannay, the Commanding Officer of the Depot, was appointed to command the new unit, being gazetted "Temporary Lieutenant Colonel while commanding".'[6]

The relatively small Depot Barracks at Dorchester could not cope with the rear details of young soldiers, those unfit for active service, and the 5th Battalion. The latter was therefore sent to Grantham to join 11th (Northern) Division. Training was hard, as K1 formations, such as the 11th Division, were ordered to be ready for operations overseas within six months. However, as autumn progressed, the Battalion suffered a reverse, when trained former 3rd Battalion soldiers were recalled and sent to replace casualties suffered by 1/Dorsets at Mons and on the Aisne.

The Dorsets' historian recorded the usual problems with uniforms:

Civilian costume was originally almost universal, but as various issues were made of different items, the most anomalous mixtures appeared, such as the combination of a bowler hat with a khaki tunic and flannel trousers ... Some ancient blue garments were unearthed and for a time Grantham 'swarmed with warriors only lacking broad arrows to make them look like convicts'. However before long the whole battalion was completely turned out with proper khaki, with noticeable effects on its general smartness and efficiency.

The 6th (Service) Battalion, the Dorsetshire Regiment was formed in Dorchester on the departure of the 5th to Grantham, under Lieutenant Colonel Rowley DSO, who was posted to form the depot with only an adjutant and quartermaster to help. With the assistance of the Dorset Constabulary, over 1,000 men were received and marshalled into companies in a single week. Only 300 of the volunteers were from Dorset, some of these having volunteered in small groups of 'Pals' from the county's towns and villages. Most of these local groups formed 'D' (or as they preferred 'Dorset') Company. The remainder of

Men of C Company 5/Dorsets during a ten-minute halt on a route march near Grantham in early 1915.

the Battalion came from the more populous cities and regions of England. Thus it was that 400 Londoners, a similar number of Yorkshire men and 73 South Wales miners joined the 6/Dorsets. The Regimental History hints that not all these men were happy to be in a regiment not of their home area. However, as group identity developed, a loyalty to company and battalion grew that transcended a mere title. After two weeks at Dorchester, a short train journey took the new battalion to Wareham, where they became the only 'local' battalion in 17th (Northern) Division, and forging the battalion began in earnest.

Seven ex-regular majors had come out of retirement when called for, and five of the subalterns were masters at Sherborne School, who happened to be officers in the School's Officer Training Corps. The few men with military experience in the battalion were essential during 'the early days of drill and inculcation of military manners and martial bearing'. Some of these officers and NCOs brought out of retirement 'proved to be strong enough and young enough at heart to be eventually able to accompany the Battalion on active service'. The remainder of the battalion's 'NCOs below the rank of sergeant were civilians, and were appointed by appearances [and no doubt background]. The system worked well.'

The county and people of Dorset nurtured the new battalions by providing 'comforts' (individual clothing and items to make life in camp more comfortable) and musical instruments for a battalion band. The band was formed under the eye of the 'indestructible' Company Sergeant Major 'Mac' Macmullen, who had rejoined the Regiment from retirement in Bridport. The bandsmen also trained as stretcher-bearers and did much valuable work on the Somme.

At the end of the war, an officer calculated that the 6th served 1,216 days in France and that the battalion's

> *roll of dead claims men from thirty-seven English counties, and*

The Warrant Officers and Sergeants' Mess 6/Dorsets in 1915.

others came from Scotland, Ireland, Wales and the Channel Islands.
Two hundred and seventy officers and nearly five thousand men joined
as reinforcements

This was the equivalent of replacing the original 1,000 men five times over, with the 6th losing a high proportion of these men on the Somme in 1916.

Deployment

The first battalion of the West Country regiments to see action was 1/Dorsets, who embarked at Belfast docks for France with the 5th Division on 14 August 1914. They fought at Mons, Le Cateau and on the Aisne. 1/Devon, who had crossed to Le Havre in August, found almost 600 reservists waiting for them. However, with the Jersey garrison battalion being 'unattached' to a division in peacetime, the Devons initially became a lines-of-communication battalion. Their first 'battle' was to restore order when a hastily recruited Royal Engineer labour battalion of Glaswegian dockers 'had run amok and were in possession of the town of Nantes'. Order restored, the Devons joined the 3rd Division, who were fighting alongside the Dorsets in the 5th Division on the Aisne, before both battalions marched north in the 'Race to the Sea'. By the end of October 1914, the German Schlieffen Plan had failed, the war of manoeuvre was over, a line of trenches had been established, stretching 475 miles from the North Sea to Switzerland.

Moving north, 1/Devons fought at Givenchy and Festubert, while the 1/Dorsets marched on to Ypres, where they fought over winter. 2/Devons crossed to France with 8th Division in November and fought briefly in the Ypres Salient, alongside 1/Dorsets, before moving to the Neuve Chapelle area.

Under-equipped and suffering a steady stream of casualties, the three battalions fighting in France and Flanders endured their first terrible winter in the trenches. With no respite in sight, 2/Devons were in action during the Battle of Neuve Chapelle in March 1915, and in May 1915 1/Devons and 1/Dorsets had the dubious distinction, on Hill 60, of being among the first troops to be attacked with gas, without breaking and running. Exhausted from the Second Battle of Ypres, the two battalions were transferred, with the 5th Division, to take over trenches on the Somme from the French. Meanwhile, 8/ and 9/Devons crossed to France in time for the Battle of Loos, and moved to the Somme from Festubert in February 1916. 2/Devons and 6/Dorsets, who both remained fighting in trenches to the north, arrived on the Somme at the end of March 1916.

1 Lieutenant Colonel A. L. Ransom *1st Battalion Dorsetshire Regiment in France and Belgium, August 1914 to June 1915*. Privately published

2 Halfway through mobilization, the age for overseas deployment was lowered to nineteen.

3 Major C.H. Dudley Ward *History of the 1st Battalion, The Dorsetshire Regiment 1914-1919*.

4 C. T. Atkinson *The Devonshire Regiment 1914 – 1918*.

5 In Devon, men could also choose to serve with the Royal Navy and Royal Marines.

6 C. T. Atkinson *History of the Fifth Battalion The Dorsetshire Regiment 1914-1919*.

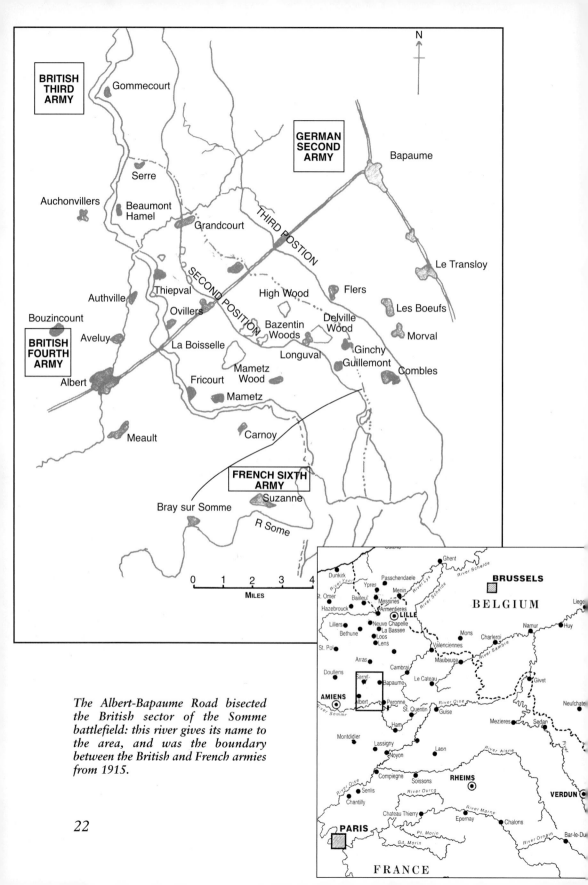

BRITISH THIRD ARMY

Gommecourt

GERMAN SECOND ARMY

Bapaume

Serre

Auchonvillers

Beaumont Hamel

Grandcourt

THIRD POSTION

Le Transloy

SECOND POSITION

Thiepval

High Wood

Flers

Authville

Ovillers

Les Boeufs

Bouzincourt

Bazentin Woods

Delville Wood

Morval

BRITISH FOURTH ARMY

Aveluy

La Boisselle

Longuval

Ginchy

Guillemont

Combles

Albert

Fricourt

Mametz Wood

Mametz

Meault

Carnoy

FRENCH SIXTH ARMY

Bray sur Somme

Suzanne

R Some

0 1 2 3 4
MILES

N

The Albert-Bapaume Road bisected the British sector of the Somme battlefield: this river gives its name to the area, and was the boundary between the British and French armies from 1915.

22

Ostend

Ghent

Dunkirk

River Scheldt

BRUSSELS

Passchendaele

Ypres

River Lys

Menin

River Scheldt

BELGIUM

St. Omer

Bailleul

Messines

Armentieres

Liege

Hazebrouck

LILLE

Namur

Huy

Lillers

Neuve Chapelle

La Bassee

Mons

Charleroi

Bethune

Loos

Valenciennes

River Sambre

St. Pol

Lens

Arras

Cambrai

Maubeuge

Le Cateau

Givet

Doullens

Serre

Bapaume

AMIENS

Albert

Peronne

River Oise

Neufchatel

River Somme

St. Quentin

Guise

Ham

Mezieres

Sedan

Montdidier

Lassigny

Laon

Noyon

Compiegne

River Aisne

Soissons

RHEIMS

VERDUN

Senlis

River Ourcq

Chantilly

River Marne

PARIS

Chateau Thierry

Epernay

Chalons

Bar-le-Duc

Pt. Morin

Gd. Morin

River Ornain

FRANCE

Chapter Two

The Somme: 1915

The 1st Battalions of both West Country Regiments moved south with 5th Division, from the fighting at Hill 60, in the Ypres Salient. They joined the Third Army forming on the Somme during August 1915. With New Army divisions now arriving in France in significant numbers, the British agreed to take over fifteen miles of trenches from the French. This would enable the French to release experienced divisions for the Allied autumn offensives at Loos, Artois and Champagne. The sector taken over by the British was quiet, and it was intended that it would remain so, with the Third Army maintaining a defensive posture. 5th Division took over responsibility for 4,000 yards of deep and comfortable trenches from the French 22nd Division, in a sector of the line between Beacourt and Carnoy. The Battalions were used to the shallow muddy trenches or breastworks of the Ypres Salient, and the Devons' historian commented '... they found the new line much more elaborate in construction and much more habitable than any they had yet held'. The 5th Division's history[1] commented that:

> ...the trenches [all eight to ten feet deep] were well supplied with dug-outs and shelters; many of these latter gave protection against the lighter natures of shells, whilst some were even furnished with bunks made of timber and rabbit wire, and lined with wood – comforts hitherto undreamt of.

However, it was found that the fighting qualities of the trenches were inadequate.

> Parapets, it is true, hardly satisfied the Devons' standards; much work was needed to make them bullet proof, and the French did not appear to have troubled much about constructing snipers' posts and machine-gun emplacements and making good fire steps. Both sides had been obviously letting sleeping dogs lie, and working and carrying parties had been allowed an immunity which the British were hardly prepared to continue.

It was 'several months before they realized the peculiar disadvantages of a chalk country in heavy rain'.

Topography

The Germans had occupied the dry high ground in the Département of the Somme during the 'Race to the Sea' in 1914. They had dug positions on the naturally defensible chalk heights between Arras and the River Somme. Each steep spur was crowned with a German redoubt, and each upland village became a fortress, producing a series of defensive lines based on the range of the Maxim machine gun. On average, the villages consisted of 150 buildings, most of which had cellars that formed the basis of the network of underground

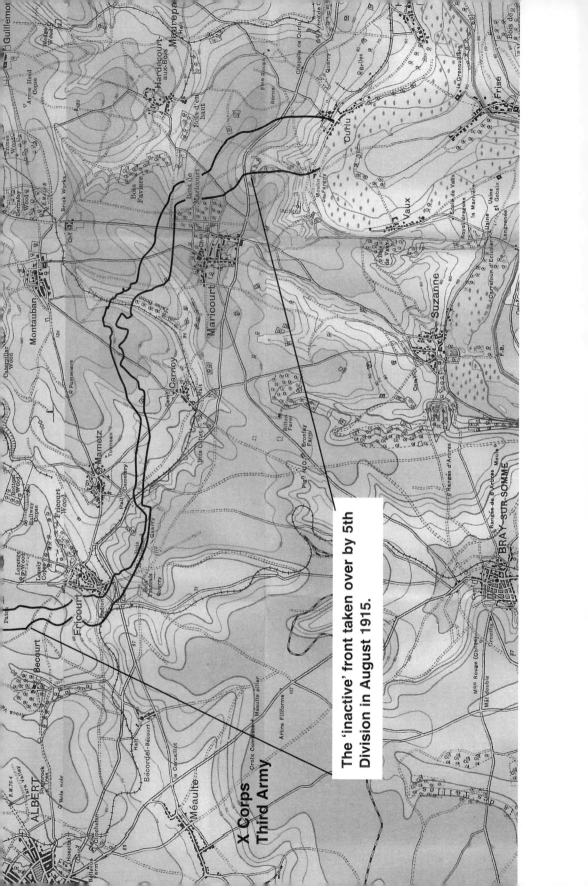

The 'inactive' front taken over by 5th Division in August 1915.

X Corps
Third Army

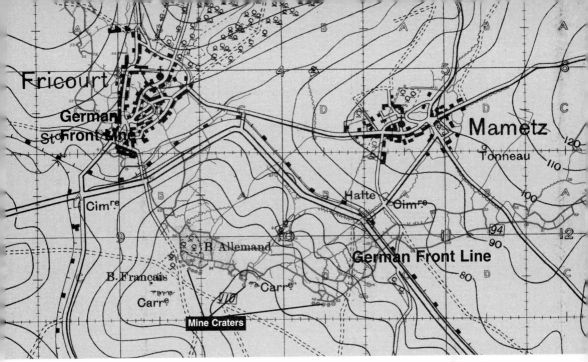

Printed trench maps replacing earlier French and hand-drawn maps showing the German positions in detail and their own in outline (or, as in this case, not at all) were issued during the winter of 1915-1916.

tunnels and chambers in which the German infantry sheltered. The river valleys of the Somme and Ancre are steep and about 500 – 700 yards wide. The ground in the valleys is peaty: prone to flooding in winter and easily churned into a morass by repeated shellfire. These valleys were distinct obstacles to movement, even if their rivers had been only 5 to 7 yards wide.

The terrain of the Somme's chalk uplands is remarkably similar to that of Salisbury Plain, which was familiar to most of the Regular soldiers. The views in the open country were extensive, with no hedges and only small villages and woods to obstruct the view. With shellfire removing the few natural features, navigation, even over short distances by day, became difficult. The woods were mostly mature but overgrown, but soon fell victim to shell fire.

The abiding impression of the British soldiers on the Somme was of constantly fighting uphill against the Germans in dominating positions. Even when the Fourth Army was established on the Pozières Ridge, the Germans still managed to make the most of the terrain by adjusting their positions to include all vantage points.

The portion of line that the 5th Division took over was similar, except that unusually

> *observation was excellent from our positions, the whole of the enemy's front-line system and much of his rear areas being plainly visible; in this respect we had the superiority, as, owing to the high ground in rear of our positions, practically the whole of our back area was free from enemy observation, except from balloons and aeroplanes.*

This helps to account for the events on this flank on 1 July 1916.

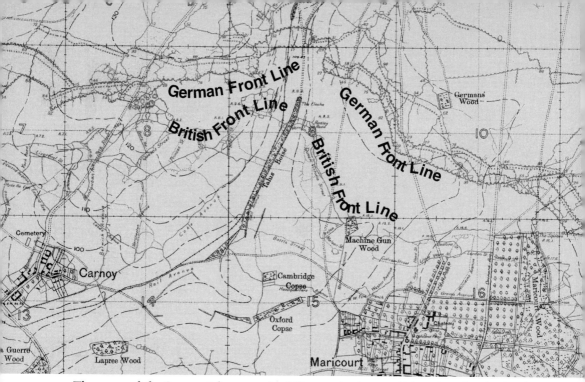

The areas of the Somme taken over by 1/Devons in August 1915. Note the depth of the German positions.

Early Days on the Somme

The first time 1/Dorsets came into the 15 Brigade's sector, they took over the C1 Sector trenches from 1/Cheshires, opposite Fricourt, in the Bois Francais area, while 1/Devons, serving with 14 Brigade, occupied trenches in front of Carnoy. For a short time, the divisional sector was increased to 8,000 yards, including Maricourt on the northern bank of the River Somme, as the final French troops departed for Artois and Champagne. Sergeant Major Shephard described the move forward and occupation of the trenches during a 'miserable and bewildering night', when the Battalion found it difficult to locate the communications trenches in the pitch-black and unfamiliar country. Shephard, a Regular Army soldier, was Company Sergeant Major of B Company, and recorded in his diary[2] the first day on the new front:

> We were all soaked and the trenches were over our knees in water and mud ... our sector is a perfect maze.

> Spent the whole morning exploring the trenches we hold. After three hours, I got a good idea of our position. We have two companies in the firing line. A Coy on our right joining up with the West Ridings and on our left are the Bedfords. C Coy is in support and D in reserve. These two Coys bring up our food and trench stores and do fatigues. Our (B Coy) sector of trenches is the E [left] Sector and each communicating trench (boyau) and fire trench (tranchee) is named in French after someone. We have the Boyau Garibaldi, Boyau Sergeant Lonches, the Tranchee

26

Capitaine du Page etc. We got busy renaming these trenches. In our sector is 'la Bois Francais' i.e. 'The French Wood'. This seems to be named so in sarcasm, as the wood is non-existent, a few poles here and there.

The 5th Division's battalions moved in and out of the line, taking over different sectors and getting to know the trenches, the surrounding country and the rear area. In contrast with the daily attrition rates on an active front, casualties on the Somme were at first light. 1/Devons reported that 'the casualties for August only amounted to thirteen, for September sixteen and October eight'. Major Shute, having reported for duty as Second in Command 1/Dorsets, wrote home on 10 September:

The Regiment are coming out of the line at Susanne, a very quiet spot, and there they have only one casualty, the whole time they have been there [seven days]. The lines are about two thousand yards apart; they cannot get closer – very bad ground marshes.

A group of infantrymen in a forward trench, fusing their newly issued grenades or 'bombs'.

Eventually, 5th Division settled down to a pattern of reliefs where two brigades were in the line at any one time, with the reserve brigade occupying billets and barns in villages to the rear. Normally, there were two battalions per brigade in the line, leaving the other two carrying out labouring duties, training, and resting. In these circumstances, the battalions regained their efficiency and (as a low priority) they were brought back up to strength and were able to undertake some training in the rear area.

Mines and Mining

Having occupied the Hill 60 area of the Salient, the West Countrymen were familiar with mine warfare. At this stage of the war, the opposing sides, unable to break the enemy's line opposite in conventional attack, sought to gain advantage by tunnelling under the enemy, and placing charges to blow away a portion of his line. This would either be as a part of a local 'bite-and-hold' attack or, as will be seen, as the opening move of a major offensive.

In late 1915, mine warfare had not developed into the well-controlled military science that it later reached with the attack on Messines Ridge in 1917. The official historian explained[3]

> *The work done in 1915 might be described as the first phase of British mining. It was one of local interests, depending to a great extent on the demands of the infantry in the front trenches. The proximity of the opposing forces invested with great importance small local objectives, such as salients which flanked No Man's Land, or ruins and natural features which gave cover to machine guns and sniper.*

Mine warfare was developing into a complicated art, as the offensive mines as described above, were complemented by defensive mine shafts and tunnels that were dug to intercept and blow-in enemy offensive mines. At Fricourt, in 5th Division's area, both sides engaged in active mine warfare. Sergeant Major Shephard noted in his diary that the British trenches in the Bois Français area were regarded as 'a very dangerous place, as it is known to be heavily mined and we expect it to go up any moment. The whole place is honeycombed with mines, and the enemy is doing the same, probably more. We can hear the digging underneath us.' The official historian explained:

> *... it can be readily understood that any sounds thought to come from underground were regarded as proof of enemy mining. Thus there often arose conflict of views, some troops demanding the destruction of enemy strongholds, whilst others were equally insistent in their immediate demands for immediate protection from enemy mining. The general result was the development of numerous small workings, started in haste from shallow shafts in the front system of trenches.*

The mine shafts and tunnels were built by the specialist Tunnelling Companies of the Royal Engineers, each 344 men strong, supported at any one time by 216 infantrymen from the local brigade, who provided the unskilled labour. The mines varied in length according to the width of No Man's Land and the ground needed to conceal the 'mine head', its spoil and associated activity. Typically, a mine in the Fricourt / Carnoy area was 300 to 400 yards long, and in the chalk rock the 4'6"-by-2'6" tunnel was only revetted where strictly necessary. Huge material resources were needed to construct mines, in addition to the significant demands on manpower. The infantry did most of the heavy work of carrying wood etc. forward and spoil back from the diggings to dumps out of sight of the enemy. Spoil had to be taken well to the rear in order to keep the location of mine heads secret, otherwise it would be blown in by enemy artillery. To add insult to injury, the West Country regiments did the carrying while in reserve or 'resting'.

The speed at which digging progressed depended not only on resources and the quality of the rock but also on the proximity of the workings to the enemy. In the chalk rock of the Somme, silence was essential as the tunnel approached the enemy line. Two men, supervised by their Engineer, would be working at the chalk face. One would lever blocks of chalk out with his bayonet, while the second would catch the block before it thudded on the ground, and pass it back to other men whose job it was to remove the spoil.

Quoted in the Devons' history is an unnamed regimental officer's description of the infantry's role in support of the mining efforts at Bois Français:

> The mining fatigues one had to do when out of the line were about the worst thing in the war. They meant spending eight hours out of the twenty-four, in the line, carrying wet sandbags full of mud from the mouth of the shaft down a very wet sticky communication trench to a dump about a hundred yards to the rear. They were often enlivened by mine werfer and rifle-grenades, but otherwise there was little to make it anything but a tedious job. It was rather annoying, when the battalion had captured this section of the German trenches, to find that the careful and methodical Germans had a tunnel running back from the Bois Francais, along which the spoil from the mines was run back on trucks, dry and safe.[4]

Sergeant Major Shephard complained with passion and at length, in his diary entry for 13 August about duties in the mines:

> We have also to find parties for mining. This is a great muddle and causes a lot of grumbling. The infantry soldier's actual pay is 1/- daily. Engineers get 3/- daily and extra pay for special jobs such as mining.
>
> What actually happens is that our men do the work with a man of the

British infantrymen supervised by a Royal Engineer officer remove spoil from a mine. Note the stethoscope used to detect enemy counter-mining operations.

Engineers to every fifteen of ours to superintend, yet our men get no extra pay, neither will the 1st Bn Dorsets Regt get any honour when the mine is finished and successfully exploded. The Engineers will get that. We have the men mining who are more skilful than the Engineers who superintend. We do not blame the Engineers. They do their work well in all cases, but the War Office authorities are to blame in putting men to work as Engineers with no extra pay. The men do not trouble so much about the pay. It's the principal of the thing.

The war underground was every bit as dangerous as it was on the surface. The Dorsets' war diary for 17 August records: '1 man in working party killed by foul gas while working in a mine shaft'. There was also an ever-present danger of breaking through into a German tunnel, or having one's own sap blown in by an enemy camouflet charge.

Sergeant Major Shephard records an average of two enemy and friendly mine detonations per month in his diary during the period August to December 1915. The entry for Thursday, 14 October describes one such detonation:

At 5.15 p.m. the enemy suddenly opened a very heavy rifle fire [causing the British to reinforce the front line], we stood to arms. Nothing moved until 10 minutes after, when a very powerful mine was exploded by the enemy on our left in a trench which the A and SH had just taken over. Our trenches rocked severely. Heavy fire continued accompanied by artillery for about 10 minutes longer when it gradually subsided. We sent two platoons to reinforce the firing line.

The mine had been dug too short and missed the target. Even so, a length of trench was blown in, eleven men were listed as missing, two killed and a further six wounded. By the standards of the time on the Somme, this was a high casualty rate. As Shephard wrote: 'This shows vividly the uncertainty of trench warfare'

The Autumn

Once the Battle of Loos (25 September to 8 October 1915) was over, the tempo of operations, that had already steadily increased since the arrival of the British on the Somme, started to build noticeably. Contributing to the growing number of exchanges of fire was the fact that all three brigades were in the line, and that there had been an increase in the allocation of artillery ammunition to both the British and Germans. The latter had been suffering a shortage of shells every bit as bad as the British, and according to 5th Division intelligence, had restricted their fire on the Somme to two rounds per trench sector per day during August and September.

The Devons' historian wrote:

In October, things became brisker. The Germans seemed to have an increased ammunition allowance and indulged in occasional but comparatively ineffective bursts of fire, usually called 'hates.' They made little effort, however, to dispute no-man's-land with the British patrols, which became increasingly enterprising.

During the autumn, the Dorsets' war diary started to detail exchanges of fire between the opposing trenches, as the following exert indicates:

> *4 Nov. Situation quiet. Trenches in wet and muddy condition.*
>
> *5 Nov. Bombs thrown by West Bomb Thrower[4] at enemy working party in trench opposite our 62 Trench.*
>
> *6 Nov. Our artillery successfully ranged on point opposite 63 Trench, where enemy trench mortar was located.*
>
> *7 Nov. Quiet.*
>
> *8 Nov. 5.30 p.m. enemy fired trench mortar and within 15 seconds our artillery fired at point previously located.*

Exchanging machine-gun fire was now a regular feature of life, as it was elsewhere on the British front it served to keep both sides out of sight, below ground level, and made entering No Man's Land far more dangerous. Major General Kavanagh, who had taken command of the 5th Division as it moved to the Somme, was very keen on the value of sniping, and had

> *In addition to ordinary service and telescopic-sighted rifles, obtained three elephant rifles which were distributed along the front; to the uninitiated these weapons were as dangerous to the firer as to the target, and several men who thoughtlessly sniped with them found themselves at the bottom of the trench with a feeling as though a mule had kicked them;*

German infantry in late 1915, before the issue of steel helmets. Note the variety of equipment and bandoliers of extra ammunition.

A carrying party bringing up warm food for the troops in the front lines. This service only worked in the relatively quiet conditions where the Germans did not overlook the British communication trenches. The profusion of telephone wires and alarm rockets indicate that this was probably the area of a front line company HQ.

they were, never-the-less, excellent weapons for the destruction of loophole plates, and when used on one occasion against a ration party carrying hot soup up a German communication trench, the results were startlingly effective.

The Germans were not the only enemy that the British troops on the Somme had to face. As the weather deteriorated, the deep comfortable trenches they took over in August became a distant memory as the 'disadvantages of defences dug in chalk' began to show. The Devons' history records that:

November brought heavy rains, and in consequence additional work. Soak pits had to be dug, trench floors drained and lined with stones, the sides of the trenches, which in dry weather had stood firm with little revetting, began to cave in and needed constant attention.

The Dorsets' war diary entry for 3 December stated 'One man killed by collapsing trench. Trenches in very bad state' and on 10 December 'One man killed by collapse of a dugout'. Meanwhile, 5th Division's history describes the Somme mud that flowed into the trenches after a period of heavy rain:

Work was carried on incessantly, and the task was a heartbreaking one; the mud stuck to the shovels or scoops, and could not be thrown out of the trenches, whilst water appeared to remain at the same level whatever attempts were made to drain away. At times the mud was so bad that men got stuck in it, and were totally unable to get themselves out without assistance, and frequently their boots were pulled off their feet in the effort of walking. On many occasions trench reliefs were carried out over the top of the trenches to avoid the interminable delays and the exhaustion caused by the journey along the communication trenches.

The second winter of the war looked as if it would be only marginally better than the first.

The routine of winter in the trenches was broken by Christmas Day 1915. A part of 1/Devons spent the day in the trenches, where under the prevailing relatively quiet conditions on the Somme they received as much traditional Christmas fare as possible. However, orders had been issued that on no account was any truce to be held with the enemy, and 5th Division's battle police were deployed to ensure that there was no repetition of the previous year's Christmas Day No Man's Land truce. After their experiences with German gas on Hill 60, a truce was unlikely, and one battalion diarist wrote that 'there cannot be any goodwill between our troops and the despicable enemy troops opposite us'. The Dorsets were, however, out of the line, and the B Company festivities were recorded by Sergeant Major Shephard:

Rose at 6 a.m., supplied party for work on Peronne Avenue, guards etc ... Busy morning preparing for Xmas dinner etc. We fixed up rough tables and in old barns for the Coy. MENU: Breakfast, Ham and pickles. Dinner, Roast beef, cabbage, potatoes, carrots, Xmas pudding, apples and beer, good supply of cigarettes.

For the dinner, as is customary, the Sgts waited on the men. They had a good feed. The Drums came round and gave us a tune and our Colonel came round to wish all as happy an Xmas as possible.

After the men had finished we went to our room, all the Sgts of the Bn together, and had dinner... Very good dinner, singsong after. We were competing in a Divisional cross country run at 2.30 p.m. No shelling or bombs today ... After parading a fatigue party at 6 p.m. went to canteen, thence to QM Stores until midnight when I had to parade another mining party. ... Fini of Xmas day on Active Service.

32nd (New Army) Division

As part of the policy of mixing the experienced Regular Army battalions with Kitchener's Volunteers, four battalions and a brigade headquarters from the 5th (Regular) Division were selected for exchange with those from 32nd (New Army) Division (K2)[6]. Consequently, on 31 December 1915, 1/Dorsets left 15 Brigade and joined HQ 14 Brigade and 2/Manchesters (both also from 5th Division) further north in the la-Boisselle-to-Thiepval sector of the line. 14 Brigade's two Kitchener Battalions were 19/Lancashire Fusiliers who were more commonly referred to as 3/Salford Pals and 15/Highland Light Infantry (or the Glasgow Tramways Battalion).

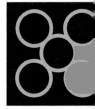

32nd Division Sign
(Red circles on black. Not worn as a
sleeve badge by the infantry)

1/Devons remained with 5th Division on the Somme until the end of February 1916. In a late winter blizzard they rushed north to join VI Corps to relieve the French between Arras and Lens, thereby releasing French troops to reinforce Verdun where the Germans were attacking in great force. 1/Devons eventually returned to the Somme in late July 1916, at the height of the battle.

1/Dorsets, having joined an inexperienced Division recently arrived on the Western Front, were honoured by being selected to run the Divisional School at Frenchcourt. On 21 February, they began training the officers and non-commissioned officers of the New Army battalions in 'open warfare' tactics, in anticipation of the resumption of a 'war of manoeuvre'. Being the 'School Battalion' was a welcome change of routine for the Dorsets, and it did much for the soldiers' self-esteem to be held up as experts and as an example to the newcomers. Using shallow trenches, flags and tapes, the soldiers of the 32nd Division went through increasingly complicated exercises, starting with platoon attacks and culminating with full brigade attacks, complete with supporting arms. However, the month spent at Frenchcourt passed quickly, and 1/Dorsets were soon on their way back to the front to take over one of the most infamous spots on the entire Western Front.

14 Brigade, 32nd Division
(Red diamond. The other brigade sy…
were a triangle and a circle)

Battalion Bars – 1/Dorset
(Green bars. Second battalion of 14
Brigade, 32nd Division)

1 *The 5th Division in the Great War.* Hussey and Inman.

2 A photocopy of the diary is available at Leeds University Research Centre. However, extracts were published under the title *A Sergeant Major's War*, edited by Bruce Rossor and published by The Crowood Press. 1987.

3 *Military Operations, France and Belgium, 1916, Vol I.* Edmunds.

4 8/ and 9/Devons took over this sector in March 1916 and eventually captured the section of German line described. Therefore, the 'unnamed' officer was almost certainly one of theirs.

5 A spring-loaded frame, similar to a clay-pigeon trap, designed to throw hand grenades into the opposing trenches.

6 See Becke's *Order of Battle of Divisions* Parts 1 and 3B for full details.

Chapter Three

1916: Preliminary Operations and Preparations

The move of 1/Dorsets to join 32nd (New Army) Division, in the trenches below the heavily defended Thiepval Heights, took the Battalion to a new environment. The line here had the River Ancre to its rear. The right flank included the village of la Boisselle, and, heading north, crossed 'Mash Valley' before climbing the Ovillers Spur and descending to the Nab at the bottom of the narrow 'Blighty Valley' (see map on page 38). From here, the Front cut diagonally up to the dominating salient, known as Leipzig Redoubt, where the line took a more northerly direction, past Thiepval and the heights crowned with the Schwaben Redoubt, to the Valley of the River Ancre.

It was on 4 March 1916 that the Dorsets arrived back in the 32nd Division's rear area. Lieutenant Charles Douie[1], Commander of 1 Platoon, A Company, describes their march to Millencourt:

> *In a blinding snowstorm we marched heavily laden up the hill. On reaching the summit we became exposed to the full force of the storm that swept over us in a white fury ... The men marched uncomplaining; from time to time, a song would be taken up or a joke passed down. Soon I caught the infection of the prevailing hilarity. Chapman, my servant, marched behind me, silent and unperturbed.*
>
> *Our first halt left A Company in an exposed position on a hill. We were glad when it ended. A blizzard is more tolerable when one is moving. ... By the time that we reached Hencourt, the snow had abated. We marched through, as if on parade, so that the assembled crowd composed of other Regiments might appreciate that the Dorsets Regiment did not notice snowstorms and had never heard of fatigue.*

In Millencourt the Battalion became the reserve to 14 Brigade, who were in the trenches around la Boisselle.

The Glory Hole

A handful of points along the Western Front, such as la Boisselle, earned a particularly evil reputation. These points were invariably where local advantage was to be gained by holding a feature; the opposing lines were very close together, and exchanges of fire were seemingly continuous. The Glory Hole at la Boisselle met all these criteria in abundance. Astride the Albert – Bapaume Road, at the point where the front line cut through the outskirts of the now-ruined village, the opposing trenches were on average a little more than thirty yards apart. On the flanks of the village, white chalk mounds marked the position of a series of overlapping mine craters. In places, the infantry on

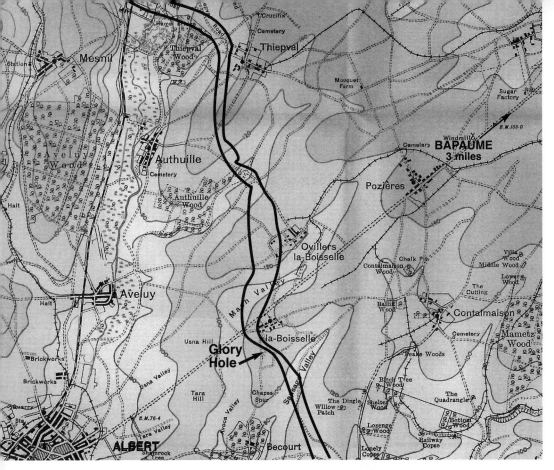

opposite lips of the craters, were as close as 15 yards. The presence of the craters was testimony to the consistent deadly bickering, first between the French and Germans, and now with the British. Major Shute, the Battalion Second in Command, commented on the state of la Boisselle in a letter home: 'You wouldn't believe what a shambles the village in front of us is. There is no semblance of any house left, and every tree is broken. There are a few bricks, about ten feet high, where the church stood.'

Lieutenant Douie describes his recce of the Glory Hole trenches before taking over this section of the line for the first time.

> In the afternoon, I and a companion went forward to inspect the mine craters, which my company was to take over in the course of the night. We passed down our front-line trench towards the ruins of the cemetery through which our lines ran. East of the cemetery was the heaped white chalk of several mine craters. Above lay the shattered tree stumps and litter of bricks, which had once been the village of la Boisselle. We progressed slowly down the remains of a trench and came to the craters, and the saps, which ran between them. Here there was no trench, only sandbags, one layer thick, and about two feet above the top of the all prevailing mud. The correct posture to adopt in such circumstances is difficult to determine; we at any rate were not correct in our judgement,

as we attracted the unwelcome attentions of a sniper, whose well aimed shots experienced no difficulty in passing through the sand-bags. We crawled away and came in time to a trench behind the cemetery, known as Gowrie Street. Liquid slime washed over and above our knees; tree trunks riven into strange shapes lay over and alongside the trench. The shattered crosses of the cemetery lay at every angle about the torn graves, while one cross, still erect by some miracle, overlooked the craters and the ruins of la Boisselle. The trenches were alive with men, but no sign of life appeared over the surface of the ground. Even the grass was withered by the fumes of high explosive. Death, indeed, was emperor here.

An intermittent bombardment was going on, we all became aware at the same moment that a Minenwerfer *bomb had been projected directly at us. It rose high in the air, and I for one was certain that it would land directly on us and blow us to pieces. Nothing is so destructive as a* Minenwerfer *bomb which hits its mark; indeed, a man becomes as though he had never been born. I watched it, stupefied rather than afraid. Movement was impossible in the liquid mud. There was a swish over our heads; the bomb just cleared the trench and exploded with a deafening crash above us. We did not observe another* Minenwerfer *bomb till a man fell off the fire step of the trench with commendable speed. This bomb had been aimed with greater accuracy, and fell right into the trench. It would have killed several of us but for the happy circumstances that it failed to explode.*

Lieutenant Douie again at the rear of the Battalion column, led 1 Platoon forward to relieve 2/Manchesters at the Glory Hole on the night of Thursday 9 March 1916.

Lieutenant Charles Douie

We marched into Albert, over the railway bridge, past the ruined cycle factory, and so through the square under the shadow of the shell-torn church, with the image of the Virgin and Child at a miraculous angle from the tower, and out on the Bapaume Road. At the light-railway crossing beyond the town we halted again under a great Calvary to inquire for some promised gum-boots, which were unhappily not forthcoming. On our right were the remains of a house, whose shelter looked most inviting, and a battery of artillery, well concealed, in action. We proceeded slowly up a long and unpleasantly exposed stretch of broad route nationale, which extended bleak and haunted to the skyline. On one side were shelters scooped out of the bank, and some dugouts where the [179th] tunnelling company, working on the mines at la Boisselle, kept their stores. The road was under constant shellfire, but was protected from direct observation from the German lines by a rise, on the summit of which were the riven trunks of five tall trees.

In front of A Company was Sergeant Major Ernest Shephard, who was chivvying along the soldiers of B Company. With vastly more experience, he took a more phlegmatic view of the occupation of the trenches.

Marched for trenches in the afternoon ... We picked up guides from

Manchesters at the level crossing in Albert, and picked up gum-boots [too few for the whole battalion] *at the same place. A few yards up the Albert-Bapaume Road we entered our communication trench called St Andrew's Avenue. We finally arrived and relieved the D Coy of 2nd Manchesters in the "Counter Attack Trench" (i.e. close support) called St Andrews. The right sector is the worst, where trench is nothing but the forward edge of mine craters, 15 yds from the enemy, in a terrible state. Left sector is not as bad – drier, and in places 200 yds from enemy.*

We, [B Company] *as the close support Coy, have to reinforce both Coys* [in the frontline] *in case of attack, 2 platoons to the right, 2 to the left. We do no carrying fatigues, but supply working parties for the trenches. A Coy is in reserve at a point some way behind, called USNA Redoubt. They carry all meals, rations, etc, for the Bn. Had a look round our position*

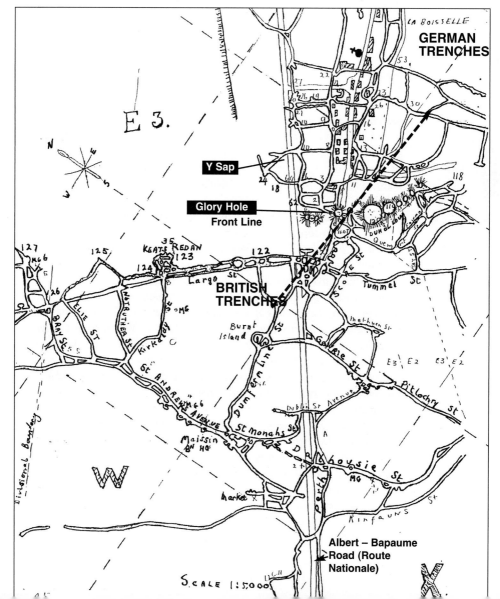

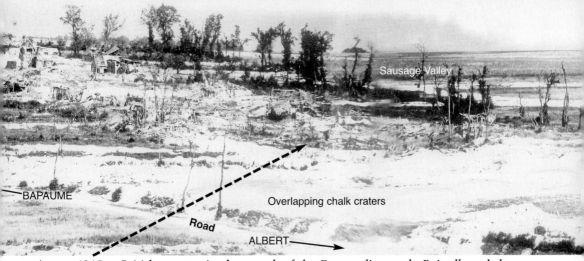

Labels on photograph: BAPAUME, Sausage Valley, Overlapping chalk craters, Road, ALBERT

August 1915, a British panoramic photograph of the German lines at la Boisselle and the Glory Hole craters. Arrowed line indicates the same view as indicated on the map opposite.

before dusk. It would be difficult to imagine a more confused tangle of trenches than our position, and the position of the enemy. Immediately in front of right sector is the village of la Boisselle which the enemy holds. We hold the cemetery. I have never seen a place as completely smashed as this village, not a wall standing. This point had been the scene of some desperate fighting, and had been won and lost six times, finally by the enemy.

It is a dominating position, which if lost by the enemy prevents them observing the effect of their fire in this area. Therefore they are continually blowing up mines under us, and trying to nibble forward as much as possible to make the ridge behind the village more secure.

We had a few 'oil cans' over at 6 p.m., also we found that Fritz has our trench well in line. They sweep machine guns along all night, just tipping the parapet. Started to snow at 8 p.m.

He continues in the same vein to describe the German reaction to the Dorsets' efforts to repair the trenches and Royal Engineers' mining activities, which were more developed here than anywhere else on the Somme.

We have several saps being worked on there, and the least noise, talking or hammering by our men, brings over a shower of bombs, rifle grenades, and trench mortars, which the enemy do chiefly to try and blow in sap heads and hinder as much as possible our mining.

Luckily the enemy are not sure where the trench we man runs, or we could never hold it. As it is, most of their heavy mortars drop behind us in the cemetery. Waking up the dead with a vengeance.

No one is allowed to go to sleep on any account there. The 'Glory Hole' is only 15 yds in places from the enemy, and the enemy are all under it. They can be heard plainly sapping away as hard as they can go. However, our Sappers are under them so I don't suppose they feel any more comfortable than we do, but they certainly have the best of us in trench mortars. Apparently, they have got about 40 guns against our (Blank) very few...

Sergeant Major Shephard's description of life in the trenches is less colourful than Lieutenant Douie's but they would both agree that 'Here death held sway, and the life of a man is numbered in days, not years'. Conditions were so bad at the Glory Hole that the companies were rotated through the front, support and reserve trenches on an almost daily basis, and the battalion would only remain at the front for four to six days before relief. The casualties that 1/Dorsets suffered during each of its periods in the line at la Boisselle more than made up for the light casualties suffered since arriving on the Somme.

Douie describes one inter-company relief at the Glory Hole:

> At two in the morning came the order to move. Two is not an hour of the night at which I normally feel at my best, but unhappily during war it is quite the usual hour for relieving trenches. I became happier when we moved off. We came to Dunfermline Avenue, where the mud was so deep that I was constrained to warn my neighbours against the dangers of submarines. I took over Trench 121, which lay to the left of the craters and was the normal approach to them. The outgoing company was undisguisedly glad to be off, and provided lurid tales of the events of the preceding thirty-six hours.
>
> My most vivid memory of the night is that of two very old soldiers addressing the German Army in familiar, if deplorable, language; while a machine gun swept the parapet of the trench from end to end, their heads remained silhouetted against the skyline, and, so far as I could see, did not move up or down during the two hours of their watch.

Raiding and Being Raided

Raids were a feature of British trench warfare, as it was thought that patrols sent out to dominate No Man's Land and raid enemy positions would foster and maintain an offensive spirit. A successful raid was also good for a battalion's morale. However, in the early spring of 1916 there were other pressing reasons to conduct raids. Chief amongst these was that the French were under pressure from the German attack at Verdun. They had requested the British to raise the tempo of their operations and mount minor attacks or raids on the enemy lines. The intention was to fix German divisions in their defensive positions so as to prevent them becoming available to support the attack at Verdun.

The Official History[3] describes the tactical aims of raiding:

> The essence of a raid is that the raiders should enter the enemy's trenches by surprise, kill as many of his men as possible and return before counter-measures can be taken. Special tasks may be added, such as obtaining prisoners for 'identification', damaging mine shafts, destroying a length of trench or post which is giving particular trouble but cannot be permanently held if captured. The number of men employed was usually 10 to 200.

However, at this stage of the war, raiding was far less developed than it became in later years, when the West Country soldiers took part in many successful enterprises that contributed to British domination of No Man's Land.

The Y Sap Raid

While out of the line, 1/Dorsets received orders to mount a major raid against the German-held Y Sap on the northern flank of la Boisselle. The mission they were given was to test the enemy position's strength and to seize a prisoner in order to confirm the identity of the German battalion holding the village. The raid was to be led by Captain Algeo, a pre-war Regular officer, who now commanded A Company. His second in command was one of the Dorsets' most experienced and effective officers, Lieutenant Mansel-Pleydell, the Battalion's Intelligence Officer. His presence highlights the important intelligence nature of the raid. The other two officers were Second Lieutenants Blakeway and Clarke. Twenty men from each rifle company were selected for the raid.

When the Battalion marched for the trenches, on 21 March, the raiders were left behind at Millencourt to prepare for the attack, which was to take place on the night of 25 March. Preparations were thorough. The plan was for a party of 28 men, under the command of Second Lieutenant Blakeway to attack the Y Sap that jutted out north from the village's main defences. To the right, Lieutenant Mansel-Pleydell was to enter the enemy trenches near la Boisselle Point. Lieutenant Clarke was to remain in No Man's Land with a section of 10 men in support. A further 10 men were to remain in the Largo Street trenches as a reserve. Orders were given and men allocated to their officers; rehearsals began on a taped-out representation of the la Boisselle trenches. Having been through the attack innumerable times in daylight, it was practised at night until all ranks knew the attack inside out.

Meanwhile, at the front, Major Shute, the Battalion's second in command, was preparing the remainder of the Battalion and its trenches for the raid. The Regimental History reprints Major Shute's notes, which gives an idea of the detail required to prepare for the operation:

Captain Algeo photographed in 1912.

> *Practice carrying wounded up Kirkaldy Street.*
>
> *Thermos for the doctor.*
>
> *One Hundred Buckets (for bombs)to be painted so as not to be visible at night.*
>
> *Signal lamp for Capt Algeo and one for headquarters.*
>
> *Be prepared for counter attack. See plenty of ammunition and bombs in Lago Street. Extra Lewis gun there, too.*
>
> *Trench ladders for getting out of the trenches.*
>
> *Leather hedging gloves for wire cutters.*
>
> *Extra bandages.*
>
> *Drummers to assist stretcher-bearers.*
>
> *Four extra machine guns to be brought up.*
>
> *[Officers] Servants dugout to be cleared and used for prisoner escort party.*
>
> *One telephone with each company, two in signals office, one in dressing station, and one in fire trench. Extra telephone in front line with direct communication to RA.*
>
> *Rockets [signal] ready for SOS, in case line to RA broken.*

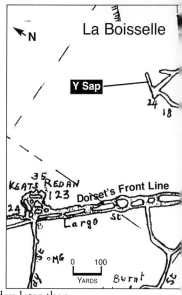

La Boisselle

> *Hot meal for raiding party at 1015 p.m. Tea and rum for ditto on return from raid.*
>
> *Knife rests ready to put out where we make the gaps in our wire.*
>
> *Bayonet men at the exits of trenches.*
>
> *Lozenges to be issued to prevent coughing.*
>
> *Patrol to go out an hour before raid.*
>
> *Should enemy be found to be ready – immediate retirement.*
>
> *Warn adjacent trenches re bombardment.*
>
> *Final orders to Thwaytes re sentries for guiding through wire.*
>
> *No patrols to go out after 1130 p.m.*

According to the Battalion's history, on a wet morning: 'The raiders rejoined the Battalion in the line on the 26th March', a day later than planned. Over the preceding days, both sides' artillery had been active. The British guns and trench mortars did their best to create viable gaps in the enemy wire, which had taken longer than planned, while the German artillery harassed the British in their trenches. Lieutenant Douie was holding the right sector, which included the mine craters. 'The days preceding the raid were distinguished by shell fire of an intensity which in itself might have expunged the word "quiet" even in the trench diary.'

The Germans had learnt of the Dorsets' raid. Despite constant spy scares in the rear area, it is most likely that the Germans had recognized the signs of an impending attack or gained information from listening posts pushed out into No Man's Land. However, the Germans had also developed a device that enabled them to intercept British telephone conversations. Douie commented that on the day of the raid:

> *Throughout the afternoon experienced soldiers, among whom I was not numbered, could tell that news of our impending attack had reached the German Intelligence, as we were subjected to harassing fire, and registration by new guns on our support and communication trenches.*

Back at Millencourt, a party of Dorsets, for the sake of deception, pretended to go through the routine of training on the taped-out trenches, 'and carried out the usual nightly performance there, putting up [Very] lights, throwing bombs, etc,' in case spies were watching. Meanwhile, at la Boisselle, as darkness fell, the firing slackened and patrols left the Dorsets' lines. According to Douie, 'it was found that the Germans were repairing the gaps cut by our artillery in their wire, and bursts of machine-gun fire were directed on gaps to keep them open'.

An unusual silence set in around la Boiselle and the Glory Hole. Douie continued:

> *The night was still, to a degree which no night had been before. The broken posts and wire which marked the boundaries of No Man's Land and the white chalk of the mine craters were agleam in the moonlight ...*

Yet not a shot was fired ... the deathly silence did not augur well.

Sergeant Major Shephard recorded that the Dorsets' patrols came in at 11.30 hours and reported that there were no enemy in No Man's Land. In B Company's position at Usna Redoubt, 'At 10 p.m. the party had dinner. I supplied various parties to carry stretchers, bombs, etc., 11 men as orderlies, and a party of 12 to escort prisoners to the rear. ... At 11.15 p.m. the party left the redoubt.' The Battalion stood-to-arms at 12.15 a.m and according to Douie 'as the Colonel passed down the line I noticed the grave anxiety on his face'. The raiding party crept out in to the narrow silence of No Man's Land. A silence, 'broken only by the rattle of machine gun fire from Ovillers', across Mash Valley to the left.

The raid was initiated by the Engineers blowing three small mines placed in tunnels beneath the German lines. Sergeant Major Shephard described them as 'feeble, and did very little damage'. Once the mines had exploded,

... the British artillery opened up a heavy fire on the 2nd, 3rd, and reserve lines. Enemy very much awake, they opened up an intensive volume of fire in very short time. Heavy artillery on Albert, Usna Redoubt and counter attack trench, whiz-bangs, trench mortars, bombs, machine gun fire etc, on our front trenches and intervening ground over which our attacking party of eighty were moving.

According to the post-action report, the two groups of attacking troops 'got through the gaps in the wire entanglements' although a lot of loose wire had been laid in them and reached the Y Sap and German front line'. These they found abandoned, deepened to fifteen feet and filled with a mixture of loose and tightly nailed barbed wire. It was a trap, designed to ensnare the raiders, who were deluged with bombs and assorted trench mortars. The history continues, 'At some spots bombs were thrown back, but nothing could be done in the face of such a hail of missiles. The signal to retire [the sound of a hand-cranked siren] was given at 12.45 a.m.'

Casualties were very heavy. About half of the raiders regained the British line with their clothing ripped to shreds. Shephard, controlling the stretcher-bearers, noted: 'At 2 a.m. forty were still missing. At 2.30 a.m. the bombardment lessened a good deal and search patrols and stretcher bearers went out to find and bring in remainder.' Douie commented,

Our wounded were everywhere, and time and time again survivors went out to bring them in. It seemed incredible that anything could live out there ... A young subaltern stayed behind to help a wounded man out of the German trench and in the act was killed on the wire.

Shephard reported that 'Four were found dead in the enemy trench, hopelessly tangled in wire, and impossible to move owing to heavy bombing.'

Armed with some intelligence on the enemy opposite, Shephard considered that the raid could be regarded a qualified success.

Information gained shows that the enemy 28th Reserve Division, who apparently held the Fricourt – Authuille front until recently, has been

withdrawn, probably to Verdun, and the 26th Reserve Division who held the Authuille – Serre front are ready to move to Verdun. Other information too confidential for entry in this book.

It was also some time before it came apparent that the three mines set off to initiate the raid were in fact large camouflets, which according to Major Shute were: 'a great success, although it seemed such a rotten job at the time. It must have smashed up all their galleries and pretty badly, too, as they have done no further mining since.'

Despite the raid's meticulous preparations, losses had been significant. Field security had let the raiders down; a hard lesson had been learnt by 1/Dorsets that was to be repeated on a grander scale on 1 July 1916. However, as some consolation, Field Marshall Haig mentioned the Battalion and its raid in his dispatches.

'In the cold light of dawn', the morning after the raid, Lieutenant Douie peering through a trench periscope could see 'a dark speck on the German wire beyond the craters'. It was the body of his friend Second Lieutenant Noel Blakeway, 'a young and most gallant subaltern', who had been killed attempting to rescue his wounded soldiers.

German Raids

As divisions arrived on the Somme, 1/Dorsets' sector of the line moved north to the Thiepval area. Here, on the heights around Authuille, above the Ancre valley, the Battalion was involved in the 'constant bickering'[2] that characterized the fighting on the Somme in the first half of 1916.

After a month's rest and training, the Battalion returned to the line in early May, now under the command of Major Shute[4]. Raiding was now a regular event and had developed into a 'tit-for-tat' pattern. 15/Lancashire Fusiliers (1/Salford Pals) of 96 Brigade had conducted a raid on the night of 5-6 May. Unfortunately for the Dorsets, they had relieved the Salford Pals during the following evening, when a counter raid was expected. According to the Battalion's history however,

Major Shute had taken precautionary measures to keep his men under cover as much as possible. At 11 p.m., the enemy opened a heavy bombardment on the Thiepval sub-sector, which soon became intense. C and D Companies were in the front line, and Battalion headquarters found all telephone wires cut except to C Company; communication was therefore very slow.

The German bombardment included a small proportion of the new German gas shells, which caused a few casualties amongst the Dorsets and forced them to put on their gas masks which were still relatively crude. With localized clouds of gas still dissipating from their trenches, in the darkness, the West Countrymen were, to face the Germans with strictly limited vision.

At 11.30 hours, D Company, on the Battalion's left, were attacked by approximately three platoons of Germans. Effective flanking fire from C Company prevented one of the enemy platoons from breaching the wire in front

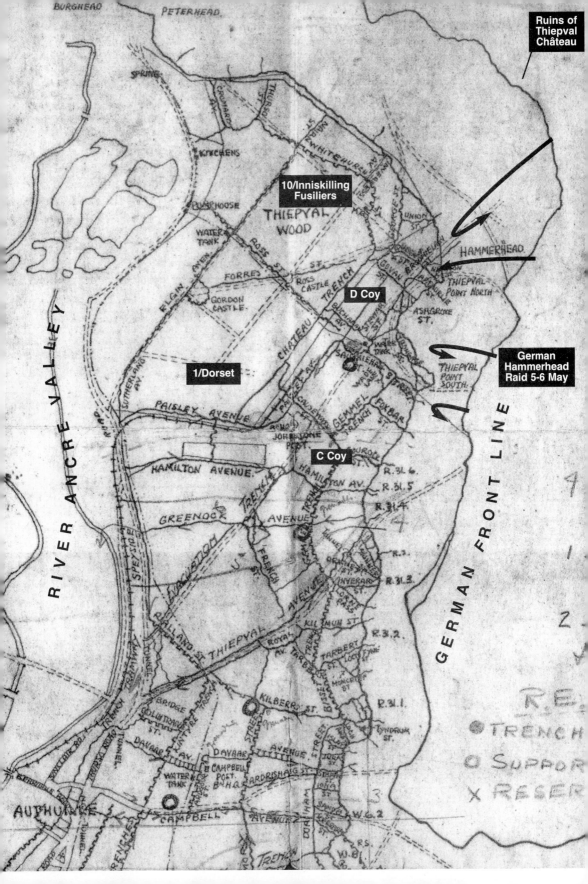

BURGHEAD · PETERHEAD.

Ruins of Thiepval Château

SPRING

KITCHENS

BUSH HOUSE

WATER TANK

10/Inniskilling Fusiliers

THIEPVAL WOOD

FORRES

GORDON CASTLE

ROSS CASTLE

ROSS ST.

ELGIN OVEN

SUTHERLAND AV.

CHÂTEAU

D Coy

UNION

HAMMERHEAD

THIEPVAL POINT NORTH

ASHGROVE ST.

GOVAN

1/Dorset

WATER TANK

PAISLEY AVENUE

THIEPVAL POINT SOUTH

GEMMEL ST. FOXBAR

TRENCH

JORDAN ONE POST

HAMILTON AVENUE.

HAMILTON AV.

C Coy

R.31.6.

R.31.5

R.31.4

GREENOCK

AVENUE

INVERARY

R.31.3

R.31.2

SPEYSIDE

THIEPVAL AVENUE

KILMUN ST.

TARBERT ST. LOCHGAIR

ROYAL AV.

MONCRIEFF ST.

KILBERRY ST.

TYNDRUM ST.

R.31.1.

BRIDGE STREET

COLINTRAIVE ST.

DAVAAR AV.

DAVAAR

AVENUE

WATER TANK

CAMPBELL POST. Bn HQ.

ARDRISHAIG ST.

CORHAM ST.

W.6.2

AUTHUILLE

CAMPBELL AVENUE

TRENCH

W.8.1

German Hammerhead Raid 5-6 May

GERMAN FRONT LINE

R.E.
● TRENCH
O SUPPORT
X RESERVE

RIVER ANCRE VALLEY

of Thiepval Point South, but another enemy platoon 'entered what remained of D Company's trenches' around Thiepval Point North and started to bomb their way north towards Hammerhead Sap. The third group of Germans gained a foothold in the Dorsets' trench system at Hammerhead Sap but were bombed out again by D Company, supported by counter-attack from 10/Royal Inniskillin Fusiliers (The Derry Volunteers). Major Shute wrote:

> The whole of that portion of the line occupied by D Company was practically demolished by trench mortar bombs and artillery fire before the enemy raided. I had the greatest difficulty in finding out the situation. Runners were dispatched, but, owing to the damage caused by the bombardment could not get through to the responsible person required, and such information as I received was found to be incorrect.

The Germans, eventually forced out of the wrecked D Company trenches, retired, leaving behind one prisoner and one of their dead. However, the unlucky Dorsets lost 12 other ranks killed, 30 wounded and once a roll call was completed 24 other ranks, mainly from D Company, were found to be missing. Later it was established that most had been taken prisoner by the raiders.

Captain Algeo's Recce

After four days as brigade reserve in the Blackhorse Bridge/Authuile area, 1/Dorsets marched back to the trenches. They returned to the line opposite the German-held and overgrown gardens of Thiepval Château. This area was still particularly active, with well-concealed German machine guns being a particular problem. However, Diamond Wood, in No Man's Land, gave cover for some movement out of the trenches. It was here that an extraordinary event took

An extract from a panoramic photograph of the Thiepval Heights looking across the Ancre Valley to the area between the modern day Ulster Tower and Thiepval Memorial to the Missing.

place. Despite orders to the contrary, Lieutenant Mansel-Pleydell, the Battalion's intelligence officer, had, according to Shephard, gone on a solo patrol and 'brought some iron plates [sniper loopholes] back'. The following day:

> ... in broad daylight Capt Algeo went out from Hammerhead Sap and went into the enemy wood smoking his pipe quite cool, returning an hour later. At 10 a.m. this morning, without saying anything, Capt Algeo and Lieutenant Mansell-Pleydell went out from the sap. They were seen crossing No Man's Land between the sap and the wood. When nearly up to the edge of wood M-P was seen to beckon, and he and the Captain ran into wood. There was a scuffle and Capt Algeo was heard shouting 'Hands up, hands up, put it down.' A volley of rifle fire and revolver shots followed, a scream, silence. I heard the commotion and ran up to the sap. On finding out the cause I decided it was madness to attempt a rescue party, as the enemy would be waiting under cover of the wood, with every advantage. I ordered extra sentries up and no firing except at enemy plainly seen. I thought there was a chance that they had been wounded or situated in such a position that

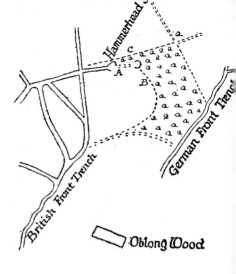

MAP 14—HAMMERHEAD SAP.

Captain Algeo's Recce. The two office were last seen at Point A headir towards Point B.

Thiepval Chateau

Geman officers question members of 1/Dorsets captured during the Hammerhead Sap raid.

they could not move. I ran to Bn HQ and reported and also asked that our artillery should be warned not to fire on the area.

The CO was very upset and gave me permission to send a man to reconnoitre to see if there was any sign of them. He also ordered me not to go myself on any account, although I wished to do so. I returned to the sap and Sgt Goodwillie (the Pioneer Sergeant) was given permission to go out and Sergeant Rogers to follow a little way behind. They went out

Château Thiepval in 1915 before it was progressively pounded to rubble during 1916.

through the valley on the left of the sap and entered the wood safely. A lot of revolver shooting took place and after ½ hour, Rodgers returned alone to say he had lost Goodwillie, as he pushed on too quickly. Rodgers heard a lot of jabbering and shooting but could see no sign of the Captain, M-P or Goodwillie, so he returned.

The CO had meanwhile come up and he ordered that no one should be allowed in No Man's Land for further reconnoitring. We kept a sharp lookout all day and at dusk sent out a patrol who reported that the enemy were working on forward edge of wood. ... The loss of my gallant Captain to the Battalion, my Company and myself cannot be estimated. He was the bravest officer I have ever met and his last thought was for the good and honour of his Company and his men.

Sergeant Goodwillie wearing the short-lived Broderick cap.

The Dorsets had indeed lost three of their best and most effective sons. Captain Algeo had turned down a posting to the staff, but Major Shute had agreed, and Algeo was to have been posted to Brigade Headquarter two days after he disappeared in the wood. Major Shute wrote of Sergeant Goodwillie, a stalwart of the Battalion: 'We were never very long in a new place before he knew where anything could be found. He provided cooking ranges and stoves in the trenches, beds and furniture for the dugouts.' It had been hoped that the three had been taken prisoner, but word was eventually received that they had been killed and were buried behind the lines.

8/ and 9/Devons' Arrival

In 1915, both 8 and 9 Battalions of the Devonshire Regiment had joined the 7th Regular Division, replacing two Guards battalions. During the winter, they left the Ginchey area and moved south, with their new division, to join the Third Army. Here, being out of the line for almost two months, as Army reserve, the Devons had the opportunity for proper rest and training before returning to the front. Arriving on the Somme in February 1916, 7th Division took over the trenches vacated by the 5th Division, including 1/Devons, in the Mametz/Fricourt area. This sector of the line was no longer quiet, but despite the problems of maintaining the trenches, 'All ranks welcomed the change from the flat country, where the ordinary infantrymen saw little more than the German barbed wire, to hills from which a fine view could be obtained'. Second Lieutenant Frank Wollocombe of A Company 9/Devon noted in his diary 'Wonderful trenches, hardly any mud, being on the side of a big hill'. The Devons also suffered comparatively few casualties in the months running up to the battle. Consequently, they 'contained plenty of NCOs and men with longish experience, and were seasoned battalions in excellent form and spirit'.

9/Devons, however, had an unattractive change of role hanging over them –

Veterans of 8 and 9 Devons, photographed in Exeter while recovering from wounds, pose alongside German guns they had captured during the Battle of Loos.

to become the divisional pioneer battalion. Second Lieutenant Frank Wollocombe made a jaundiced comment at this prospect in a letter home: 'A pioneer battalion does RE work that is too dangerous for the RE. I fear I shall never get a second star [promotion to Lieutenant] at such games. I like the ordinary trench life. I wish they would leave us alone...' Fortunately the threat was lifted, and 9/Devons remained in 20 Brigade.

In contrast with 1/Dorsets' bad luck with raids in the la Boisselle and Thiepval sectors, the Devons fared better. Describing a German raid on the outskirts of Fricourt. Lieutenant Woolcombe wrote:

> At about 5p.m. the Hun tried frightfulness on the front line, the most tremendous bombardment I have ever seen ...They then attacked the North side of the Tambour with eight parties of nine men each, each party told off for a different purpose, e.g. attacking machine guns, blowing in mine saps (for which they had enormous canisters now covered in German blood). I don't believe they were all killed, but the prisoner said so. He was in the Prussian Guard but is now in 99th Regiment, of which all were killed except one who was taken prisoner – not so bad – a nasty smack for brother Boche.

2/Devons

As 1/Devons left the Somme with 5 Division, the Regiment's 2nd Battalion arrived with 8th Division in early April 1916. After the Battle of Loos, they had spent a dull, cold, wet and dangerous winter on the Lys front to the north. Soon the experienced regulars of 8th Division, with an excellent reputation, had developed an effective method of introducing New Army units to trench warfare. Describing the 'Schooling' of 34 Division's Tyneside soldiers: on the Somme, the divisional historian wrote:

> *each incoming battalion was allotted to one of the infantry brigades of the division and was then directed to attach one of its companies to each of the four regular battalions of that brigade. The course of training was progressive. The new soldiers were sent into the trenches first as individuals supernumerary to the regular trench garrisons. When in this way they had begun to find their way about, they went in as platoons with definite if limited responsibilities of their own, next as companies and finally as complete battalions with a sector of their own to defend.*

At first, the West Country soldiers and their Geordie charges, from the Tyneside Scottish and Irish, found it very difficult to understand each other, as their accents, almost dialects, were so very different. Nonetheless, the Tynesiders and Devons parted with a mutually appreciative exchange of letters between company commanders and COs.

The Devons took over a part of the line previously held by 1/Dorsets and 32nd Division in the La Boisselle and Ovillers Spur area. In common with other battalions, they commented favourably on the dryness of the trenches, but now the area was far from quiet. In this case, the Battalion suffered casualties from snipers during its first tour, but the remaining old Regular Army marksmen in 2/Devons soon 'reduced the threat from the Germans on the high ground to manageable proportions'.

Preparations: Training

With Fourth Army's order of battle for the coming offensive almost complete, there were many more troops on the Somme than were needed to hold the line. However, with few pre-war soldiers left serving in most divisions, and with two years of trench warfare foremost in the Army's mind, training in 'open warfare' was required. It was hoped, indeed expected, that during the coming offensive General Rawlinson's infantry would break out and advance into the 'green fields beyond,' leaving the trenches as an unpleasant memory.

In May 1916, GHQ issued instructions for the 'Training of Divisions for Offensive Action'. As far as the infantry were concerned, two training requirements were outlined in the pamphlet:

> *(a) Training for the attack from trenches against a hostile system of trenches and strong points, including the consolidation and occupation of the position won.*
>
> *(b) Training for exploiting a success when the hostile systems of defence have been broken through.*

To rehearse the attack, divisions were allocated training grounds in the Amiens area. Here they marked out the enemy positions that they were to attack, with tapes, shallow trenches; and in a few important examples, they dug replicas of German trench systems, carefully copied from trench maps, air-photographs and intelligence reports. Battalions, brigades, and finally divisions practised their part in the attack under the watchful eyes of staff officers from the various headquarters. Visiting parties ensured that the tactical instructions and orders, issued by Fourth Army and its corps and divisional headquarters were applied.

Among the tactical developments of this period was the formation of specialist bombing platoons. Now available in quantity, the Number 5 Grenade or the 'Mills' bomb was emerging as a weapon increasingly relied on in trench warfare. They were a significant improvement on the various types of mostly locally manufactured grenades that had been issued to the British infantry during 1915. Once the West Country soldiers had mastered the laid down procedures of storming the enemy's trenches, including the use of grenades, they practised the general principles, battle procedure and tactics for operating in open country. For many West Country infantrymen, this involved learning a whole new set of skills.

The British Mills Bomb first issued to the Devons and the Dorsets on the Somme.

Sergeant Major Shephard described a divisional exercise in the Frenchcourt area, held on 27 April, which he realized was a rehearsal of 32nd Division's plan.

> *The scheme was as follows: General attack by our Army (the 4th) along our front. Our Division were ordered to attack a certain portion of ground with a village included. Of our three brigades, 97 Brigade are to take enemy first line and village, 96 Brigade to take 2nd and 3rd line. We (14 Brigade) have to go straight through and take enemy fourth line, and consolidate the position. Two battalions of 97 Brigade were operating as a brigade, the 96th were represented by a skeleton force. We moved off at 11a.m., the 97 and 96 Brigade having won up to the third line. We went off in artillery formation, 2/Manchester on left 19/Lancs in centre. We were on the right and 15/HLI in reserve ...We pushed straight through and took the 4th line, including German Farm [in reality Moquet Farm]. Smoke bombs were used to screen our advance a little. We were supported by artillery, machine gun, stokes mortars, etc.*

Shephard, however, went on to say 'I cannot say I relish our job, the troops taking the first line are best off. They will get all the praise and very few casualties'. The exercise had been hard on the men's feet but the reality of the attack on 1 July was to bear little resemblance to the stage managed efficiency of a divisional exercise.

In early 1916, the infantry's heavy Vickers machine guns and their crews were in the process of being consolidated into brigade companies, and were replaced by a pair of 'light' (only 26-pounds) Lewis Guns. Lieutenant Duff of 8/Devons, after limited training, was soon able to prove the value of his two guns. The Germans were again planning to raid the British trenches at Fricourt, opposite the Tambour, on 22 February. The German raiders were met by the concentrated fire of the Battalion's two guns and, unused to such firepower from the British infantry, the raiders did not press home their attack. Before long, a Lewis Gun and a section of six men, commanded by a corporal, was to be found in every

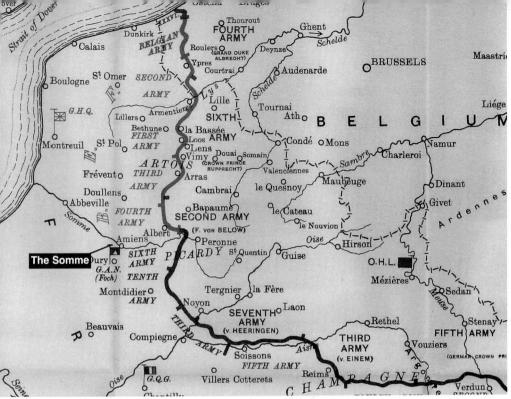

The Western Front in early 1916 after the formation of the Fourth Army on the Somme.

West Country infantry platoon.

Preparations: Labouring

The Somme was a sparsely populated area, lacking the metalled roads for the army to move on and relatively few villages to accommodate the soldiers. Consequently, there were not many soldiers to be found resting behind the lines, as the infrastructure to support a major battle needed to be built. Meanwhile, at the front line, extra communications and in some cases assault or jumping off trenches were dug in No Man's Land to reduce the distance that the first wave of assault troops had to cross at Zero-Hour.

Shortly after they arrived, 9/Devons, still under threat of becoming a pioneer battalion, were, according to Second Lieutenant Woolocombe, 'engaged in making a railway to bring up ammunition to the guns. Several [heavy] naval guns are here waiting to go up [on the railway]'. Almost twenty miles of light and full gauge railway line was laid in early 1916. As was the case in the mines, the Royal Engineers directed and supervised the infantry, who did the majority of the unskilled labouring. Later in the war, the Labour Corps and its gangs of Chinese and other Empire workers did much to reduce the burden on the increasingly scarce infantry. Lieutenant Woolcombe said of the prospect of pioneering, 'I expect it is only a craze that will pass'. The threat did indeed pass, and the Battalion, as already mentioned, remained alongside 8/Devons as a part of 20 Brigade.

Company Quartermaster Sergeants and regimental 'cooks' prepare meals for the troops in the line. Hot food in the line was a luxury not normally enjoyed once full battle was joined.

Nonetheless, other labouring tasks for the infantry in the rear area included the construction of roads and accommodation, as well as ammunition and stores dumps. In the forward area, observation and command posts were to be built, along with additional communications trenches and overbridges to facilitate the advance and provide overhead cover to the infantry.

Many of the dugouts built before the attack used a semicircular inner structure made out of 'elephant' corrugated iron sheet. Sandbags and, typically, 6 to 8 feet of packed spoil were laid on top. If the dugout was to be 'shell-proof' i.e. keep out a 5.9-inch shell, a 6-inch bursting layer of bricks or concrete would be laid before being camouflaged by top soil.

2/Devons, as the 8th Division's historian recorded, were busy on the Ovillers Spur.

> *Before the end of April, the engineers and their infantry labourers had commenced to push out towards the enemy's trenches 'Russian' saps, shallow covered ways intended* [when opened up] *to act as communication trenches when the German front line had been won. Work on dug-outs, assembly positions and bomb depots, and in construction of concrete shelters, observation posts, and dressing stations was pushed on daily in the forward area.*

Adding to the confusion of trenches in the Somme's forward area were the cable trenches, six-foot deep and as narrow as practicable, dug in an attempt to ensure that the increasingly important telephone communications would survive enemy shellfire. Meanwhile, offensive and defensive mining, which was now focused on the coming offensive, continued to be a drain on infantry manpower.

In the early months of 1916, working parties tended to suffer heavier casualties than the infantry in the front line shelters and 'funk holes'. One such casualty was Lieutenant Mansel-Carey, of the 9 Battalion, who was killed by a rifle grenade in the remains of an infamous front-line copse near Mametz that afterwards bore his name – Mansel Copse. In an attempt to reduce head casualties, particularly from airburst shells, a helmet was issued to the British Army, only shortly after the Germans received their coal-scuttle 'stalhelm'. On 19 February, Lieutenant Woolcombe recorded, 'An order has come out that we are to all wear the rotten little blue tin, supposed shrapnel-proof helmets in trenches'.

As spring lengthened into summer, it became increasingly obvious to all that the next major British offensive would take place on the Somme. Given the amount of preparatory work that they had completed and the obvious concentrations of manpower and resources around them, the West Country infantrymen were, by and large, happy to accept it at face value the assurances of coming success.

1 Charles Oswold Gaskell Douie, author of *The Weary Road. Recollections of a Subaltern of Infantry.* Douie, the son of a career officer in the Indian Civil Service; left Rugby at the age of eighteen, on the outbreak of war. He initially served in the 7/Dorsets, a training reserve battalion, before he reached the minimum overseas service age. He joined the 1/Dorsets on the Somme on 15 Feb 1916. After being wounded, he was transferred to a Munster Regiment battalion on the lines of communication in Italy. Douie went on to be Secretary of University College, London.

3 Edmunds, *France and Belgium 1916, Vol 1.*

Early 1916. Infantry sentries, looking out into No Man's Land, keep low in case of snipers, despite their newly issued steel helmets. Both soldiers also carry gas hoods slung across their shoulders.

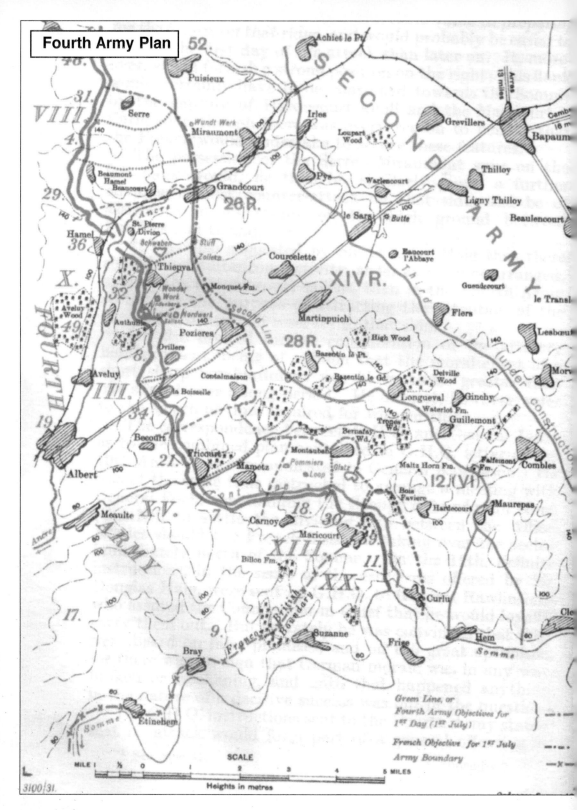

Fourth Army Plan

Green Line, or
Fourth Army Objectives for
1st Day (1st July)

French Objective for 1st July

Army Boundary

SCALE

MILE 1   ½   0   1   2   3   4   5 MILES

Heights in metres

3100/31.

Chapter Four

Fourth Army Plan and the Preliminary Bombardment

The architects of the Allied plan for 1916, Field Marshal Joffre and General Haig.

The Battle of the Somme had its genesis in late 1915, following the failure of the disjointed Allied autumn offensive. In November, Prime Minister Asquith and his French counterpart met, and agreeing that the Allies needed to work together more closely, formed a 'mixed permanent committee designed to coordinate the action of the Allies'. Shortly afterwards, the newly appointed commander of the BEF, General Sir Douglas Haig, met the French Chief of General Staff, General Joffre, at the Chantilly Conference. The latter was very much the senior partner and despite Haig's insistence that his armies should not be tasked to mount attacks to wear down the Germans, the French general issued the following instruction:

I have directed the General Commanding the Group of the Armies of the North to make a study of a powerful offensive south of the Somme ... This study is part of a general plan drawn up for the French Armies as a whole and will permit me to determine the points against which our principal effort will be made in the coming spring ... the French offensive would be greatly aided by a simultaneous offensive of the British forces between the Somme and Arras. ... it will be a considerable advantage to attack the enemy on a front where ... activity ... has been less than elsewhere.

The original plan was for a phased joint attack on a front of 45 miles, astride the Somme. To the north, the British were to attack with as many divisions as they could make available, up to a 'possible maximum of 25 divisions' while south of the river, the French Sixth Army was to attack with 39 divisions on a front of thirty miles.

Operations on the Western Front would complement offensives by the Italians and the Russians.

Delays in equipping, training and deploying the New Army divisions ruled out preliminary British attacks in the spring of 1916. This suited Haig, who, at the beginning of his command had not yet accepted that he would have to fight a war of attrition. His natural instinct was to believe that he could break through the German line in a continuous, rolling attack, and resume open warfare. However, it was the German attack on Verdun, designed to 'bleed the French Army white', that fell on Joffre's army on 21 February and did most to shape the eventual Allied plan for the Somme. Such was the ferocity of the battle that 'the mincing machine of Verdun' had to be 'fed' by a constant supply of fresh divisions to replace shattered French formations, which had to be withdrawn to a quiet sector to rebuild.

By late spring, with the Germans fighting their way through the network of forts towards Verdun, Joffre's only wish was to relieve pressure on the French Army, who he believed were 'near breaking point'. By June, Joffre was demanding that the British attack, but he could only spare sufficient French divisions to attack on an 8-mile front astride the Somme. The British were to lead the offensive with the 25 divisions available to General Rawlinson's Fourth Army and Gough's Reserve Army. The initial British attack was to be mounted by 13 infantry divisions, with two further divisions of General Allenby's Third Army mounting a diversionary attack on the German salient at Gommecourt.

Despite the change of concept from a massive joint Anglo/French attack by 64 divisions, confidence grew in the coming offensive, as 'the flower of British manhood' arrived on the Somme with the New Army divisions. Even the older and more experienced soldiers, who, in most cases, did not share what has been characterized as the 'naive optimism' of the Kitchener Volunteers, were impressed by the quantity of manpower and material being assembled for the offensive.

General Rawlinson, however, did not share the confidence of the lower levels; nor did he share Field Marshal Haig's expectation that a breakthrough could be achieved or exploited, although he accepted Haig's plans for the rolling capture of the enemy defensive systems. As the only infantryman among the three army commanders involved, he expected to mount deliberate attacks on each successive enemy position[1].

General Rawlinson

58

The Fourth Army Plan

With the Germans on the high ground overlooking the mass of British troops, little attempt was made, or was indeed possible, to hide the intent to launch an offensive on the Somme. General Rawlinson made a plan for his Fourth Army based on a number of assumptions. First, that the inexperienced New Army divisions, who made up the bulk of his Army, were only capable of executing a limited number of detailed instructions. This led to a simplistic, deliberate and inflexible plan. Rawlinson and his staff justified this approach in Fourth Army Tactical Notes:

> We must remember that owing to a large expansion of our army and the heavy casualties in experienced officers, the officers and troops generally do not now possess that military knowledge arising from a long and high state of training which enables them to react instinctively and promptly on sound lines in unexpected situations. They have become accustomed to deliberate action based on detailed orders.

Rawlinson's second assumption was that the power of the British artillery, now generously supplied with ammunition, would destroy the enemy trenches and defenders up to 2,000 yards behind the German front line. The plan eventually issued was for a five-day preliminary bombardment of the German first and second defensive systems by 1,537 guns, of which, however, only a small proportion were of the heavier calibres. The British infantry assault on a 24,000-yard frontage was to be launched in conjunction with the French on the southern flank. The first day's objectives included large portions of the German second position, which on the left flank required the infantry to take objectives such as the Pozières Ridge: for example, 1/Dorsets' objective was 4,000 yards behind the enemy front line. In the southern sectors, however the objectives were less deep, with 7th Division (8/ and 9/Devons) having objectives beyond Mametz to a depth of 1,200 yards.

Most of the Fourth Army's five infantry corps were to attack with two divisions, with a third division prepared to take trench systems in depth. Over the following days, a series of plans had been made for the capture of the remainder of the second and the whole of the embryonic third defensive system and the formation of defensive flanks to hold open 'the breakthrough'.

Having broken the German lines, it was then planned that the infantry and four cavalry divisions of Gough's Reserve Army would launch themselves into the gap and plunge into the enemy's rear. Though planners were keen to exploit any success that presented itself, their general wish was to exploit northwards to outflank the Germans facing the BEF around Arras. This, it was hoped, would unhinge the entire German front and lead to a resumption of open warfare, where Haig's much-prized, but largely inactive, Army reserve of five cavalry divisions could be employed.

Zero-Hour was set for 07.30 hours on Z-Day. The British would have preferred to attack almost three hours earlier, at dawn, but the French had insisted on a later time in order to ensure the accuracy of the final hours of intense artillery bombardment. The result was that, while the Allied gunners had a clear view of their targets, the German machine gunners could also clearly see the advancing British infantry.

Leaving their trenches, Fourth Army's Tactical Notes required infantry to:

... push forward at a steady pace in successive lines, each line adding impetus to the preceding line. Although a steady pace for assaulting troops is recommended, occasions may arise where the rapid advance of some lightly-equipped men on some particular part of the enemy's defences may turn the scale.[2]

The first sentence of this paragraph is often used as evidence of simplicity and overconfidence in the power of the bombardment. However, the reality was, as we shall see, that the lightly equipped men, sent forward to take important objectives, became casualties and the heavily laden succeeding waves were easy prey for any German machine guns that survived the bombardment.

The Bombardment

Too little ammunition and too few guns have been identified as prime reasons for the failure of the British offensives in 1915. With the Chantilly Plan came the intention to stockpile sufficient guns and shells to destroy the enemy and his trenches in the five-day preliminary bombardment of unprecedented power. The 7th Division's historian commented 'During these seven days the British gunners sent into the enemy's positions more shells than had been fired in the first twelve months of the war'.

The bombardment started on 24 June, five days before the planned date of the attack, which was to have been 29 June. The fire plan for each day U, V, W, X and Y-Days was detailed. On U-Day the bombardment opened with 2-inch medium trench mortars starting to cut the enemy wire, while medium batteries fired counter-battery missions in order to suppress the Germans' response to the bombardment and the assault. For the remainder of the artillery, the orders were for 'no increase [in rounds fired] beyond normal, except for registration [of targets]'. However, overnight the process of harassing the enemy rear area began overnight, as the Official History quoted 'with the object of preventing replenishment of ammunition, food and water'.[3]

The enemy's response, according to the Official Historian, 'was generally feeble ... When he did reply, fire was intensified, he was given four shells for every one of his, and if that did not stop him, larger guns and howitzers turned on'.

On V-Day, the bombardment-proper started with fire missions on trenches, strong points, OPs and machine-gun emplacements. Among other tasks, the 18-pounder field guns joined the process of cutting the enemy wire, by firing shrapnel[4] shells into the Germans' protective belts of barbed wire and forward trenches. Meanwhile, the heavy guns[5] concentrated on the Germans' underground forts, built beneath the villages that bisected the German line. The bombardment was to carry on 'all day and at intervals during the night by all nature of howitzers'. From U-Day onwards, the fire plan required the gunners to fire a 'concentrated bombardment for 1 hour 20 minutes' using every gun

Massive dumps containing millions of shells were difficult to conceal from the enemy.

available. The time of this particularly heavy bombardment varied from day to day, with the idea of accustoming the enemy to expect an unpredictable period of heavy fire. However, on Z-Day (the day of the attack) the bombardment would only last one hour and five minutes before Zero-Hour in an attempt to achieve some tactical surprise. The plans for W, X and Y-Days were to follow a similar pattern as the previous days, with batteries coming out of action for planned periods for cooling the guns, maintenance and rest. Observation posts (OPs), balloons and Royal Flying Corps (RFC) aeroplanes were to ensure the accuracy of the bombardment by direct observation and air photography. Meanwhile, the British trenches and normal billets in the villages behind the front line were manned as thinly as possible.

At night, the brigade machine-gun companies thickened up the barrage with their .303-inch Vickers Guns, while some of the artillery gunners rested. The

61

machine gunners' tasks, including on occasions the infantry battalions' Lewis guns, were to fire sweeps across No Man's Land, to stop the Germans mending the wire cut during the day, and indirect fire on to the approaches to the German communication trenches. The nightly bombardment was specifically aimed at 'the physical and moral exhaustion of the enemy'.

Expectations of the bombardment were high, as described by 8th Division's historian:

> Hope ran high that the result would be so to pulverize the enemy's defences that a legitimate chance would be given to the infantry to press forward to success. So far as the infantry themselves were concerned, all had been done that experience could suggest or ingenuity and foresight could devise.

However, the effect of the bombardment was mixed. For instance, the skilled task of cutting the enemy wire allocated to the 18-pounder field guns of the New Army divisions was in many cases beyond the abilities of the relatively inexperienced gunners. Setting the fuse correctly was vital; too short and the shell would burst over the wire with a much reduced effect; too long and the round would explode with little damage in the ground below the wire. However, even perfectly timed fuses that exploded in the midst of a belt of wire were seen on occasions to lift dense masses of barbed wire up, only for the wire to drop back in place having suffered no visible damage. To cut the enemy wire, the artillery observation officers needed to observe the fall of shot. Consequently, the Germans did their best to lay their wire out of sight of the British trenches. Patrols sent out by the 2/Devons during the night to check the progress brought

The British medium artillery in action during the bombardment.

in word of mixed results. A Battalion intelligence report recorded:

Patrols report that there are sections of enemy wire on the Battn front that seen to be largely untouched by the barrage but there are viable gaps. These are not straight forward and only a few yards wide. If they are not improved, their inadequacy will lead to bunching of the men in the attack.

Despite the evidence, the confidence of senior commanders in the bombardment, the plan and its results was undiminished.

Other targets for the field, medium and heavy guns, which concentrated on the defended localities such as trenches and strong points, seemed to be working, as wrecked or blown-in trenches could easily been seen. However, this was largely surface damage, as the Germans had built deep dugouts in the chalk hillsides that proved to be impervious to all but a direct hit from the heavier shells, and the British had too few heavy guns. In contrast with Allied practice, every German soldier had a place in a deep dugout. With signs of the coming battle being obvious in early 1916, German orders had been given that each shelter was to have at least seven metres of chalk above it and some were found to be up to fifteen metres deep. In addition, there were to be a minimum of three exits from each dugout, which would ensure that the troops were not trapped by a surface collapse of a single exit. Proof that the Germans were surviving the bombardment was given in a 2/Middlesex patrol report dated 25-26 June 1916. A raiding party went out on to the Ovillers Spur, where they and 2/Devons were to attack. As they approached, 'the deep dugouts in the enemy's lines were found full of Germans singing and apparently in good spirits notwithstanding our bombardment'. However, that was after only two days of British artillery fire. For the Germans, safe below ground, the *Trommelfeuer* (drum-fire) of the bombardment was at first an annoyance. Gradually, however, as the firing went on, the relentless hammering of shells began to wear on the minds of the soldiers below ground. Inevitably, there were psychological casualties. Some Germans, reportedly 'went mad under the strain', which worsened as food ran out and as shellfire started to damage water and electricity supplies. Matters were made worse as troops due to come out of the line had to remain in position, as reliefs could not get through.

Another factor affecting the results of the bombardment was the failure of a significant number of shell fuses, as witnessed by the annual 'iron harvest' of duds, turned up by the plough for over eighty years after the battle. The Official History states that the Fourth Army fired 1,508,652 rounds of all calibres, during the bombardment. However, up to thirty per cent failed to explode, and sadly, the failure rate among the heavier calibre shells, as we shall see, had a particular impact on the effectiveness of the British heavy artillery. These failures largely resulted from the faulty manufacture of the shells' fuses: the products of a hastily expanded armaments industry and the rushing of intricate fuses into full production.

The weather over the period 26-28 June was bad; therefore, the fireplan had to dwell[7] for forty-eight hours and with a strict allocation of ammunition, the rate of artillery fire slackened. Consequently, 'the enemy were given an

An 18-pounder field gun in action during the bombardment. This gun was the workhorse of the divisional artillery.

unexpected and, to him, invaluable opportunity to get food and water, and reinforcements to his front line garrisons'.[8]

Despite the general confidence and the scale and intensity of the bombardment, some individuals expressed concerns. However, in the Discipline and Morale paragraph of the Fourth Army Tactical Notes was a general warning that deterred commanders and their men from voicing their concerns, and staff officers from listening to them,

> *Finally, it must be remembered that all criticism by subordinates of their superiors, and of orders received from superior authority, will in the end recoil on the heads of the critics and undermine their authority with those below them.*

Despite this warning, concerns were expressed, if only, as in the case of 2/Devons, in the form of patrol reports. Sadly, such reports were largely ignored.

Gas

The Germans had introduced gas as a battlefield weapon in 1915 at the Ypres Salient. Two battalions of West Country infantry had been the first British troops to be attacked with the new weapon, when in positions directly opposite Hill 60 on 1 May 1916. 1/Devons and1/Dorsets, unlike others to be so attacked in the days before, did not panic, break and run. However, despite the initial impact of gas, it had largely lost its fear factor and had not been as effective as hoped during the Battle of Loos. Worse, it had on occasions proved to be a double-edged weapon, when gas clouds blew back onto the attacking British infantry. Consequently, gas was initially relegated to a subsidiary role on the Somme.

By 1916 gas masks were increasingly effective, but soldiers fighting in them were at a disadvantage.

In 1916, offensive gas was still largely delivered from pressurized cylinders dug into the friendly front line, as shells and mortar bombs were in short supply and were regarded as not very effective. Needless to say, the arrival of Special Brigade detachments, with what Lieutenant Ransom described as 'their loathsome apparatus', was not welcomed by the resident infantry, who could find themselves the unintended victims of their own gas. Enemy shellfire could burst the gas cylinders before release, or a light or gusty breeze could bring the gas back into their own trenches.

The preliminary fire plan included the release of gas at various junctures, provided that the wind was steady at a minimum of four miles an hour and was at least forty-five degrees from the line of the British trenches. These conditions were generally not met on the nights of U and V days, and the only gas officer to authorize release of the mixture of phosgene and chlorine gas belonged to 4th Division, who during the hour of their gas attack were heavily shelled in response. During 26 June, there was a more general release of gas on divisional fronts, when the increasingly windy weather permitted the deadly mixture to be released. The gas and accompanying smoke and shrapnel caused 'the enemy in each case to retaliate with artillery fire, but without serious effect'. The physical effect of the gas on the Germans was minimal, causing few casualties despite their inferior gas protection equipment. Just to the north, around Arras, gas was used as a part of the deception measures during the period 25-27 June. *Leutnant* Ernst Junger recalled:

> *A whitish wall of gas, fitfully illuminated by the light of the rockets, was moving over Monchy. As a strong smell of chlorine was noticeable in our cellar, we lit fires of straw at the entrances. The acrid smoke nearly drove us out of our refuge, and we were forced to clear the air by waving coats and groundsheets.*

It was not until the introduction of gas shells in quantity, and the development of delivery systems such as the electrically fired Livins Projector, which was designed to deliver concentrations of gas into the enemy's position, that gas again became a significant battlefield weapon.

Final Preparations

In the run-up to the battle the assault troops were as far as possible to be rested, but according to the Official Historian:

> *Rest, even when training was over, had only a comparative meaning for the officers. Nominal rolls of carrying and water parties and for other essential duties had to be prepared; equipment inspected and checked; maps examined and bearings worked out and explained to officers and NCOs responsible for maintaining direction; the plan of action expounded as far as necessary to NCOs signallers and runners; the times of the artillery lifts and the meaning of the various Very light and rocket signals committed to memory or written on scraps of paper in a manner indecipherable to the enemy.*

Lieutenant Douie was one of the officers of 1/Dorsets who went forward to recce the route that the Battalion was to follow from its position as a part of 32nd Division's second echelon. He brilliantly captures the moment and the battalion orders that followed.

From Blackhorse Bridge the way south lay along the bank of the river [Booker's Pass] towards Aveluy. Passing this way I found a [18-pounder] battery in action in a green meadow leading down to the Ancre. I felt a certain envy of the gunners; they looked so clean and free from care, and they lived in quarters so much better than those of the infantry ... I turned to enter Authuille wood. Not yet had gunfire seriously thinned the trees nor deprived them of their foliage, and the wood was cool and green ...The wood of Authuille held its presage of things to be, for it was thronged with fatigue parties busily engaged on completing bridges [across trenches and defiles], gun positions and ammunition dumps. On the eastern edge I came to our front line. Concealed emplacements held guns, which were destined to fire over open sights at Leipzig Redoubt when the time came. For the present, they were silent.

A heavy 15-inch howitzer preparing for action, well concealed in a wood behind the front line.

I came to a bridge over a defile which our plan of attack required us to cross, and examined it with interest. Its span was less than ten yards. A few days later the bridge, marked with unerring accuracy by the German machine gunners ...

My reconnaissance completed, I moved away from the emplacements and into the wood; a moment later the rush and roar of shells resounded through the trees ... I crossed again the shell-scarred meadow bordering the Ancre and turned aside to the gunners whose lot I had envied as I went up the line. I had no occasion to envy it now. The emplacement was a shambles; the gun would never fire again.

It was late afternoon. The officers of the Regiment were assembled in a dug-out looking over the Ancre at Blackhorse Bridge. Plans for the attack were gone over in detail by the Adjutant; duties were allocated. Everything was businesslike and matter of fact. I have known orders for a field day in England to be given in a more portentous manner. The proceedings were marked by no high seriousness, and occasionally degenerated into hilarity when a duty of unusual difficulty or danger was allocated. This reached its climax when a young officer received instructions that his duty was to convey a Bangalore torpedo [a metal pipe filled with explosive] up to and beyond Mouquet Farm, to place it under the wire of the German third line, and, having exploded it, to consolidate beyond this somewhat advanced position. ... Four subalterns were allocated a duty to them more distasteful, to remain in regimental reserve. One of them, confused and distressed beyond measure by this unexpected blow, raised his voice in protest. The Adjutant, ignoring a breach of discipline caused by such great provocation, hurriedly passed on to the next order. The subaltern sat unheeding and inconsolable, with bowed head.

Preparations for the great offensive were complete.

1 The third German position was barely begun until well into the planning phase.

2 Appendix 18, para 12 to the *Official History, France and Flanders 1916 Volume 1*.

3 *Military Operations, France and Belgium 1916*, Volume 1. Appendix 19.

4 Invented during the Napleonic War by Lieutenant Shrapnel. This type of shell was packed with lead balls, which surrounded a bursting charge. The whole was contained in a casing only thick enough to survive the forces on the shell during firing.

5 III Corps heavy & medium artillery consisted of 1 x 15", 3 x 12", 12 x 9.2" & 16 x 8" Howitzers and 1 x 12", 1 x 9.2", 4 x 6", 8 x 4.7" & 32 x 32-pounder guns (Total sixty-eight guns or one heavy or medium gun per forty yards of frontage).

6 *Official History*. Page 302.

7 Halting the fire plan's progress but maintaining fire at a lower rate.

8 *The 8th Division in War*. Published by the Medici Society Ltd. 1926.

Chapter 5

2/Devons' Attack on Ovillers

Of the five West Country battalions in action on the first day of the battle, 2/Devons was one of the two Devonshire battalions that attacked or 'went over the top' in the first wave at Zero Hour. They had arrived on the Somme to join the Fourth Army at the end of March, with 8th Division, who joined III Corps. Along with the remainder of the Army, the Devons worked hard training and preparing for the great offensive. Meanwhile, the Germans, with only the questions of time, date and boundaries of the British attack to determine, continued to strengthen their position.

The German Positions
Opposite III Corps, the Germans, 26th Reserve Division occupied positions on three spurs that ran down from the Pozières Ridge. The two fingers of high ground of significance to 8th Division and the Devons were the Ovillers Spur and the la Boisselle Spur. Both were crowned with German-held villages that had been developed into fortresses within the front line trench systems. The Official Historian commented that:

> Owing to the enemy's front position being on the forward slopes, it was completely exposed to fire ... but the enemy front line was singularly well adapted to defence, being sited, as the ground demanded, as a series of salients and reentrants being particularly strong.

Behind the front line lay two intermediate lines and further in depth, was the incomplete Second Position. Here the trenches and wire were both less well developed, and consequently lacked the comprehensive defensive properties of the front line system. A further three miles back were the beginnings of a Third Position, which was being worked on as German time resources were available. In July 1916 it was still patchy, but was clearly marked out for development.

Realizing that they were astride what was likely to be the Fourth Army's axis, the German 180 (10th Wurttemberg) Regiment put a great deal of effort into improving the area's defence. They dug the usual deep shelters, linked up the strengthened cellars of Ovillers with the fighting trenches and ensured that their positions were covered by overlapping arcs of machine gun fire. These guns were sited in considerable depth and were very well camouflaged, with many battle positions remaining unlocated by the British. 180 Regiment was holding the front line from

Above: A German Maxim machine-gun section pose for the camera in the rear areas.

Right: 23 Brigade's attack on the Ovillers Spur.

Left: A German officer photographed in a well, made trench at Ovillers before the battle.

70

the Ovillers Spur to Leipzig Salient with two battalions, each with three companies in the first and second lines of trenches, with individual companies covering a frontage of approximately 400 yards. Their fourth companies occupied the support line, while the reserve line was occupied by a company from the Regiment's third battalion, with the remaining companies being positioned in the Intermediate Lines. Approximately 1,800 men were facing 8th Division's infantry element of 9,000 men. Calculating the number of enemy machine guns that 8th Division was facing is more complicated, as the machine gun's effective range was over 2,000 yards. However, up to six guns belonging to 110 Regiment, dug into the hillside behind la Boisselle, were able to sweep 8th Division's positions and No Man's Land in the Ovillers area.

British Plans

III Corps was to attack between the Nab and Mash Valley with 8th Division on the left and with 34th (New Army) attacking astride la Boisselle. 19th Division was Corp's reserve, initially located around Albert. This division's task was to move up, securing the forward divisions' gains, to complete the capture of the German's third position and deepen the penetration.

8th Division was to attack with all three of its brigades, each with two battalions in its leading wave. The Division's New Army brigade, 70 Brigade, was on the left, attacking the northern flank of the Ovillers Spur rising from Nab Valley. In the centre of the Spur, 25 Brigade was to attack the crest line. This brigade was considered to have the easiest initial objectives, as they were not so likely to be engaged by flanking machine-gun fire. On the Division's southern flanks, 2/Devons, with 23 Infantry Brigade, had to attack what was perhaps the strongest part of the enemy line. The divisional history[1] describes the ground in the following terms:

... no division was more difficultly placed than 8th Division. Except for a short

71

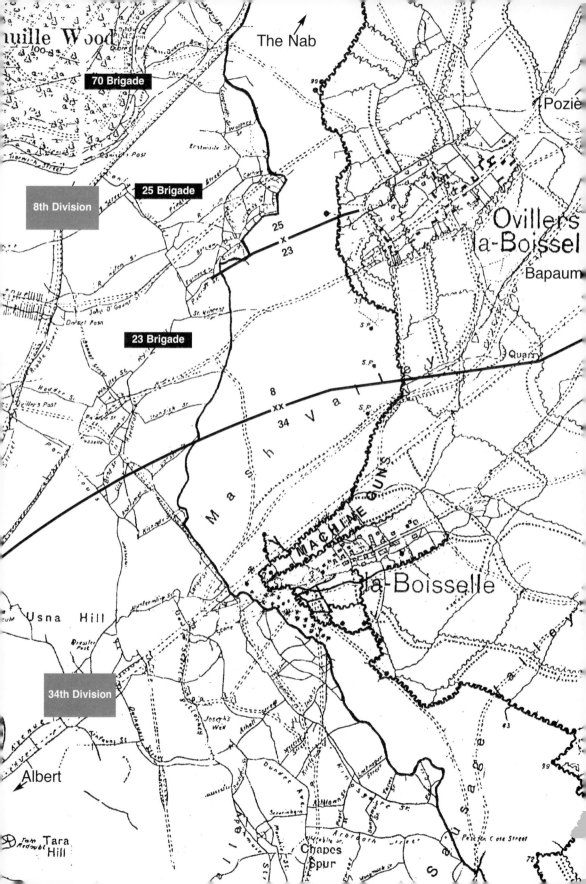

space in the centre of the section, no-man's land was everywhere exceptionally wide. Particularly was this the case on the right, where both our own and the German lines were somewhat recessed. Here the 23rd Infantry Brigade had before it an appalling stretch to negotiate before it gained contact with the enemy trenches. Furthermore, the advance of the right brigade [23 Brigade] lay up a valley [Mash Valley], dominated to the left by the higher ground of Ovillers and on the right even more dangerously threatened by the German Salient at la Boisselle. If all went not well elsewhere [i.e. the 34th Division], it was obvious that both from Ovillers and from la Boisselle spur a deadly flanking fire could be brought to bear on our troops as they struggled up that desolate valley towards their distant objective. ... The village of Ovillers was a solid and terrible obstacle. It will readily be appreciated that unless the results of the final intense bombardment covering the assault were such that the defence was for the time being completely out of action, and unless the progress made by troops on either flank was rapid and successful, the 8th Division was likely to find its task beyond the powers of human accomplishment.

8th Division's objective lay beyond the village of Pozières, some three miles distant. However, as far as the 8th Division were concerned, they had been impressed by the barrage, and 'hope ran high that the results would be so to pulverize the enemy's defences that a legitimate chance would be given to the infantry to press forward to success'.

The essentials of Brigadier General Tuson's plan for 23 Brigade, to attack with two of his four battalions, had been laid down by 8th Division. He decided 2/Devons and 2/Middlesex were to provide the leading assault waves, who were to break into the German front line trench system, fight through the southern portion of Ovillers and capture the enemy's two intermediate lines. At this point, the Brigade's reserve battalion, 2/Scottish Rifles and 2/West Yorkshire, following closely behind the leading battalions, were to take the second and third objectives, in the German Second Position and around the village of Pozières respectively.

2/Devons' commanding officer, Lieutenant Colonel Sunderland, had also been given comprehensive orders, and had little to do other than allocate his troops to the specific tasks given to him in his orders. He decided to attack with A and B Companies, who were to advance in columns of platoons (i.e. in four waves), at a distance of fifty paces apart. This formation, one of those recommended in Fourth Army Tactical Notes, was adopted because of the distance of the objectives behind the German front line. They were to be followed by C and D Companies. A part of each of these companies detailed as carrying parties, who would bring up defence stores, such as pickets, sandbags and ammunition, in order to consolidate trenches taken by the assaulting infantry. Also planned to move up behind the assault waves were sections of Vickers guns from 23 Brigade's Machine Gun Company, Royal Engineers and artillery observers. During the initial stages of the attack, Battalion Headquarters were to remain in the trenches at the junction of Rycroft Street and Farness Street, as instructed by Headquarters III Corps. This was so that they could report the progress of the attack, as the chain of command depended on field telephones. Once away from the cable head at the end of the deeply dug -in lines, they could only pass their reports by vulnerable runners or unreliable pigeons. However, commanders were confident that the infantry could reach their objectives without the intervention of Battalion Headquarters, as the well-schooled companies knew their part in the battle, having repeatedly practised the attack on the divisional training area. The Devons' Battalion Headquarters would cross No

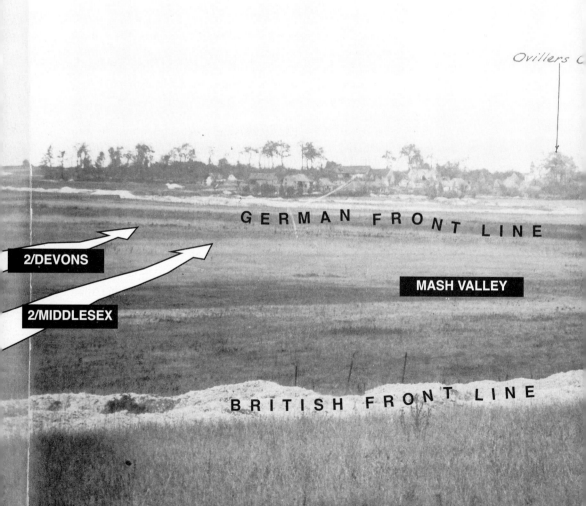

Man's Land during the consolidation phase, with signallers laying line as they went. In subsequent phases, Battalion Headquarters would follow a bound behind the forward troops, ready to command in what was accepted would be a more fluid battle.

Before the Attack

On 6 June, C and D Companies of 2/Devons had taken part in an important preliminary operation: digging New Trench. They went out into No Man's Land and deployed to cover a large working party, which dug a 'jumping-off trench' designed to reduce the width of No Man's Land. The first the Germans knew about the digging of the trench was in the morning, when they saw the heaps of chalk soil that formed the trench's parapet. The distance between the British and German lines had

A photograph taken from Usna Hill in late 1915 looking across Mash Valley to the Ovillers Spur.

2 Grands arbres jumeles
(now cut down)

Pozières →

been reduced from an average of almost 800 yards to 500 yards in the sector to be attacked by 2/Devons.

Another measure designed to reduce the danger presented by the 'appalling stretch of no man's land' was the digging of Russian saps. The Official History describes their construction and intended use.

> Three tunnels had been constructed on the III Corps front to provide covered communication across no man's land after the assault, ... [two of which] were in the 8th Division area, one north of la Boisselle and the other to a point opposite Ovillers. These tunnels were 8' 6" high and 3' 6" wide at the bottom and 2' 6" at the top. They had been dug through chalk at a depth of 12 to 14 feet, the last 150 feet being excavated with bayonets to prevent any sound of working reaching the enemy.

Once taken, the Russian saps would be connected to the German front line and would be used by follow-on troops to cross No Man's Land. By taking this subterranean route, they would avoid enemy barrage fire that was designed to isolate the British assault force while the Germans prepared to counter-attack and destroy them. Subsequently the shallow tunnel could be opened up and used as a communications trench.

On the eve of the attack, just as they were starting out for their assault positions, the Devons received General Sir Henry Rawlinson's less than inspiring message to the Fourth Army.

> In wishing all ranks good luck, the Army Commander desires to impress on all infantry units the supreme importance of helping one another and holding on tight to every yard of ground gained. The accurate and sustained fire of the artillery during the bombardment should greatly assist the task of the infantry.[2]

2/Devons duly occupied their assembly positions in New Trench, in front of the main defensive line. Moving up had been a slow business, as the men had to negotiate the frequent ninety-degree turns in the communication trenches, many carrying awkward loads. The process was further delayed by the drawing of additional ammunition and stores from dumps en route. However, as recorded by the regimental historian, 'They had been waiting in readiness for several hours before, at 06.25, a tremendous bombardment opened'.

As already recorded, a heavy artillery and mortar fire had opened for one hour twenty minutes, at various times every day, since the beginning of the bombardment. On 1 July, however, the shellfire was to be fifteen minutes shorter than normal, ending at 07.30 hours, in order to achieve some tactical surprise. At most points along the front, the British artillery barrage halted briefly, at 07.22 hours, while the artillerymen re-laid their guns from the enemy's frontline trenches and wire to engage depth targets including the German intermediate lines. Their fire on the enemy front line was to be taken over by the 2" and 3" trench mortars that fired an eight-minute hurricane bombardment. However, due to the

Formed from the infantry of the Brigade, including 2/Devons, a platoon of 23 Trench Mortar Battery pose with an unknown Devon officer and their 3-inch Stokes mortars.

width of No Man's Land facing 2/Devons, 23 Trench Mortar Company were out of range of the German lines. Therefore, a few field guns remained firing on the front line, but this was no replacement for the mind-numbing weight of mortar fire employed elsewhere.

Across No Man's Land, the enemy were waiting. A German officer from 180 Regiment wrote:

> *The intense bombardment was realized by all to be the prelude to an infantry assault sooner or later. The men in the dug-outs therefore waited ready, belts full of hand-grenades around them, gripping their rifles and listening for the bombardment to lift from the front defence zone on to the rear defences. It was of vital importance to lose not a second in taking up position in the open to face the British infantry, which would advance immediately behind the artillery barrage. Looking towards the British trenches through the long trench periscopes held up out of the dug-out entrances there could be seen a mass of steel helmets above the parapet showing that the storm troops were ready for the assault.[3]*

At 07.28 hours, just before the barrage lifted from the enemy front line, the 2/Devons, with the 2/Royal Berkshires (25 Brigade) on their left and

2/Middlesex on the right, climbed out of New Trench. Captain Andrews led the forward platoons of A and B Company across no man's land towards Ovillers. Even though the line ahead of them was being pounded by mortar fire, the divisional historian wrote that 'they were subjected to a searching fire from rifles and machine guns'. Meanwhile, C and D Companies moved forward to the now-vacated assembly trenches and prepared to follow in two waves at 50 yard intervals. The leading assault waves were little more than 100 yards from the enemy wire when the mortars lifted from the German trenches.

Zero-Hour

The German observer in 180 Regiment's lines continued his account:

At 7.30 A.M. the hurricane of shells ceased as suddenly as it begun. Our men at once clambered up the steep shafts leading from the dugouts to daylight and ran singly or in groups to the nearest shell craters. The machine guns were pulled out of dug-outs and hurriedly placed in position, their crews dragging the heavy ammunition boxes up the steps and out to the guns. A rough firing line was thus rapidly established. As soon as the men were in position, a series of extended lines were seen moving forward from the British trenches. The first line appeared to continue without

The entrance to a German dugout and surrounding barbed wire somewhere on the southern slopes of the Ovillers Spur.

German machine-gun team manning their Maxim on an improvised low sledge mount.

end right and left. It was quickly followed by a second line, then a
third and fourth. They came on at a steady easy pace as if
expecting to find nothing alive in our front trenches.

At Zero-Hour, the Devons' companies amidst the dust of the
bombardment 'got up and went forward in waves to the assault at the
pace laid down in Army Instructions to Infantry, '100 yards in 2
minutes'. Despite some reservations, commanders' confidence that the
barrage would destroy the German defences was generally accepted, and
most believed that they would simply advance and occupy the German
line. However, with the Germans having survived the bombardment, to
succeed, the Devons would have to have occupied the enemy line before
the defenders could get up from their deep dugouts and establish a
proper firing line. The Wurttembergers of 180 Regiment were waiting:

*A few moments later, when the leading British line was within a
hundred metres, the rattle of machine gun and rifle fire broke out
along the whole line of shell holes. Some fired kneeling so as to get
a better target over the broken ground, whilst others, in the
excitement of the moment, stood up regardless of their own safety,
to fire into the crowd of men in front of them. Red rockets sped up
into the air, as a signal to the artillery, and immediately afterwards
a mass of shells from our batteries in the rear tore through the air
and burst among the advancing lines.*

A and B Companies were caught in interlocking and overlapping arcs of
machine-gun fire from Ovillers to their left and from la Boisselle to their
right. According to the Devons' after-action report, Lieutenant Colonel
Sunderland could see very little of the action. 'At first and for some little
time owing to mist and dust caused by our shell fire, it was difficult to
realize what had happened ... The lines appeared at first sight to be
intact...' Catching a glimpse through the swirling clouds of morning mist
and lingering smoke and dust from the barrage, the Commanding

Officer, could just make out rows of his men lying down. He demanded 'Why aren't they advancing?' The Adjutant, Lieutenant Tillett, peered through his binoculars and turning to Lieutenant Colonel Sunderland he replied 'They're all hit, sir!' The battalion's report recorded 'The lines appeared at first sight to be intact, but it was soon made clear that the lines consisted of only dead or wounded'.

The survivors bunched as they made their way forward through the gaps in the enemy's wire. According to the Official Historian, 'the original wave formation soon ceased to exist, and the remains of companies became mixed together, making a mass of men, amongst which German fire played havoc'. The German eyewitness wrote:

> *All along the line, men could be seen throwing up their arms and collapsing, never to move again. Badly wounded rolled about in their agony, and others, less severely injured, crawled to the nearest shell hole for shelter. ... The extended lines, though badly shaken and with many gaps, now came on all the faster. Instead of a leisurely walk they covered the ground in short rushes at the double. Within moments the leading troops had advanced to*

German machine-gun crew.

within a stone's throw of our front trench, and whilst some of us continued to fire at point-blank, others threw hand grenades among them.

The Devons' report recorded that 'only a very few reached the German lines alive. Some of these managed to effect an entry into the German trenches, where they put up a determined fight against enormous odds and were soon killed'. The toehold that the Devons had gained could not be reinforced, as the curtain of fire that the German artillery put down in the middle of No Man's Land halted C and D Companies who were following up behind them. They too were driven to ground by the German machine gunners, who then switched their fire to the support battalion, 2/West Yorks, who moved forward at 08.25 hours. Meanwhile, the British barrage was still proceeding into the depths of the German position as planned, leaving the infantry without the assistance of suppressive fire. Consequently, the attack ground to a halt, and few of the supports, C and D Company 2/Devons along with A Company 2/West Yorks, ever reached the German line. However, it is thought that at least one mixed group of Devons and West Yorks may have 'reached the second trench, two hundred yards beyond' the front line.

Despite individual acts of heroism, determination and footholds gained in the enemy front line, by 09.00 hours, the attack of the 8th Division had failed along the length of its front. The extent of German success is indicated by the fact that two battalions of 180 Regiment held the entire 8th Division, and that they only had to call on part of one reserve company during the day. At 09.30 hours, Major General Hudson instructed commanders of 23 and 25 Brigades to gather their men and repeat the attack. He insisted until it was pointed out that a repeated bombardment would hit their men, some of whom were thought to be stranded in the enemy position.

Later in the Day

As late as 14.30 hours, observers' reported that 'bomb fighting' was going on in the German lines.[4] However, for those remaining out in No Man's Land, it was fortunate that the shell holes, which had earlier hindered the movement of advancing men, now provided cover from enemy fire. The Battalion report recorded that:

No accurate information could be ascertained as to the exact number of casualties the Battalion had suffered, although it was clear that there were very few left who had not been hit; the enemy began to snipe at our wounded. When it was quite clear that we were not holding the front line trenches, 2/Scottish Rifles were moved forward to the 'New Trench' and were told to hold themselves in readiness to advance.

Meanwhile, many lightly wounded Devons, such as Sergeant Major

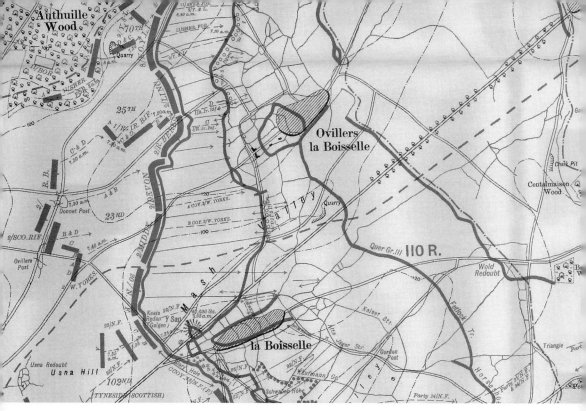

Brigade's attack on Ovillers Spur.

Bauer and three men, spent much of the morning sniping at the Germans from No Man's Land. In their case, 'they established themselves in a shell-hole seventy yards from the German lines and fired away till they had expended all their ammunition'. However, the German artillery played up and down No Man's Land seeking and killing already wounded men and presenting a wall of fire to a renewed attack.

The Devons' Medical Officer, in his Aid Post dugout in the reserve line, after the initial rush of walking wounded, had few casualties to deal with. The reason why is explained in the Battalion's after-action report:

> Our wounded still continued to crawl in to the New Trench but great difficulty was found evacuating the wounded to the Regimental Aid Post, as the trenches were too narrow to allow a stretcher to pass and also the trenches had been so knocked about that in many places one was exposed to hostile machine gun and shell fire.
>
> The Medical Officer went down to the New Trench and bandaged all the wounded, while the stretcher bearers and parties of regimental pioneers from Headquarters carried the wounded back to the Aid Post on their backs and in waterproof sheets. By this means all our wounded which it was possible to get at were removed to the First Aid Post where the MO redressed their wounds. The supply of [RAMC] orderlies for removing the

wounded from the Aid Post was not good. Several messages had to be sent asking for orderlies to be sent up to remove the wounded.

The sad fact is that many casualties succumbed to their wounds, who would have survived if evacuated promptly. Many, lay in degrees of agony until, eventually, the British barrage, which was running to the original fire plan, was brought back to the enemy front line. Under its cover, many men regained the British line, and more returned under the cover of darkness. The Germans, once all fighting and firing had died down, did little to hinder 8th Division's efforts to clear casualties from No Man's Land. The Battalion report recorded that 'During the day wounded and unwounded crawled-in, in small numbers. The unwounded were organized into parties by company. ... By this time [20.00 hours] about forty men not including Headquarters had been collected.' This figure of forty gives an indication, not only of the scale of casualties, but also of how effective enemy fire was in completely neutralizing the Battalion's combat effectiveness.

As the scale of the disaster became apparent, offensive operations were cancelled. The Devons' Commanding Officer wrote,

A Lewis gunner photographed in the Ovillers area.

About 4 p.m. all Adjutants were ordered to report at Brigade Headquarters. The Brigade Major started to dictate orders to the effect that the Scottish Rifles would take over the front line and the remainder of the other battalions of the Brigade would move into the support trenches. While taking down the orders, the 8th Division informed the Brigade that the whole Brigade would be relieved that night, and that orders for the relief would be issued. Adjutants then returned to their battalions and COs were ordered to re-organize their battalions.

Shortly afterwards the Devons learned that they were to be replaced in the line by 12th Eastern Division, called up from Fourth Army Reserve. The remains of the Battalion marched back to its familiar but now very empty billets in the village of Millencourt. During the night, the Medical Officer and Senior NCOs from each company remained in the front line to receive men coming in from No Mans Land or who were found by patrols. By dawn, most of the wounded who were to return had done so, but the last badly wounded Devon was not brought in for almost three days after the attack. So badly shattered was the 8th Division's infantry when they were relieved during the night of 1-2 July that they left the Somme the following day to join the First Army, whose front was quiet.

The casualty figures that were eventually compiled show the one-sided nature of the battle, which to all serious intents and purposes was

The ruins of Ovillers; only the remains of hedges and piles of rubble.

over within forty minutes of 'Zero'. 'The 8th Division suffered 5,121 casualties, the 180th Regiment only 280 – a proportion of eighteen to one in favour of the German defenders.'[5] 2/Devons eventually assembled about 300 officers and men. Eleven officers and 221 men were killed or missing and 194 men were wounded; in all, 431 casualties out of an attacking strength of approximately 800 men in action. The proportion of the casualties who were killed is unusually high, and is a reflection of the fact that, unable to be recovered from No Man's Land, a high proportion died of their wounds.

Analysis

What went wrong? The Regular Army soldiers of 23 Brigade lost no time in analyzing the day's events. With the Battalion safely out of the trenches, 'the CO and Adjutant then proceeded to Brigade Headquarters where a conference was held by the GOC 23rd Infantry Brigade, on the operations and the best methods of overcoming the difficulties which had been met.' All agreed that there had been an overestimation of the fire effect of the British Artillery, on deep dugouts and wire in particular, and on the German defensive system as a whole. Following on from this misappreciation was the decision to send over men who were to advance at a steady pace with 'Ported Arms'. This allowed the virtually unscathed Germans to man their wrecked trenches above their dugouts and shoot down the lines of advancing British infantry. Thirdly, the Artillery had yet to learn the technique of controlling a creeping barrage. In July 1916, the artillery operated in a series of timed lifts, which unless the attack went to schedule, left the infantry without support when most needed. 23 Infantry Brigade's post-action report stated:

> A bombardment on some given line may be of value in damaging the enemy's defences and preventing supports from being sent up; but if the line in question is 1,000 yards behind the line from which our assaulting troops are being held up, as was the case on July 1st, the position is very far from satisfactory. To prevent reinforcements from reaching the enemy is but of minor value if we are ourselves unable to maintain our hold on the enemy's front line. I consider ... that no barrage should lift until the infantry concerned have notified that they are ready.[6]

Another factor was that success by the 8th Division was dependant on the equal success of 34th Division's attack immediate right of the 8th, across Mash Valley, on la Boisselle. The German machine guns had not been destroyed, and the devastating enfilade fire on the Devons' flank made maximum use of the weapons' characteristics.

A further reason for the attack's failure became clear when the British eventually took Ovillers: they found a translation of a British operation order. Even if deception and concealment of the preparations for the offensive had been of a higher standard, German intelligence had already made such attempts pointless. A breach in field security had delivered into the hands of enemy commanders the complete British plan! In addition, the Germans were able to confirm the time of the attack, as they had tapped the British wires in the area of la Boisselle and had taken down Haig's message to the troops, which had been passed by a New Army brigade major over the field telephone, in contravention of instructions. Once again the lessons of concealment, deception and field security were relearnt at a tragic cost.

The 1 July 1916 was a tragic day for 2/Devons. The casualties they suffered on this occasion were only surpassed at Bois des Butts, during the Second Battle of the Aisne, two years later. The first day of the Somme was, for the 2/Devons, a mind-numbing disaster, with nothing to show for their casualties.

Epilogue

Over the following days Ovillers, though no longer on the main Fourth Army axis of advance, saw further fighting. 12th Eastern Division took over the line at Ovillers at 05.40 hours on the morning of 2 July. However, there was to be no immediate renewal of the attack, but the remains of the village were comprehensively bombarded, while across Mash Valley, 34th Division continued their attack on la Boisselle.

Field Marshal Haig's message to the troops on the eve of the attack had been picked up by the Germans.

12th Eastern Division attacked Ovillers before dawn on 3 July. They gained the enemy front line, now lightly held but the Germans concentrating in the second-line shelters counter-attacked and drove them back from all but a few short stretches of their line. The British had again suffered from German machine-gun fire from the hillside behind la Boisselle. With the Germans eventually pushed back from la Boisselle, the attack on Ovillers was resumed on 7 July. This time, despite heavy casualties, 12th Division did gain a part of Ovillers and fought through the village over the coming days.

During this period, the depleted 1/Dorsets, whose operations on 1 July 1916 will be covered in the following chapter, returned to the front line, organized as two companies, to hold trenches just to the north-west of Ovillers. The Dorsets' historian wrote:

> *Refreshed by their short respite, the Battalion relieved the 9th Essex (12th Division) in the western part of Ovillers on the 8th. Ovillers, and the front-line system of trenches round it, had been so pounded by the bombardment that it was impossible to indicate the actual line held by our troops; no land marks remained. At best the position held was no more than a shallow foothold. The troops*

*occupied a series of shell holes linked up by a shallow trench. The
weather was bad; incessant showers of rain hampered all work and
movement.*

As soon as the Dorsets had arrived, the Germans, who were at close
proximity, started an exchange of bombs, and the Dorsets suffered four
casualties, the first of many while simply holding the line during full
battle. Meanwhile, in response to one of the problems identified on Z-
Day, Captain Fenton's company were employed in support of 12th
Division's attack, carrying and evacuating the wounded. This was yet
another task for the infantry until the RAMC could be expanded. After
'a few shell holes were won' 1/Dorsets were relieved of their unenviable
position, during the night, by 16/Lancashire Fusiliers.

Fighting continued in Ovillers, which was now garrisoned by soldiers
of the 3rd Prussian Guard, the remainder of whom eventually
surrendered the ruins to the 48th Division on 17 July.

An officer moving up to the new front line beyond Ovillers in mid-
July took a route up Mash Valley and across the line of 2/Devons'
advance.

Presently I saw a likely trench across the valley, and having no

British infantry occupying a captured German trench at Ovillers.

news of Bickersteth, decided to risk it. I went on in front of the party to pick the way. There was mud in the bottom, though the sides were white chalk and a few corpses at that repulsive stage when skin turns slimy black, so I followed the example of the men, climbing out and following the parapet.

It was then, turning back, that I knew what novelists mean by a 'stricken field'. The western and southern slopes of the village had been comparatively little shelled; that is, a little grass still had room to grow between the shell holes. The village was guarded by tangle after tangle of rusty barbed wire in irregular lines. Among the wire lay rows of khaki figures, as they had fallen to the machine guns on the crest, thick as the sleepers in Green Park on a summer Sunday evening. The simile leapt to my mind at once of flies on a paper. I did not know

Scene of operations to the west of Ovillers.

then that twice in the fortnight before our flank attack, had a division been hurled at that wire-encircled hill, and twice it had withered away before the hidden machine-guns. The flies were buzzing obscenely over the damp earth; morbid scarlet poppies grew scantily along the white chalk mounds; the air was tainted with rank explosives and the sickly stench of corruption.[7]

1 *The Eighth Division in War 1914 - 1918*, Boraston and Cyril, The Medici Society Ltd, 1926.
2 The Devonshire Regiment 1914 - 1918.
3 Quoted from Schwaben in the *British Official History*.
4 *Official History*.
5 *The First Day on the Somme, 1 July 1916* by Martin Middlebrook. Republished by Pen & Sword Books, 2002.
6 Public Record Office WO 95/1579.
7 Charles Edmund Carrington *A Subaltern's War*, published under a pseudonym Charles Edmunds by Peter Davies Ltd., 1928.

Chapter 6

1/Dorsets' Attack on Leipzig Redoubt

Dramatic value can hardly be found in the annihilation of the flower of an English county by a death which came whining and screaming through the trees, dealt by an enemy whom no one could see.

Lieutenant Douie *The Weary Road*

At dawn on 1 July 1916, another West Country Battalion was preparing for battle a mile to the north of Ovillers. The officers and men of 1/Dorsets, having been amongst the first arrivals on the Somme, were familiar with the enemy positions on the Thiepval/Pozières Ridge. Having raided the enemy line and themselves been raided, they were under no illusion as to the enemy's determination and the strength of his positions.

The German Positions
The Wurttembergers of the German 26th Reserve Division, who had checked 2/Devons at Ovillers, were also holding this section of line as far north as Beaumont Hamel, having been in position on the naturally

German infantry posing in a front line trench. The box set in the sandbags on the right is a grenade store.

strong Thiepval Heights since 1914. However, impetus to improve defensive positions had been given by the arrival in 99 Regiment of Major von Fabeck, in the spring of 1916. Across the divisional front, dugouts were deepened and strengthened, while further back deep underground complexes were built in which the German reserves were to shelter. The resulting network of trenches and strongpoints presented a formidable challenge to the British attackers.

Dominating the area where the West Countrymen of 1/Dorsets were to attack was the Leipzig Salient. This was a particularly strong defensive redoubt[1], built around a small chalk quarry and held by 3rd Company, I/Battalion 180 Regiment. Here, the German line changed direction from approximately north – south to an east – west alignment and was the enemy's vital ground in the area north of the Albert – Bapaume Road. It was defended by 'numerous machine guns that completely commanded no-man's-land to the south and west'. From the salient, the Germans also had a panoramic view deep into the British rear area. Its capture would not only deny enemy artillery observers a valuable position, but would also give the British X Corps a vital foothold on the Thiepval Spur.

The German front line in this sector was formidable, with deep and well-built trenches, thick belts of wire, and supporting machine guns in protected and camouflaged positions. In addition, the enemy's forward defences were complemented by a network of positions that gave strength in depth, such as the *Wundtwerk*. Named after its designer, Oberst Wundt, this redoubt, known to the British as the 'Wonder Work', was on the surface a self-contained network of trenches, surrounded by wire, while below ground, dugouts deep in the chalk provided shelter from British artillery fire.

32 Division's plan and the main German positions.

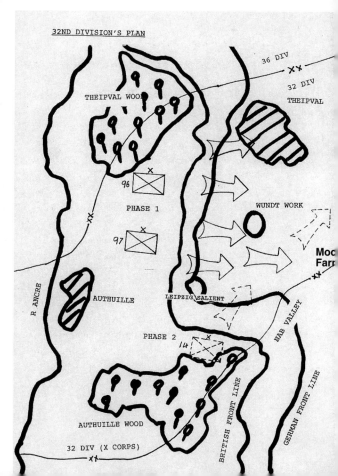

British Plans

X Corp's plan was to assault with two divisions. The 36th (Ulster) Division, on the left, was to attack astride the River

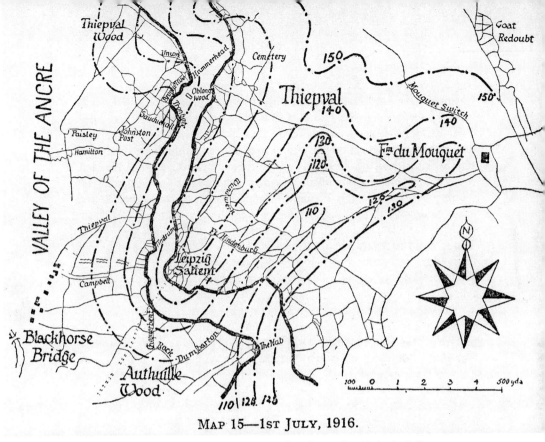

MAP 15—1ST JULY, 1916.

A map from the Dorsets' Regimental History showing the Thiepval to Leipzig Salient area.

Ancre to the north of the village of Thiepval. Meanwhile, 32nd (New Army) Division was to make its initial attack on the Corp's right between Thiepval Village and Leipzig Salient. The 49th (West Riding) Division, were X Corps Reserve, positioned in Aveluy Wood, immediately to the west of the Ancre. (see map on page 93)

Major General Rycroft's plan for 32nd Division was to attack 1,850 yards of the north/south running line between Thiepval and Leipzig Salient with 96 and 97 Infantry Brigades. 96 Brigade to the north or left, was to attack the fortified village of Thiepval and the 'Wonder Work'. 97 Brigade, on the right, were also to attack the enemy line as far south as the tip of the Leipzig Salient. The first assault wave of four battalions were to clear the enemy's front, support and reserve trenches to a depth of about 700 to 800 yards (First Objective). Their support and reserve battalions were then to expand their lodgement to a depth of 2,500 yards (Second Objective). When orders were finally issued to 1/Dorsets on 22 June 1916, they found that 14 Brigade was 32nd Division's reserve, earmarked to advance through the southern face of the Leipzig Salient, from Authuille Wood. In the second phase of the attack, 14 Brigade was to pass through 97 Brigade and 'mop-up' the remaining defenders east of Leipzig Salient and then advance in a north-easterly direction to take Mouquet Farm. This was a headquarters location[2] and

91

strongpoint in the German second line, some 3,500 yards behind the German front line. The Division's third and final objective for the day were the German trenches some 500 to 800 yards further on, including Goat Redoubt, which, optimistically, was to be secured by 10.10 hours, just two hours forty minutes after Zero-Hour. At this point, X Corp's plan was for the 49th Division to pass through the 32nd and complete the breakthrough[3] by advancing towards the village of Courcelette. This would open the way for General Gough's Reserve Army and cavalry who would roll up the German line in a northerly direction.

The Eve of the Attack

In the days preceding the great assault, 1/Dorsets were out of the line at the village of Senlis four miles behind the battle area. Their stay in this village was longer than anticipated, as the attack was delayed by two days on the evening of 27 June. Keeping the men occupied for the extra days involved inter-company competitions such as tent pitching, with marks being awarded for speed and correct and effective pitching; C Company won the prize of fifty francs.

The Dorsets eventually left Senlis for the front on 30 June at 20.20 hours, having, according to Company Sergeant Major Shephard, struck camp at 19.00 hours and paraded for a short address by the Commanding Officer, Major Shute. He 'asked us to particularly avenge Captain Algeo and Lieutenant Mansell-Pleydell. He said he firmly believed they were murdered by the Huns. "No prisoners for the Dorsets".' Leaving the village, 'hundreds of troops turned out to cheer us on our way, on through Senlis...' and on to roads crowded with men and transport. On reaching Aveluy Wood[4], they halted near a 12-inch gun. Shephard commented that 'a most terrible gunfire going on, gun flashes quite blinding and noise deafening'.

After passing through the wood, crossing the Ancre by Blackhorse Bridge was the next challenge for the Dorsets. Lieutenant Douie described it as only suitable for men and mules. It was, however, being used as a principal crossing for all the transport of a division about to enter battle. The Blackhorse Dugouts, in the steep bank above Brooker's Pass and the river, were inadequate for the number of troops trying to use them. Consequently, most of the men had to sleep in the open. The men had little sleep as they were subjected to shelling for most of the night. Sergeant Major Shephard described the scene:

> Going over the bridge we had very near escapes from heavy shells close by. We arrived at dugouts at 1 a.m.[5]
>
> Saturday 1st July 1916.
>
> Place nearly all crammed, only 4 dug-outs for the Company. 2/3 of us slept outside, enemy sending over heavy shells and shrapnel all around us. A heavy shell caught a store containing flares, etc; a big fire caught some petrol and Bangalore Torpedoes[6]. Some

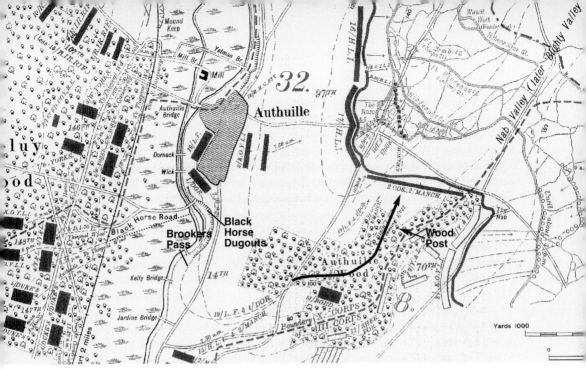

An extract from the Official History (with annotations) including details of the Dorsets' moves. However, it contains one of the rare errors in this series of maps, which is corrected by the arrow.

KOYLI [King's Own Yorkshire Light Infantry] *were there, 10 were killed by the shell and 2 burnt to death. Fire continued until dawn. I got no sleep. It was bitterly cold. Had a limited walk round at 4 a.m., roused troops as all breakfast to be finished by 6.30... At 6.30 a.m. our artillery were bombarding intensely, a most awful din.*

Lieutenant Douie recalled the Dorsets' last moments in Brookers Pass:

Under the bank the regiment paraded on the fateful morning of July 1, when the thunder of our barrage was such that orders could not be heard.

Zero-Hour – Z-Day

The Dorsets were preparing to lead 14 Brigade's left column in its march to the front, while 96 and 97 Brigades left their trenches to assault the German line between Thiepval and Leipzig Redoubt. Sergeant Major Shephard, as CSM of B Company, was at the very rear of the Battalion column:

At 7.30 a.m. we moved to the attack by companies at 200 yds intervals[7] in order C, D, A, B. We took the track in rear of the batteries by Brooker's Pass, turned left on and over the road, into Authuille Wood and followed the Dumbarton Track ... enemy sending heavy shrapnel all over the place searching for us ...We had a number of casualties there, and passed by a number of killed and

93

wounded from our leading companies. We had a terrible dose of machine-gun fire sweeping through the wood, could not understand why.

97 Brigade's attack on Leipzig Salient got off to a good start. This was largely a result of Brigadier Jardine's insistence that 15 and 17/Highland Light Infantry (HLI) were to be through the German wire and within thirty yards of the shells falling on the enemy trenches at Zero-Hour. This insistence was based on his experience as a liaison officer with the Japanese during the Manchurian War, where he had seen this tactic being used to good effect. It worked very well, and the Highlanders were on the Germans before they could emerge from their dugouts. Having successfully established a foothold in the redoubt, the HLI advanced across the open slope to their next objective, the Hindenberg *Strasse*, 150 yards beyond. However, the enemy had survived the bombardment in their dugout, and Brigadier Jardine had no answer to the concentrated 'machine guns in the "Wonder Work", which caused such heavy casualties that the attackers were compelled to halt'. In addition to the German machine guns in the *Wundtwerk*, those positioned in the *Nordwerk* crowning the Ovillers Spur, which 8th Division were unsuccessfully attempting to capture, had also survived the bombardment. These guns were now raking Authuille Wood with their fire. The machine gunners could not see 14 Brigade moving up through the wood but knew that they would be interdicting the second echelon of the British attack.

Fifty yards inside the northern edge of Authuille Wood, there is a deep, wide depression barring the way, which Lieutenant Douie described seeing during his recce.

I came to a bridge over a defile which our plan of attack required us to cross, and examined it with interest. Its span was less than ten yards. A few days later the bridge, marked with unerring accuracy by the German machine gunners, was heaped with our dead and wounded so as to be almost impassable; a platoon forty-eight strong on one side emerged with a strength of twelve.

Reports of how long the Dorsets had to wait in the wood under machine gun and artillery fire varied from fifteen minutes to two hours. Again, this disparity results from the fact that Sergeant Major Shephard was at the rear of the Battalion's column and would have had to await the move of the remainder of the Battalion. His account continues:

Had to wait nearly 2 hours on the track waiting for the brigade ahead of us to get forward, most infernal noise all the time, had a rough time from enemy artillery. Finally, we got to Wood Post. This lies on the forward edge of the wood, a lot of killed and wounded there. Here we had to wait again. I went forward to see what was happening.

The significance of Dumbarton Track's exit from the wood was appreciated by the enemy and was consequently also marked for special attention.

1/Dorsets in the Attack

At 08.45 hours, the Dorsets advanced from Wood Post in a dispersed 'artillery formation,' but as they emerged from the cover of the trees, the leading platoons were shot down by the *Nordwerk* machine guns. Company Sergeant Major Hodge of C Company recalled:

> *The first Sections to go were met by a hail of bullets, and so well was the fire directed that many casualties occurred. Sections following met the same fate. This was rather discouraging, as we had not reached our own line, let alone the enemy's! Suddenly we heard someone playing a flute, and then we heard the strains of our Regimental March-past. Drum Major Kerr had gone forward with the sections, and while others were gaining ground by short rushes he was calmly walking in the open, playing the troops onwards. He continued to play well-known tunes, until his left arm was shattered by a bullet.*

The advance of the following companies was halted, and patrols were sent out to right and left to locate alternate exits. The northern edge of Authuille Wood, however, formed an important part of the British defences and was heavily wired along its entire length. No other viable exits could be found and using an exit further away would have involved crossing boundaries, which required authority. This, in view of the detailed movement plans and the need to keep up with the timetable dictated by the artillery fire plan, would not have been given. The Dorsets, therefore, had no choice but to cross 120 yards of machine-gun and artillery fire swept ground to the British front line. The German recorded that the essence of their success was 'the wonderful effect of

Infantry in No Man's Land taking cover from enemy fire. In such circumstances, keeping men moving forward is the single greatest leadership challenge for NCOs and young and inexperienced officers.

the machine guns, which, without exception, thanks to the well-built machine-gun emplacements, were all able to go into action when the attack began'.

Sergeant Major Shephard goes on to describe his crossing of the gap between the wood and the British front line:

I saw the last platoon of A Company going over the open ground in front of the wood to our original front line trench, a distance of about 120 yds. Half of this platoon were killed and almost all of the remainder wounded in the crossing and I at once realised that some part of the attack had gone radically wrong, as we were being enfiladed by batteries of enemy machine guns from the ridge to our right front held by the enemy [the Nordwerk].

I saw the Adjutant at this moment, and sent a signal to our leading [B Company] platoon to advance. We were told to cross as quickly as possible. I went on ahead, Gray the Company Orderly behind, and No 5 Platoon behind him. How I got over I can not imagine, the bullets were cracking and whizzing all round me. I got bullet holes through my clothing and equipment in several places and was hit in the left side. The ground was covered with our dead and wounded men. When nearly over I dropped into a shell hole for breath and to see how the platoon was getting on. Gray was shot dead alongside me, and very few of No 5 Platoon were left. I pulled two wounded men of A Coy into the shell hole for cover and then went on again, and got to a communicating trench. This I could not get into, as it was simply crammed with troops from all units in utter confusion, some badly wounded and others dead. I pushed on half left and got into our fire trench, which was almost level from shellfire in places. From here I directed my Company behind to cross further to the left where the fire was not so hot, never the less they grew very thin in the crossing.

The Regimental History summarized the situation: 'Half of the total casualties of the day occurred while passing this narrow stretch of open country to the front line'. The Dorsets found the British trenches occupied by 150 other ranks and no officers from 11/(Lonsdale Battalion) The Border Regiment. Lieutenant Butcher wrote in the Battalion war diary that the 'numbers of killed and wounded added to the congestion, and lateral movement was practically impossible, except over the top, until we managed to organize matters, and move the men further to the right'. Despite the confusion in the trenches, '... the object of the battle was not lost sight of and six officers, followed by about sixty men [led by Captain Lancaster], went forward at once, across the shell storm in No Man's Land, to the enemy line'. Shephard continued his personal diary account:

I joined my Company Officer (2/Lt Webb) and tried to find out from men of other units what the situation was. These were chiefly

*men of the Battalions of 97th Bde ... most could only say they were
the only survivors of their Bn, but we got news that some of our
own Bn had gone on to the enemy trenches, but no one knew
exactly what portion of enemy trench or trenches were in our
possession. There were NCOs and men from C, D and A Coy in
with us. We gave orders for these to get ready to push on to the
enemy line, meanwhile 2/Lt Mainhood came up and I got No 6
and 7 platoons together and they went over.*

However, Major Shute, who had just arrived in the front line, stopped
Sergeant Major Shephard from taking the survivors of his last two
platoons across to the captured trenches. He realized that, while the
commander wished the Dorsets to advance through the salient, the
situation had changed radically. Major Shute, therefore, held back the
last two platoons of B Company, having deduced that he should hold
the, British line, now undefended, until he could gain more information.
Having only been at the front for a matter of minutes, while standing up
to direct the reorganization of Borders, Dorsets and the leading elements
of the Lancashire Fusiliers, Major Shute was wounded. Lieutenant
Butcher, who had come forward with his Commanding Officer, now
took command of the situation in the front line.

Leipzig Salient

Meanwhile, across No Man's Land, of the six officers and about sixty
Dorset's soldiers who set out from the British lines, only one officer and
about twenty-five men reached the German trenches. They immediately
joined a few Pals from 11/Borders and the remnants of 17/HLI (The
Glasgow Commercials), who had taken Leipzig Redoubt. It was during
this period of fighting that Sergeant Turnbull, with a group of soldiers
from 17/HLI, earned his Victoria Cross by single-handedly keeping
severe German counter-attackers at bay with bombs 'thrown by his fine
cricketer's arm'. He held the Germans until the Dorsets arrived, but was
killed by a sniper in a lull in the battle. On arriving in the German
trench, the Dorsets began expanding the lodgement to the right by
bombing the enemy out of each individual traverse of their trenches. The
German historian wrote that 'The 3rd Company, 180th Regiment, was
practically exterminated in hand-to-hand fighting' in Leipzig Redoubt.
Sergeant Major Shephard recorded in his diary an account of the
Dorsets' action in the enemy position, as recounted to him by survivors:

*This party was commanded by Capt Lancaster. He got wounded
but held on and our men did very good work there. They bombed
and captured a very large portion of enemy second line, and
completed the capture of enemy 1st and 2nd line up to the
Hindenburg Fort on the right and Leipzig Redoubt on the left.
Very strong position held them up. We lost a lot of men there, but
we have satisfaction over them as they killed a large number of the*

enemy. The enemy troops against us were the Prussian Guards ...
they only came there two days ago and lost heavily[8]. Enemy
trenches choked with their own dead.

They say enemy trenches are very substantial and wanting
nothing. Good dugouts fitted luxuriously with electric lights,
boarded and even wallpapered, plenty of good food, cigars, wines,
in fact everything required.

During the afternoon, 14 Brigade joined the attack from Leipzig
Redoubt, having sent 2/Manchesters across No Man's Land via Russian
saps, taking with them plenty of ammunition. They reinforced the mixed
battalions fighting in Leipzig Redoubt and could be seen bombing
forward. However, with the enemy trenches strongly held and shrapnel
balls beating down on them from 'a continuous roar of exploding air
burst shells over Leipzig Redoubt', their attack lost momentum.

The Leipzig Redoubt was the only piece of enemy territory held by
the 32nd Division at the end of the day. The Russian saps continued to
prove their worth, with one being opened up as an instant
communication trench and the other retained as a tunnel providing a
secure covered route for messengers and limited resupply.

Other small lodgements were gained between the Leipzig Redoubt
and the Nab by small groups of Dorsets. Such lightly held toeholds
succumbed to German counter-attacks during the afternoon. Of the men
who crossed No Man's Land into Leipzig Salient, few returned; some
were wounded and taken prisoner; most, however, were killed. It was a
very small party of survivors who returned from Leipzig Redoubt to
rejoin the battalion that night.

Holding the Line

Since mid-morning, the 1/Dorsets had been split in two groups,
separated by the 'shell storm in No Man's Land'. Back in the British
front line, B Company's two platoons were mixed with the remnants of
the Lonsdales. Brigade Headquarters eased the confusion by sending a
message ordering 19/Lancashire Fusiliers back to Authuille Wood and
confirmed Major Shute's decision for the Dorsets to consolidate where
they were. Lieutenant Butcher and his small group of Dorsets held the
old front line along with men from 11/Border who had lost all their
officers.

Lieutenant Butcher's entry in the war diary summarized the action
over the next few hours:

Arrangements were made for a concerted attack upon the
German position at a given signal, a patrol was sent out to
ascertain exactly which trenches were held. Also as our own guns
were still firing on the German trench it was necessary to wait till
this barrage had lifted before we advanced.[9] Before this plan could
be carried out the officer commanding the Right column decided to

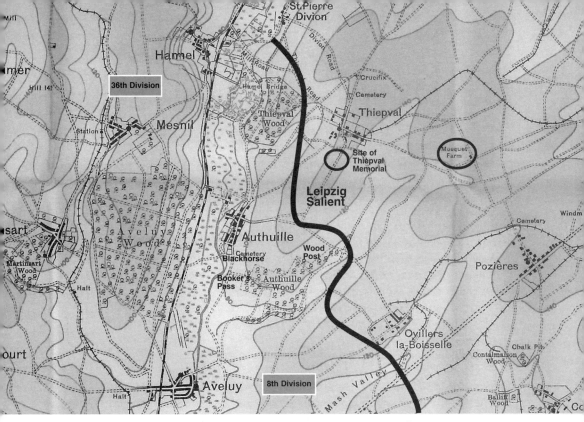

A section of the layered topographical map showing the Dorsets' area of operations.

> *withdraw the 19th Lancashire Fusiliers and the 11th Border Regt from our front line trench, leaving the 1st Dorsets to hold the line. At that time we had in addition to the Adjutant – three 2/Lieutenants and eighty-five other ranks in the trench*[10]. *Soon after 1p.m. these men were sorted out into companies, a commander allocated to each company, sentries were posted and the two remaining Lewis guns in action, and we became a definitely organized unit.'*

The Battalion had the entire front line to occupy from the Nab to Chowbent Street, almost opposite the tip of the Leipzig Redoubt. The Dorsets were apparently not in touch with flanking units and therefore extremely vulnerable to counter-attack. The Germans, however, had no intention of leaving the positions that had served them well, and limited themselves to counter-attacking lodgements in their line. Sergeant Major Shephard described the measures taken to hold the line:

> *I took charge of trench from Chequerbent St to the left of 'The Nab'. CSM Stehr took from my left to Chowbent St. CSM Pedder of C Coy had been killed and CSM Mills slightly wounded in leg. My wound was not very deep. I stuck a bandage on and managed to keep going.*
>
> *A lot of casualties in my trench. The enemy are enfilading us*

with heavy shells, dropping straight on us. A complete trench mortar battery of men killed by one shell, scores of dead and badly wounded in trench. Every move we make brings intense fire, as trenches so badly battered the enemy can see all our movements. Lot of wounded in front we got in, several were hit again and killed in trench. We put as many wounded as possible in best spots in trench and I sent a lot down, but I had so many of my own men killed and wounded that after a time I could not do this. Sent urgent message to Brigade asking for RAMC bearers to be sent to evacuate wounded, but none came, although Brigade said they had been despatched. Meanwhile, the enemy deliberately shelled the wounded between the trenches with shrapnel, thus killing or wounding again most of them. Our own Regimental stretcher bearers worked like niggers to take cases away.

We were told to hold on tight. We needed to; literally, we were blown from place to place. Men very badly shaken. As far as possible we cleared trenches of debris and dead. These we piled in heaps, enemy shells pitching on them made matters worse.

Counted all Dorsets at 1 p.m. Total 53 all ranks.

During the afternoon, the Adjutant estimated that sixty more men joined the Battalion who had been detached on duties or become detached from their platoons during the advance. Their arrival, however, only temporarily boosted the Battalion's strength in the face of the continuing enemy bombardment and the resulting casualties. At 17.00 hours, Major Thwaytes came up to join the Battalion from the Left Out of Battle[11] details and found that the Dorsets had suffered a further thirty casualties. Shephard wrote: 'Wounded suffering agonies. I got them water from bottles of the dead; a few managed to crawl away to the Aid Post in the Wood. At dusk we got more wounded in from the front.'

Word from Brigade Headquarters reached Major Thwaytes shortly after his arrival that the Dorsets were to be relieved by 15/HLI. This Battalion was stopped from advancing while still well back in Authuille Wood and had consequently suffered few casualties. Sergeant Major Shephard recorded that:

The HLI arrived at midnight. I handed care of wounded to them, and took remnants of B and C Coys, only ten NCOs and men, back via Mounteagle and Rock St, through Wood Post and over the same track (Dumbarton through Blighty Wood), down to Crucifix Corner. Arrived there at 1a.m. on

Sunday 2nd July.

Had a halt there, then on as ordered, to Authuille defences in Kintyre St. Got to top of hill, when we met a messenger, orders to go to Blackhorse dugouts for night, arrived there at 2 a.m. No dugouts available, place crammed with troops of another

ergeant Major
rnest Shephard.
pre-war
egular soldier
rom Lyme Regis.

division[12]. Very cold had some sleep for an hour. Terrible bombardment going on all the time. ... A number of our men came in at 4 a.m., some had been mixed up with other units, others had to lie in shell holes unable to budge owing to machine gun fire, some from various jobs ... and a number from the enemy trenches on relief by 15th HLI.

During the following day, more men rejoined the Battalion from No Man's Land, from other units and from the Left Out of Battle (excluding the transport details). This boosted the Battalion's strength to six officers and 317 other ranks. The casualties suffered by the Battalion have been variously quoted as between 450 and 490 other ranks and twenty officers. At least half of this number were hit in the desperate dash from the defile in the Wood to their own front-line trench. Shephard commented that 'Had we lost so many in actual grip with the enemy, we should have felt more satisfaction'. He went on to note his opinion of a commander who had ordered the attack to continue after it had patently failed, 'if our General did know and yet decided that we should carry on, he is not fit for his job'.

The assault by 32nd Division had indeed failed. It is worth noting that both the 8th Division (2/Devons) and 32nd Division grumble in their respective accounts that the failure of their attack was due largely to machine-gun fire from across their respective divisional boundaries.

The Second Day

Despite heavy casualties, the battle was not over for the Dorsets. After a brief rest in the Blackhorse dugouts at Brookers Pass, the Battalion was assembled at 07.30 hours on 2 July, in Kintyre Trench north-east of Authuille. Sergeant Major Shephard wrote: 'On arrival there we had a roll call of the Bn. After all were in, I mustered ninety all ranks, out of two hundred B Company soldiers who went into action. I lost 111 all ranks ... all my platoon sergeants and three platoon officers'. From here, the Dorsets moved up to the front line and spent most of the day carrying forward bombs, other natures of ammunition and all sorts of trench stores to the hard-pressed 15/HLI.

After a hard day's labour, the majority of the Battalion were just settling down in the reserve trenches above Authuille 'for a decent sleep at 8.30 p.m.'; the previous two nights rest had been short and largely sleepless. However, despite rumours that the Division was to be relieved, there was to be no immediate rest for the exhausted Dorsets, as orders arrived. According to Shephard, Company Sergeant Majors,

... were sent for and told to be ready to move in 1 hour for trenches to relieve 17th HLI. I sent a sergeant to take over our portion of trench. Our Bn is to hold our original front line from Chequerbent Street to Tindrum Street as support to 2nd Manchester in the enemy trench in front between the Leipzig and

Hindenburg Forts. The 15th HLI are relieving Manchesters at
3a.m. and are to make an attack to capture the forts. We act as
supports to them with 19th Lancs and Manchesters in reserve.
Stood by for orders which came at 1.30 a.m.

With the arrival of orders, the weary West Countrymen again went into
the routine of briefings and battle preparations for the third day of the
battle.

3 July 1916

Following the failure of the attacks north of the Albert/Bapaume Road,
Fourth Army was to concentrate its efforts south of the road.
Meanwhile, General Gough, who had taken over command north of the
road, had an overarching mission, which was to prevent the Germans
from being able to concentrate their reserves against the Fourth Army.
Gough recorded his operational instructions which Sir Douglas Haig
gave him verbally:

The Reserve Army would not carry out any grand operations,
but that we were to make every effort to progress by 'Sapping' as
he termed it, on the left of the Fourth Army and gradually enlarge
the breach in the enemy's front.

14 Brigade's attack on 3 July was the first part of this plan. The
immediate tactical aim of the attack was, as Sergeant Major Shephard
wrote, to capture the *Wundtwerk* and the Hindenburg Redoubt, which
would improve the British position by taking them up on to the Thiepval
Spur. This, as fully intended, was an aim that the Germans were bound
to react to.

Shephard describes a chaotic move forward, which exemplifies how,
in war, even the simple becomes difficult:

We moved up via Campbell Av and got blocked there by a
company of Cheshires[13] with 'wind up'. Hell's own bombardment
going on by our artillery preparatory to the attack, and enemy
retaliating heavily all round us. Got clear of Cheshires and cut
across the new MG Trench. Here we found half of our men had got
cut off by Cheshires and lost touch. Waited an hour trying to
connect up, nothing doing so I sent on what we had and went back
to find others. I found nine of them and they said the remainder
were sure of the way on, so I decided to get the nine up. Got to
Oban Av and up to the front trench expecting to find others there.
Most terrible fire from enemy on the trench from howitzer shells
dropping dead in trench, also the enemy were using gas shells,
which almost stifled us. Evidently by intense shelling from enemy,
they have news of our attack and shelling this trench to prevent
troops from getting up. Shells dropping all round us, hairsbreadth
escapes. LCpl Lillington and Jenkins killed by one shell. The trench
almost level with ground. Finally got to Chowbent St, still no sign

of our men so came to conclusion they had all been killed and buried by debris in trench. I turned into Chowbent, worked way to junction Bury Av and through Hough St to Oban Av, met no one, so I put the men in a shelter for a rest, while the HLI passed up to relieve Manchesters.

Now almost break of dawn. At 4 a.m., the remainder of lost party came up, so I decided to hold Hough St (instead of fire trench) and I put two groups on duty there. Later I found my OC Coy at the Aid Post and found that he had, on arrival with the first party, decided not to hold fire trench owing to intense fire, and he had put his party on duty in Chequerbent St on the right of Hough St. Time now 6 a.m., devilish row going on ahead.

The attack started at 6.30 a.m. I went along the fire trench and put out another post in the new communicating trench across the salient from Chowbent to Iona St. From there I had fine views of the attack. Apparently, the HLI are getting on all right, as they have not asked for our help yet. We are getting a lot of heavy shells and machine gun fire. I return to Coy HQ at 11 a.m. to find the OC in a great stew over my absence [not surprising, as Lt Webb was twenty years old and his military experience totalled barely a year. He was also the Company's only surviving officer]. They thought I had been killed and reported me as 'missing' to Bn HQ.

Lietenant Butcher (Adjutant), the RSM, company sergeant major and colour sergeants of 1 Dorsets in 1916.

Had breakfast. Enemy brought down one of our aeroplanes at noon. ...

14 Brigade's attack from Leipzig Salient had been delayed and was eventually delivered late and by too few troops. They succeeded in gaining a foothold in the German line but were thrown back by a violent counter-attack and barrage fire.

Sergeant Major Shephard continued his account:

Heavy shelling continues all day. At 7 p.m. message to say we are being relieved by 1st Wilts tonight, so sent guides down and made all preparations. They arrived at 9.30 p.m. and we got out fairly easily as enemy eased down a little at that time.

Under the cover of darkness, the West Country soldiers of 1/Dorsets marched back to Senlis. 'We pushed on and got in by singing, quite exhausted, at 1 a.m.' Here the shattered Battalion rested for three days before they returned to hold the line in the Ovillers sector. While Sergeant Major Shephard and his fellow Warrant Officers were reorganizing the battalion, the officers spent much of the time writing letters of condolence to almost 150 grieving families.

1 Nicknamed by the Germans *'Der Granatloch'* (The Shell Hole) due to the number of shells that the dominating position attracted.
2 The forward Headquarters of the German Second Army.
  3 The 49th Division were a part of X Corps, but were under operational command of the Reserve Army for the immediate exploitation of success.
4 Readers following the battle on a modern Carte de France will note that the new map corrects the transposition of Authuille and Auvely woods in 1916.
5 *The Regimental History* records the time as 12.50 hours. The discrepancy is probably due to differing times of arrival of Bn HQ and B Coy further to the rear of the Battalion column.
6 Metal tubes packed with explosives, designed to be pushed under the enemy wire and detonated to clear a path through the obstacle.
7 The Battalion Operation Order details the spacing as 150 yards between platoons. PRO WO 95/2392.
8 This statement is at variance with German records. 3rd Prussian Guards did, however, take over the sector originally held by 26th Reserve Division some time before 8 July 1916.
9 It had taken a considerable time to stop the British barrage from continuing its lifts further into the German Position, so it was ironic that the infantry at this stage of the battle were now waiting for the artillery.
10 CSM Shephard claims that some Borders were left behind, as only the 19th Lancashire Fusiliers were ordered to withdraw to the wood to reorganize.
11 Normally ten per cent of all officers, NCOs and men were 'left out of battle' to act as immediate replacements should a battalion suffer heavy casualties during an attack. Occasionally these men formed the hard core around which to rebuild a shattered battalion.
12 49th Division, the Corps Reserve, had moved up into the areas vacated by the advancing 32nd Division in order to be well placed to advance, or now, as the situation had changed, take over the line.
13 The only fighting battalion of Cheshires was not in the area; therefore, if they were Cheshires, they were probably from an entrenching or pioneer battalion.

Chapter 7

6/Dorsets at Fricourt

South of the Albert-Bapaume Road, three West Country battalions were in action on the first day of the battle. All three were New Army battalions serving with the divisions of Lieutenant General Horne's XV Corps. 8/ and 9/Devons, whose action will be covered in the next chapter, were both with 7th Division at Mametz. 6/Dorsets were part of 50 Brigade of Major General Pilcher's 17th (Northern) Division; a division that did not have a particularly good reputation. Therefore, few were surprised to find that 17th Division were to be XV Corps reserve and were not to take part in the all important first day of the battle. However, events dictated that 6/Dorsets was to be involved in the controversial attack on the fortress village of Fricourt and the hard fighting in the valleys and woods that lay beyond.

The German Position

No sector of the German line on the Somme has been considered as poorly defended. However, the broad salient formed by Fricourt and Mametz has been considered to be 'the corner stone of the German line between the Ancre and the Somme'. As the Germans became increasingly aware that the British offensive was imminent, even strongly held sectors were strengthened. The defended villages of Fricourt and Mametz on two low spurs, separated by the Vallee de Mametz, consisted of:

> ... a maze of trenches and communication trenches twelve hundred yards in depth, and the front trench, with its many salients and flanks, was particularly well sited for defence. The villages themselves had been developed into little fortresses; there were numerous strong machine-gun emplacements and the dugouts were exceptionally fine, some of them with two storeys, lighted with electricity and, as it was said, provided with every convenience except water. The front system was backed up by two intermediate lines ... and also by the Second and Third Positions, here respectively three and six miles behind the front line.[1]

A German senior officer's dugout deep in the ground below Fricourt–Bois Français area, after its capture in July 1916.

105

Holding the forward positions around Fricourt was the 111 Reserve Regiment from 28th Reserve Division. Behind them, a battalion from 55 Landwehr[2] Regiment, under command of the 28th Division was in reserve, holding the second position.

Operations in the Fricourt area 1 July 1916. An extract from the official history mapping.

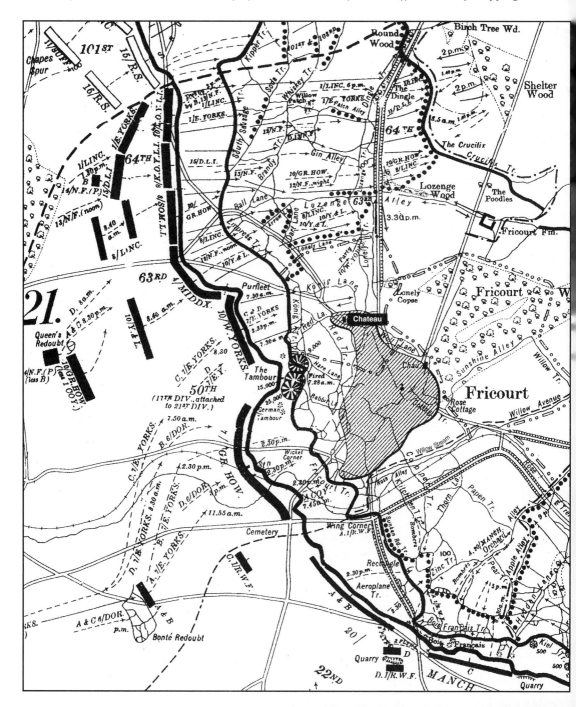

ootness sake go back! Here kom
der DORSETS

A military version of the seaside postcard, which would have been so familiar to many of the West Country soldiers, hailing from coastal resorts such as Weymouth.

British Plan

XV Corps was to attack with two divisions. The 7th was to take Mametz, and the 21st, supported by 50 Brigade, was to attack in the Fricourt area. The 'Willow Stream' in Vallee de Mametz between the two villages was to be the boundary between the divisions. The plan was shaped by the fact that Fricourt was considered too strong to attack frontally at the beginning of the battle. It was therefore to be pinched out by 21st Division's attack to the north and by that of the 7th Division from the south-west. The two divisions were to converge at a point north-east of Fricourt Château, which was marked on British trench maps as 'Fricourt Wood'.

The General Officer Commanding 21st Division, Major General Campbell, had under his command four brigades; three of his own, plus 50 Brigade, including 6/Dorsets, detached from 17th Division. General Campbell's plan was to attack with 63 and 64 Brigades to the north of the village. Meanwhile, 50 Brigade would hold the line opposite Fricourt in the initial phase, except 10/W. Yorks, who were to attack a 600 yard stretch of line north of Fricourt in order to protect the flank of 63 Brigade. The remainder of 50 Brigade were not to attack Fricourt but release gas and smoke just before Zero-Hour. As a further deception measure, three mines of between 25,000 and 9,000 pounds were exploded in front of Fricourt at a point known as the Tambour. In the next phase of the operation, 7th and 21st Divisions would advance either side of Fricourt, thus isolating the enemy in their positions, and it was hoped that the Germans would evacuate the village or surrender. At this point, 50 Brigade was to advance, clear and occupy Fricourt. Once Fricourt was occupied, the other two brigades of 17th Division were to be ready to carry out a passage of lines, through 21st Division, and take the German second position on the Bazentin Ridge.

In executing this plan, 17th Northern Division was at a disadvantage, as they had been amongst the last troops to arrive on the Somme, as late as the second week of June 1916. They had come south from Armentières on the Franco-Belgian border and had only carried out limited training in the latest assault techniques and open warfare tactics. Moreover, they had not held the line in the Fricourt area. Consequently, they had not developed a familiarity with the ground and the enemy's positions, which tended to make the orders they received a little academic, and offered greater scope for misunderstanding. As recorded in 17th Division's history:

Parties of officers were taken to points of vantage commanding good views of the German front, in order to obtain an idea of the general lie of the ground over which the advance was to be made. They saw the wide belt of trenches wrapped in smoke bursts, through which came the flashes of the explosions, and dark masses of stones were hurled high in the air. Mametz Wood was no longer green. Its leaves had been turned to brown and yellow by our high explosives. Fricourt village was crumbling into heaps of ruin. It looked as if the front line was being simply wiped out and that nothing could live under this deluge of fire.

50 Brigade, commanded by Brigadier Glasgow, held the trenches opposite Fricourt with two battalions. 10/W. Yorks were on the left, committed to their flank protection role and 7/Green Howard were on the right holding the front line. In support were 7/E. Yorks, while 6/Dorsets were a distant brigade reserve, not intended to be used in the initial stages of the battle. On the night of 30 June, the Dorsets were in billets at Ville-sur-Ancre, five miles behind the lines. The Adjutant, Lieutenant Barber recorded in the war diary that they:

... left camp at 5.15 a.m. and marched by companies to Meault, arriving there at 6.30 a.m. Just before our arrival, the guns started the final hour's bombardment. A promising morning with a thickish mist over all low lying ground. At Meault the Battalion went into billets and had breakfast.[3]

The original caption read 'Infantry sheltering in a trench'. This is certainly not a fighting trench and is more likely to be a telephone cable trench.

Zero Hour

While the Dorsets were finishing breakfast at Meault, the British bombardment of the German trenches reached its crescendo. The 17th Division's history recorded that:

> For those who waited in reserve behind the battle line on that July morning ... the impression of the early hours was one of a great victory. Reports from the fighting line told of the front trenches having been carried without much resistance.

The Dorsets saw the first prisoners coming through Meault at 10.00 hours and their war diary noted that they were 'An evil looking, unkempt crowd'. However, of concern to the waiting West Country infantry were the long columns of ambulances passing through the village, followed by a stream of walking wounded. Clearly all was not well with the attack.

Back at the front, attacking two minutes after the firing of the Tambour Mines at 07.28 hours, 21st Division's waves swept forward into the enemy line supported on the right by 10/W Yorks. The first two companies of Yorkshiremen were into the German line very quickly. The following companies however, were less fortunate, as they were caught by German machine gunners who had appeared out of dugouts below Fricourt. The Commanding Officer, the Second in Command and the Adjutant were all killed, but the battalion pressed on. The leading Yorkshiremen had disappeared into the smoke and dust where they soon became isolated and destroyed. 10/W. Yorks lost nearly 700 men during the course of the morning.

Meanwhile, 7/Green Howards were holding the line in front of Fricourt, glimpsing the battle going on to their left, through the clouds of dust and smoke. Their role was to lead the subsidiary attack on Fricourt once the village had been enveloped by the main assault. However, as recorded in his personal diary, Colonel Fife

> ... got a message to say that A Company on the right had assaulted at 8.20. I did not believe this but sent the Adjutant to find out. He reported that it was true. I could only account for this by supposing that the company commander had gone mad. Later a report came in saying that what was left of the company were lying out in front of our wire ...

Colonel Fife never received an explanation, as the company commander was amongst the 108 casualties that A Company suffered out of the 140 men who left the trenches. The fate of this company, falling to concentrated close range machine-gun fire, illustrates exactly why Fricourt was not to be directly attacked during the early stages of the battle.

With the forward trenches on the left flank of 50 Brigade vacated by 10/W. Yorks, the process of other troops moving up to replace them began. Two companies of 7/E. Yorks moved up from support to the old front line, being replaced in turn by the Dorsets in the support line. Lieutenant Barber was with the leading elements and recorded in the war diary that:

> At 9 a.m., the Battalion less two companies was ordered up to Sunken Road dugouts, near Becordel. From the north bank of the road, one obtained a grand view of the battlefield, north as far as la Boisselle and south to Mametz. Fricourt lay in the centre, buried all the morning in a thick red mist of brick dust thrown up by our shells.

By 11.00 hours, to the north of Fricourt, 21st Division had made some progress, but not enough to 'pinch out' the village, and the gap between them and 7th Division was still a mile wide. Consequently, Major General Campbell launched the reserve battalions of his 21st Division and ordered 50 Brigade to attack Fricourt, abandoning the analysis that the village was too strongly held to be attacked directly. Brigadier Glasgow, in his front line dugout, questioned the order for 7/Green Howard and 7/E. Yorks to attack, as he could see the bloody evidence of 10/W. York's failure lying in No Man's Land. It was obvious to him that there would be a repeat of the destruction on a larger scale. However, he was ordered to proceed with the attack. Zero-hour was to be 14.30 hours. As 7/E. Yorks moved up to the front line, A and C Companies, 6/Dorsets, were ordered up from Meault to Bonte Redoubt at 11.15 hours. At 12.40 hours, further deployments of the West Country battalion were ordered. Major Johnson's B Company was on the move to the Surrey Street trenches near the Tambour and D

British bombardment of the German lines in the Fricourt–Bois Français area.

Company to Kingston Avenue.

17th Division's historian described 50 Brigade's second attack of the day:

> At 2.30 p.m. the attack began, and in line after line the two Yorkshire battalions went forward, as steadily as if they were on parade. They were at once caught in barrage fire, and along the margins of the village, machine guns opened on them. In three minutes the Green Howard lost thirteen of their officers and over 300 men. They struggled on through the hostile fire, and the East Yorkshires pressed forward to help them. The ground was strewn with lines of fallen men, but numbers reached the edge of the village where their dead and wounded were soon piled in heaps. A few men actually got into the village, most were killed, wounded or captured.

At 16.00 hours, 6/Dorsets were ordered from their dispersed support positions to take over from the remains of 7/Green Howards and 7/E. Yorks in the trenches north of the Tambour. The Adjutant wrote in the Battalion's war diary that 'Everyone felt the extreme heat moving up deep communication trenches with heavy loads, without a breath of wind'. Meanwhile, at 17.00 hours, Brigadier Glasgow was instructed by 21st Division to 'try again'. Consequently, shortly after their arrival, as 50 Brigade's last intact battalion, the Dorsets' orders were changed; they were to attack at 17.30 hours, across the same ground on which the two battalions had earlier bled to death under enemy machine-gun fire. 17th Division's historian commented that in the earlier attack 'hurried orders to try to make good the situation by improvised frontal attacks against the strong points, result in inevitable failure'. Now there was to be a short bombardment followed by an advance into No Man's Land, which was already thickly strewn with the bodies of the Yorkshire infantry. The Dorsets were, however, lucky. As they were waiting in the front line for the barrage to finish, the attack was cancelled just ten minutes before they were due to go over the top. They would have surely shared the fate of those who went before them. As Captain O'Hanlon wrote '... the Dorsets were saved from the holocaust'.[4]

By 19.30 hours, the Dorsets had relieved both Yorkshire battalions. The war diary recorded: 'Relief was tedious as the trenches in the valley were deep in mud and water. Hostile shellfire increased'. At 23.00 hours, orders were received that the whole Brigade was to be relieved by 51 Brigade of their own 17th Division during that night. However, it was not until 05.05 hours the following morning that the Dorsets' relief by 7/Lincoln was complete. Captain Barber wrote:

> The Battalion was to have returned to Ville but lack of accommodation necessitated halting at Meault. The day was spent by the greater part of the battalion sitting in the main street, watching German prisoners going through.

An infantry section waiting in a shell-battered trench to go 'over the top' and resume the advance.

Although prisoners were a clear sign that there was some success on 21st and 17th Divisions' front, as they sat waiting, the West Country soldiers must have contemplated the fate of the Yorkshiremen and their own lucky reprieve from certain death.

There was, however, success at Fricourt during the morning of 2 July, as the Germans had largely abandoned the village, when they realized that they were being enveloped by two British divisions. As Lieutenant General Horn had originally planned, the ruined village was occupied with little opposition.

1 *Official History. France and Flanders 1916.* Vol 1.
2 Landwehr were the German equivalent of the Territorial Army.
3 6/Dorsets' war diary. PRO WO 95/1482.
4 *History of the Dorset Regiment 1914 – 1919.* C.H. Dudley Ward, Dorchester, 1932.

Chapter 8

8th and 9th Devons at Mametz

At the tip of the Fricourt Salient, the front lines changed direction, from their north-south orientation in the Ovillers area to an east – west alignment. Three miles south-west of the scene of the disasters that befell 2/Devons at Ovillers is the Mametz sector of the Somme Battlefield. It was also in this sector where the British, in this case Major General Watts's 7th Division, had greater fortune than was the case further north. Under his command, two New Army service battalions of the Devonshire Regiment were in action on the first day of the battle. As a part of a Regular Army division, they could benefit from the experience and support of the Division's veterans. The Devon battalions were both in Brigadier Deverell's 20 Infantry Brigade, along with 2/Border Regiment and 2/Gordon Highlanders, who were all supported by a trench mortar battery, a machine-gun company and the 18-pounder field guns of the Royal Field Artillery.

An extract from a trench map showing Mansel Copse, Rose Valley and Mametz.

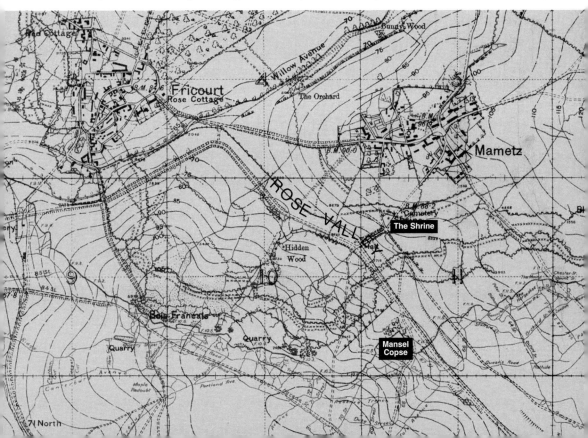

'Before Action'

Several of the renowned tales of the Battle of the Somme, that are often partly wrong or simply mistold, took place around Mametz. All three were connected with the Devons. The first involves Captain Duncan Martin, Officer Commanding Number 1 Company 9/Devons[1], who spent a considerable part of the months before the offensive in the trenches around Mansel Copse with his company of West Countrymen. It had became obvious that he would be leading his men across the broad bowl of Vallee St Martin or as the British called it 'Rose Valley,' which was dominated by Mametz on the ridge above. Repeatedly examining the ground, Captain Martin became convinced that machine guns positioned in depth at Mametz would turn the bowl in front of the copse into a terrible fireswept killing area. Of particular concern was a gun position that was suspected to be near the Shrine, in a cemetery on the opposite hillside. In fact, so concerned was Captain Martin, that while on leave in May 1916, he used his peacetime skills as an artist to make an accurate plasticine model of the Mametz-Mansel Copse area. It showed the ground, the direction of advance and the enemy dispositions that made the area in front of Mansel Copse an excellent killing area, or as Martin called it, the 'Danger Spot'.

On his return to France, Captain Martin displayed the model to his company, but it was quickly appropriated first by his Commanding Officer, Lieutenant Colonel Storey, and then by his Brigade Commander, Brigadier Deverell. However, rather than being used to illustrate the threat presented by the Shrine machine gun, as Martin had hoped, it was used by the Brigadier in his orders and briefings. When 9/Devons raised the issue of the machine gun, the Brigade Commander reiterated the accepted wisdom of the Army Commander that 'the bombardment would destroy all enemy positions'.

The second tale that has captured the imagination of those interested in the Somme is that of the poet, Lieutenant William Noel Hodgson. 'Smiler' Hodgson[2] was one of the high quality young men who volunteered to serve in the Army in 1914 at the outbreak of war. Having graduated from Oxford with a first class degree, he became an excellent and popular officer, and was awarded a Military Cross during the fighting at Loos during September 1915. At this point in the war, the MC was still regarded as a high award and none of the later comments about the devaluation of the medal in the later years of the war applies. Not only was Hodgson an excellent and accomplished officer, he was brave as well.

Lieutenant William Noel Hodgson MC.

Lieutenant Hodgson marched to the Somme with his battalion in the Spring of 1915. Here he became 9/Devons' Bombing Officer, when the Mills hand grenade was issued. Much of his poetry written on the Somme and while on home leave at Durham was published under the pseudonym Edward Melborne. His work showed few signs of the anger and criticism of the war that became the central tenet of the work of Sassoon and Graves in later years. Hodgson's work 'unaffected seemingly by the barbarities he had experienced, tended to be naïve and jingoistic in the manner of Kipling's "Recessional" though not quite as blatant'[3]. However, his poem 'Before Action,' written around dawn on 29 June (the original Z-Day) is as much a prayer as a poem predicting his death in the coming attack. The final verse of the evocative poem reads:

> *I, that on my familiar hill*
> *Saw with uncomprehending eyes*
> *A hundred of thy sunsets spill*
> *Their fresh and sanguine sacrifice,*
> *Ere the sun swings his noonday sword*
> *Must say good-bye to all of this;-*
> *By all delights that I shall miss,*
> *Help me to die, O lord.*

The German Positions

109 Regiment, reinforced by a battalion of 23 Regiment (both 28th Reserve Division) held the line west from an inter-regimental boundary at Hidden Wood. Regimental Headquarters was located in the cellars of the fortified village of Mametz. A battalion of 55 Landwehr Regiment was in depth, holding the 28th Division's second position beyond Fricourt and Mametz. The Germans had laid out their defences to take

The cover offered by sunken roads was exploited by the Germans and used to site dugouts and other shelters.

full advantage of the elevated position of Mametz and the valley that led in a north-westerly direction. This valley, 'Rose Valley', contained the D938 road and a light railway, and its slopes were infested with German dugouts that, even as the exponents of the mighty barrage conceded, would be difficult to destroy with artillery. Rose Valley was also a natural killing area (The Danger Spot) for machine guns located in the western end of Mametz. Consequently, the open 'killing area' that the valley represented effectively split the Brigade's advance into two separate attacks.

Unteroffizier Paul Scheytt recalled that not all Mametz's defenders were confident that they would survive the bombardment: 'When the British started, one of our grenadiers put on his best uniform, went to the company commander and asked indignantly, "Who has started this silly shooting? In God's name, someone is going to get hurt".' The bombardment was indeed more successful in destroying the German wire and deep dugouts in the Mametz area than further north. One reason was that from positions in the areas of the Bois Français / Hidden Wood front, Mansel Copse and from the ridge between Mametz and Carnoy, artillery observers had a comprehensive view of the village and most of its defences. Consequently, gunner officers were able to observe the fire effect, and adjust fall of shot more accurately. Another reason that has been advanced for success on the XIII and XV Corps front, including Mametz, is the presence of the French Army on the British right flank. Their more numerous heavy guns, firing reliably fused shells, could be called on to engage targets on the southern part of the British front. Even with these factors in the attacker's favour on the Mametz front, the enemy defences were still far from destroyed by the bombardment.

British Plans

XV Corp's plan was to 'pinch out' Fricourt with flanking attacks by 21st Division to the north and by 7th Division from the south. Both divisions were to form defensive flanks against Fricourt in order to contain any Germans who tried to break out. The XV Corp's divisional objectives were all limited in scope, being well short of the German second position on the Bazentin Ridge. General Rawlinson, Commander Fourth Army, planned to take each of the three German positions in separate operations, as each subsequent German line was carefully sited to be out of effective artillery range of guns, firing on the previous line. Consequently, having taken the enemy's first line, the artillery was to be moved up into the old battle area. There would follow a bombardment of the German's second position and a repeat of the infantry assault. This process was to be repeated until a final breakthrough was achieved. Rawlinson was confident of steadily pushing the Germans back, but he did not share GHQ's expectations of gaining a decisive breakthrough

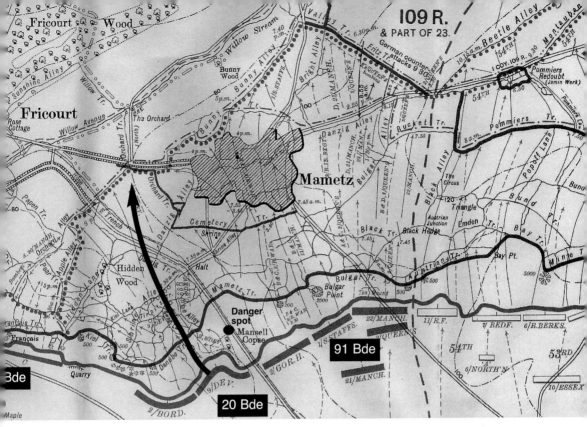

An extract from the offical history mapping showing the attack of 20 and 91 Brigades on Mametz.

early in the battle.

7th Division's plan for the assault was detailed in its operation order:

Main Attack: will be carried out by 91 and 20 Brigades.

Subsidiary attack: will be carried out by 22 Infantry Brigade, which will clear the German trenches N of Bois Francais at an hour to be decided on later, when the attack has reached its final objective. This operation will take place in conjunction with the 2 battalions of 50 Brigade, who will clear Fricourt Village and Wood...

The object of 20 Brigade will be to form a defensive flank facing NW to cover the advance of 91 Brigade...

22 Brigade's 'subsidiary attack,' to clear the trenches between Fricourt and 20 Brigade's left flank, was to be launched later in the morning after Fricourt had been 'pinched out'. Two battalions of 22 Brigade were to remain in the trenches as the divisional reserve.

91 Infantry Brigade, on the right, was to attack the eastern portion of Mametz across the hillside from the south. Success here was important, as the Division's final objective overlooked the winding Caterpillar Valley and more importantly gave good observation of the German's second position. 20 Brigade, in 7th Division's centre, were to take the

western part of Mametz and the ground towards Fricourt, where it was to link up with the 21st Division.

Brigadier Deverell's plan for 20 Brigade allocated the most difficult task to his Regular Army battalions. 2/Gordon Highlanders were to attack on the Brigade's right flank, north-west of Rose Valley, and were to breach the German wire and front line, and then attack and clear the village of Mametz. The Gordons would be fighting in the southern portion of the village, while 2/South Staffords (91 Brigade) would take the northern part. On 20 Brigade's left were 2/Borderers. Their objectives were in the direction of Hidden Wood and Fricourt rather than Mametz. Between the two Regular battalions, in the centre of the Brigade area, were 9/Devons. This battalion's task was to advance in a north-westerly direction across the southern slope of Rose Valley. The route to their objectives took them across the ground between the valley and Hidden Wood, across the road south-west of Mametz and on to Orchard Trench and its field of fire across to Fricourt. It was intended that, with the Gordons advancing along one side of the valley and with the Devons advancing along the other, the surviving enemy dugouts in the bank at the bottom of Rose Valley would be cut off and thus neutralized. 8/Devons was Brigade Reserve and were to move up into the trenches at Mansel Copse vacated by 9/Devons at Zero-Hour. There they were to await orders from Brigadier Deverell at Brigade Headquarters. Behind the infantry battalions were the Brigade's machine gunners and mortarmen, as well as pioneer and Royal Engineer companies, ready to follow up success and produce strong points, to secure gains from the inevitable German counter-attacks.

Lieutenant Colonel Story decided that 9/Devons were to assault on a frontage of approximately 400 yards, with two companies forward. Captain Martin's Number 1 Company was on the right and Number 2 Company was to assault on the left. Both companies were to attack in two waves, each having two platoons and a section of Lieutenant Hodgson's bombers in the first wave. A hundred yards behind the forward assembly trenches was the second wave, again with two platoons from each of the assaulting companies. Number 3 Company was to provide the Battalion's supports. Their tasks were firstly, mopping up behind the leading companies; secondly, providing an immediate source of reinforcement, and finally, providing depth, should the enemy counter-attack. Number 4 Company was to be the Battalion's reserve, uncommitted and available to move to assist other companies or to exploit opportunities presented to the Commanding Officer. In compliance with orders, Battalion Headquarters was to remain in its dugouts at the junction of Reserve Trench and 69 Street. It was only to move forward once the companies had reached their objectives and telephone lines were safely laid. Lieutenant Colonel Story's headquarters was, in effect, a collecting point for information, evaluation and

A bombing platoon of the Devons moving up to the front on the eve of the attack. Note that the platoon commander at the front is wearing an Other Ranks uniform jacket. If this is a Devon Regiment platoon, it is unlikely that the officer is Lieutenant Hodgson, as there is no evidence of his Military Cross ribbon that he was known to wear.

committal of the Battalion's reserves. The detail of fighting the battle was to be left to the company commanders.

The Eve of the Attack

20 Brigade's Operation Order[5] consisted of seven pages of closely typed instructions giving missions and tasks to the assaulting troops, as well as co-ordinating instructions and a wealth of administrative detail. By the time that the Devons left their billets in Bois des Talles on the evening of 30 June, they were familiar with the contents, and the men set out fully prepared as ordered. A few paragraphs from the orders will serve as an example:

> *17.EQUIPMENT.*
>
> *(a) Greatcoats and spare kits will be left in the man's pack, which will be clearly marked and stacked in a store under Divisional arrangements...*
>
> *(b) Every man, with the exception of certain specialists, will carry:-*
> *(i) Rifle and equipment less pack.*
> *(ii) Two bandoliers of SAA in addition to ammunition carried in his equipment (220 rounds in all).*
> *(iii) Haversack on back containing two tins of meat and 8 hard biscuits, and canteen packed with emergency grocery*

ration.

(iv) Waterproof cape or mackintosh sheet, with jersey rolled inside, fixed on to waist belt, in the small of the back by supporting straps from the pack.

(v) 3 sandbags carried under the flap of haversack.

(vi) 2 Mills grenades carried in lower jacket pockets

(vii) 2 smoke helmets.

(c) Bombers will be equipped as follows:-

Mills. Rifle Grenades. Smoke Grenades. SAA.

	Mills.	Rifle Grenades.	Smoke Grenades.	SAA.
NCO	*6*	*4*	*2*	*50*
2 Bayonet men	*1*	*2*	*4*	*50*
2 Leading bombers	*24*		*4*	*50*
2 Reserve bombers	*24*		*4*	*50*
2 Spade men	*8*	*2*	*0-*	*50*

(d) Carriers will be equipped as in (b) with the exception of two bandoliers.

In addition, most of the assaulting West Countrymen would have either carried a pick, a shovel, a billhook or wire cutters and hedging gloves. Contrary to myth, the majority of the attacking infantry went into battle no more heavily laden than infantrymen before or since. However, what has contributed to the impression that the infantry was particularly heavily laden on the first day of the Somme, is the fact that carrying parties or 'carriers' were following-up behind the assault infantry. These men, with their burdens of defence stores and spare ammunition, fell victim to the expectations of a 'walkover' by the assault wave, and the waiting German machine-gunners who, having dealt with the attackers, turned their fire on the following waves.

Another paragraph from the Operation Order concerned the wearing of badges during the attack:

22.(a) Every officer and man in the Brigade will wear a distinguishing mark, to be worn on the back and to be provided under divisional arrangements.

(b) Special distinguishing badges will be worn as follows:-

(i) For men carrying wire cutters = A white band 2″ wide on right forearm.

(ii) For all men employed as "carriers" = A red patch, 2″ deep on right shoulder strap.

(iii) For bombers (who are not badge men) = A white grenade 2½″ in length on right sleeve just below the shoulder.

With preparations complete, 20 Brigade set out for the front, just a small part of the comprehensively timed movement plan.

At 21.30 hours on the 30th June, the 9th Devons left their bivouac in Bois des Tailles. They moved forward to their forming -up positions behind the Mansel Copse front line. Throughout the British bombardment the German artillery had been active in counter bombardment. The damage caused in the Mansel Copse area was so bad that the front and support lines could not be used to form up in. Due to the German Artillery's activity in this sector there was no question of sitting on the parapet watching the shells explode on the enemy line. Instead, troops of the 22nd Brigade, who were holding the forward positions, had to dig a new trench 250 yards behind Mansel Copse. The wisdom of this move rather than making running repairs, was amply demonstrated at 0635 hrs. On the 1st July the British daily rapid fire started and the Germans, warned of the coming attack, replied with a 'furious rain of shells. These shells fell upon the old, evacuated, British front and support lines'.[6]

8/Devons had followed the remainder of 20 Brigade into its allotted positions in 'B2 Sub Sector' leaving the Grovetown bivouacs at 11.35 hours. By 03.45 hours, B and D Companies were in Ludgate Circus, which was about 400 yards behind 9/Battalion. A further 400 yards back were A and C Companies, in Lucknow Redoubt, ready to move forward.

Zero-Hour

While the Devons were preparing to advance, opposite them German machine-gunner Grenadier Emil Kury was ready for the battle:

I told my comrades, 'We must be prepared; the English will attack soon.' We got our machine gun ready on the top step of the dugout and we put all our equipment on; then we waited. We all expected to die. We thought of God. We prayed. Then someone shouted, 'They're coming! They're coming!' We rushed up and got our machine gun in position. We could see the English soldiers pouring out at us, thousand and thousands of them.

Three minutes before Zero-Hour, 20th Trench Mortar Battery's sixteen Stokes Mortars had opened a rapid fire on the enemy line, and the leading elements of 9/Devons climbed their trench ladders on to the parapet of New Trench. It took four minutes to cover the 250 yards between the assembly trench and the evacuated and, by now, wrecked front line. This distance was covered with hardly any casualties. *Unteroffizier* Paul Scheytt summed up the German mood in 109 Regiment:

We had lain for seven days under the trommelfeuer, *in a mood of blind fury because we felt so defenceless, so that, when the moment of the attack came, we felt good. At least we could get our own back. None of us thought we would be killed or wounded. Now we'd pay them back in their own kind.*

We heard the mines [at Fricourt] *go up; then it was deathly quiet for a few moments. The English came walking, as though they*

*were going to the theatre or as though they were on a parade
ground. We felt they were mad. Our orders were given in complete
calm and every man took careful aim.*

The machine gun located near the Shrine, as had been feared, survived
the barrage and opened fire at a range of 800 yards. Across Rose Valley,
Captain Martin was leading Number 1 Company down the barbed wire
strewn slope from Mansel Copse into No Man's Land. As the leading
wave reached the foot of the slope, the first sustained burst of machine-
gun fire, at the rate of 450 rounds per minute, struck. Casualties quickly
mounted. The men dashed forward into No Man's Land. Few got very
far. Captain Martin fell mortally wounded, exactly at the predicted
Danger Spot. The survivors, wounded and unwounded men, dived for
cover in shell holes. Only a handful of men made it across the 100 yards
of No Man's Land, to the German front line. Thus, the attack by
Number 1 Company, on 9/Devons' right flank, had within minutes been
broken up by the Shrine machine gun, firing from a well-concealed and
well-protected depth position. It was not a promising start.

It should be noted that these casualties were almost exclusively
inflicted by machine-gun fire, as all authorities stress that there was very
little German artillery fire in the Mametz area during the morning. XV
Corps's artillery had been exceedingly well directed during the
bombardment, and consequently the British gunners had knocked out a
significant number of the opposition's guns. Given the hilly nature of the
terrain around Mametz, ground detection procedures and air
observation of the highest order were required. Grenadier Kury reported
that during the bombardment 'We could see sixteen English balloons
and thought That's the English for you; we cannot do anything about
those. The English artillery – the English army – the masses of English

aeroplanes over our heads always.'

Meanwhile, on 9/Devons' left, Number 2 Company had more favourable ground to cross, in the bottom of a narrow reentrant leading south-west from Rose Valley. Here the low spur gave them cover from the Shrine machine gun. Consequently, they were quickly across the 150 yards of No Man's Land, taking the German front line, Danube Trench and Danube Support, with few casualties. 'Number 2 Company', in the words of the Divisional history, 'forged ahead, disappearing over the skyline and out of sight of the watchers at Brigade Headquarters', to take the [south-western] portion of Shrine Alley south of Rose Valley. By 08.00 hours, the remnants of Number 1 Company and the Battalion's support (Number 4 Company) had somewhat tenuously secured their section of Danube Trench and had attempted to push up Coombe Alley. However, due to their severely reduced numbers, 1 and 4 Companies were well behind schedule and were later reported in the Battalion war diary as '... being held up and bombed back by parties of the enemy from Mametz'. Meanwhile, Number 2 Company, on the left, advancing parallel with 2/Borders, was almost on schedule and was bombing their way up Swag Lane. In the maze of unfamiliar trenches, groups of Germans were bypassed. *Unteroffizier* Gustav Luttgers was in action in the Mametz area with 109 Regiment:

Lieutenant Prynne, Platoon Commander in 9/Devons, on the Somme.

> We were being fired on from the rear. We thought this was our infantry, so we jumped out of our trench, all waving and shouting 'Higher! Higher!' Then we saw two or three of our men drop wounded and we realized ... the Engländers were behind us, so we jumped back into our trench. There we had a conference as to whether to surrender. One or two wanted to fight on but there were many who were over forty and unlike the younger men, these had family ties and were the first to suggest surrendering. In the end the others were swayed. We tied a handkerchief to a rifle and waved it at the English who came and rounded us up. We were very depressed but we knew that once we had surrendered the Engländers wouldn't shoot us. We could see from their faces that they were as pleased as we were that it was all over for us but they took all our watches from us.

The first prisoners sent back by Number 2 Company reached Battalion Headquarters, which had remained at the junction of Reserve Trench and 69 Street, at 07.50 hours. The first prisoners were reported as reaching Headquarters 20 Brigade at 08.14 hours.

By 09.00 hours, Number 2 Company had also come to a halt, having taken their portion of Shrine Alley and Tirpitz Trench. They were being counter-attacked by the Germans, but held their ground against the enemy bombers. However, following receipt of one of the few situation reports that reached Battalion Headquarters by runner, at 09.30 hours orders were sent to Officer Commanding the reserves, Number 3

Company:

> *The Borders are consolidating in front of Hidden Wood and our Batt'n is consolidating on the right. There is a gap between 9th Devons Regt and the Border Regt. No. 3 Coy will fill this gap and consolidate it.*

Number 3 Company crossed No Man's Land, where Number 2 Company had earlier attacked, and were consequently spared the fire of the Shrine Alley machine gun. Making their way forward, they successfully plugged the gap between the Devons and the Borders and took the attack forward some distance. However, 9/Devons were now faced with crossing 300 yards of open ground with Hidden Wood, to their left and front. Elsewhere in the Brigade, 2/Borders had almost reached their objectives, and 2/Gordons, on the right, had advanced but had been stopped short of Mametz. Both the Gordons and 9/Devons were having problems with the Shrine machine gun, which dominated Rose-Valley and consequently, there was a German-held salient between the battalions, along the line of the railway and overgrown road. At 10.30 hours it was clear to Brigadier Deverell that the attack had come to a halt and that it was time to commit his reserve. The Adjutant of 9/Devons, Lieutenant Hearse, wrote in the war diary:

> *At this point owing to the right flank of the Bn being held up, a message was sent verbally to Brigade asking for a coy of 8th Bn Devonshire Regt to reinforce the right. Orders were given to send B Coy 8th Devons who were then in Reserve Trench.*

B Company, however, followed the route taken by Numbers 1 and 4 Companies, and suffered the same fate. Captain Mahaffy, the company commander, was soon badly wounded while leading his soldiers forward, as were all his officers. Lieutenant Colonel James noted in 8/Devons' war diary:

> *OC B Company moved his troops via Mansel Copse into the hollow on the Bray Fricourt Road* [the Danger Spot]. *This company did not move again* [from Mametz Trench] *as a whole until 4 p.m. when all its officers had been wounded and CSM Holwill assumed command.*

According to Lieutenant Colonel James, who complained in the war diary that following the committal of A Company:

> *Colonel Storey (9th Devons) ordered the advance of B Company to support the right of 9th Devons. ... No information of this move was given to my Battalion Headquarters. They moved in the direction of the Halt. The four officers of this Company were either killed or wounded and I got no information as to the whereabouts of this company until late in the evening...*

A Company, led by Captain Tregelles, advanced through the corpse-strewn Mansel Copse and Danger Spot. Here Tregelles was also hit. He was described as 'an officer of remarkable quality and devotion to duty, who had inspired his company with his spirit'. The loss of three out of four company commanders who crossed No Man's Land via the Danger Spot adds credence to the calculation[7] that the most dangerous rank to hold in the British Army on 1 July 1916 was that of captain.

In Support of the Gordons

At approximately 10.30 hours, Brigadier Deverell gave orders for D Company 8/Devons to be prepared to deploy, under command of the Gordons as additional support. It was clear that this battalion had met stubborn resistance. D Company were ordered to remain in their assembly trench for the time being, ready to move at short notice; but at 10.45 hours, Lieutenant Colonel James recorded: 'Officer Commanding D Company reports two of his platoons sent forward to support the left of the Gordons', i.e. alongside Mansel Copse and the Danger Spot.

One of the platoon commanders, Second Lieutenant Davidson, was hit early on in the advance. However, as the Gordons' Regimental History records, these two platoons, inspired by Sergeant Tucker, 'carried out some useful mopping up' of enemy who had emerged behind the advancing Highlanders, their dugouts missed as the infantry fought their way through the tangle of wire and trenches. The following account by Grenadier Emil Kury illustrates the difficulties of clearing

An infantry company advancing across the German trenches towards Mametz. They are either from 2/Gordons or D Company 8/Devons.

trenches and dugouts:

> *I was wounded quite early in the morning and remember lying semiconscious and seeing British soldiers jumping over our trench but we were not rounded up and several of us took shelter in a dugout. Once during the morning, an English grenade came down and exploded with a loud crash. No one was hurt and one of my comrades said 'Pardon me' as if he had made a rude noise. We laughed. A second grenade followed and again no one was hurt. Then an English soldier came down but we hid in a dark corner and weren't seen. It was many hours later that one of our men went out with a white handkerchief and we were taken prisoner by two soldiers from the Devonshire Regiment. They were very friendly and the doctor who attended to me asked me where I came from. When I told him 'Freiburg', he told me that that was where he had studied and asked me about certain girls that he knew there.*

Not all the Germans in the dugouts were wounded and not all were as passive as Grenadier Kury. Sergeant Tucker, at the insistance of Colonel Gordon, received a well-earned Military Medal for leading the fighting in support of his battalions.

Colonel Storey's Recce

Back on 9/Devons' front, the situation late in the morning in Mansel Copse, No Man's Land, and on the shoulder of Rose Valley was far from clear to Lieutenant Colonel Storey. With hindsight, it is clear that about half of the four companies of Devons committed to the battle had crossed No Man's Land and fought their way forward to Shrine Alley west. Here small groups of officers, NCOs and men were doing their ill-coordinated best to reach their objectives. However, in Mansel Copse, the shell holes of No Man's Land's and in Danube Trench, a number of unwounded men, lacking leaders to take them forward, had gone to ground. As recorded in 9/Devons' diary,

> *Later in the morning, all communication having been cut and runners failing to get through, the Commanding Officer decided to proceed to Mansel Copse and investigate the situation. He found that No. 4 Coy had been held up by heavy machine gun fire and that all officers and senior NCOs of this Coy had become casualties.*
>
> *One Lance Corporal was found and sent forward with some men from Mansel Copse to collect the remainder of the Coy who were lying in the line beyond, in front of the Copse. He was given orders to take them forward and join up with A Coy 8th Devons. This NCO (Lance Corporal Beal) pushed on with his men and joined up with forward troops.*

Reinforced, the mixed groups of 8 and 9/Devons saw off further German counter-attacks from Mametz and pursued them up Shrine

Alley. Lead by Lieutenant Hodgson, bombing sections fought their way forward from traverse to traverse, towards the Halt and up towards the Cemetery, Shrine and Mametz. A machine gunner positioned near the Halt recalled:

> There were five of us on our machine gun when I saw an English soldier about twenty metres away to our left. Then our eldest soldier, a painter from Pforzheim who had five children, was shot in the forehead and dropped without a word. Next, I was shot in the chest. I felt blood run down my back and I fell; I knew the war was over for me. He shot three of us before I even had the chance to use my rifle. I would like to meet that English soldier. He was a good schutzen.[8]

It was during this stage of the fighting that Lieutenant Hodgson was killed, having been hit in the neck while bravely carrying forward green canvas buckets full of grenades to resupply his bombers. His death added poignancy to the prediction he seemed to make in his final poem. The regimental historian recorded, in a departure from his usual reserved style, that 'Lieutenant Hodgson was a particularly fine officer, a most inspiring personality with a great hold on his men, and nearly as much liked and respected by the 8th as his own Battalion'. Few were surprised that he had died playing a leading role in the attack on the key German position at the Shrine. Colonel James wrote in his war diary that:

> A machine gun was found at the Shrine, which had fired a great quantity of rounds. The enemy had taken advantage of this high bank to make it an impregnable position advanced on by a bombing party down to Combe Alley or along the bottom of the bank.

With the removal of the Shrine machine gun, positioned to dominate the centre and right of 20 Brigade, the tempo of the operation began to increase. Up to this point, only isolated parties of Highlanders had penetrated the defences of the fortified village of Mametz. Now the Gordons, supported by the Warwicks and by 8/Devons, joined by its last two platoons, were able to assemble sufficient combat power to properly clear Mametz. This time the Devons were not involved in the dangerous business of clearing dugouts in support of the Gordons, but leading the attack with the vigour of fresh troops. The regimental history describes the fight for Mametz:

> In this advance, fine work was done by Sergeant Cater, who took charge of the supports and took them forward to join in the attack, and by Lance-Sergeant Clay[9], an old soldier who had done good service in South Africa. He set a splendid example, rallying and steadying his men and leading them forward after their platoon commander had fallen. When the platoon was held up by uncut wire and Sergeant Clay asked for volunteers to cut it, Private

Wadsworth darted forward and started cutting. He was hit, but went on, and before a second bullet finished him had cut a large gap and let his platoon go on ... The Gordons supported by D Company and the R Warwickshires took Mametz.

Afternoon

By early afternoon, with the Shrine in British hands and Mametz being cleared, 9/Devons was hours behind schedule and still only half-way to their objective, but they had broken coherent German resistance. Nonetheless, many of the German defenders of 109 Regiment proved to be determined fighters. 20 Brigade ordered C Company, 8/Devons, forward early in the afternoon. Colonel James wrote:

3.30 p.m. C Company, my last company in Reserve Trench were given orders to proceed to Hidden Wood via Mansel copse. This company sent two platoons over the top of Reserve Trench but Lieutenant Saville seeing numerous casualties took the remainder of the company via 70 Street and proceeded to his objective with practically no casualties at all.

Late in the battle, Lieutenant Saville was the officer who had finally recognized the point that Captain Martin had been making about the Danger Spot and crossed No Man's Land further up the reentrant, at a point where enemy fire from the Mametz area had minimal effect. This late realization is an example of how, despite their competence in the trenches, and their personal bravery, New Army soldiers tended to lack

The village of Mametz seen across No Man's Land from Mansel Copse. The chalk marks are spoil from trenches.

Shrine

German trench lines

British Front Line

A dead German soldier, killed 1 July 1916. The photographer noted that 'he was little more than a boy'.

an understanding of one of the basic principles of soldiering: the use of ground to cover movement.

A little later, Colonel James received word that the remains of the leaderless B Company 8/Devons, who had been sent forward via the Danger Spot, were still in and around Mansel Copse and the former No Man's Land. He sent one of his 'left out of battle' officers forward:

> *4.0 p.m. I sent out 2/Lieutenant Duff to collect B Company and push on in support of C Company to Hidden Wood.*
>
> *4.20 p.m. 2/Lieut Duff reports having found remnants of B Company in Mametz Trench and is working through the trench with Gordons in direction of Danzig Support and Hidden Wood.*

This passage from the war diary gives an indication of the difficulties of fighting through and clearing a trench system. The British troops were now well and truly mixed on an inter-battalion boundary; while 'working through the trench' they came across numerous Germans missed during earlier advances through the wrecked labyrinth of unfamiliar trenches. Colonel James made the point in the war diary that:

> *The nature of the engagement was affected by mopping up parties not clearing the trenches, leaving machine guns and snipers who caused practically all the casualties. The Bank by the Halt was entirely disregarded and all dugouts in Danzig Trench were found to be occupied; the enemy using the bank above could concentrate an enfilade fire on troops advancing to Hidden Wood or Mametz. Also, the traverses being firestepped, they could shoot down the valley to our lines.*

The regimental history explained that the mixed group under Lieutenant Duff was moving through:

> *Danzig Trench, clearing the dugouts in the high banks along that trench and Plum Lane* [running parallel to Rose Trench], *and connected up with the Gordons, who had renewed the attack on Mametz. The clearing of the banks was an important achievement and yielded many prisoners, including several officers...*

Duff's prisoners included four officers, one of whom was reported to be the commander of 109 Reserve Regiment, who was found wounded on a stretcher in his own Regimental Aid Post dugout in Danzig Trench, with a broken leg.

It seems strange for Colonel James to have dispatched a junior officer such as Second Lieutenant Duff on such an important task, which would normally be beyond even the most experienced junior officer. However, Duff was a Temporary Second Lieutenant, that is to say, he was an experienced regular Army Senior NCO, who had received a month of officer training and had been commissioned and posted to 8/Devons in October 1915. Officers such as he were needed to lend much needed military knowledge and experience to a New Army battalion. For his distinguished part in the battle on 1 July, Temporary Second Lieutenant Duff earned the officer's decoration; the Military Cross.

Second Lieutenant Duff was not the only man to receive a high award for the fighting on the afternoon of the attack. Company Sergeant Major Melhuish received the DCM for his part in the action on the right of Rose Valley, having also been strongly recommended by Colonel Gordon, Commanding Officer of 2/Gordons, who went out of his way to see that the award was made.

At this stage of the battle, between 17.10 and 18.00 hours, mixed groups from 8 and 9/Devons were moving forward, against collapsing opposition to the Brigade objective along the line of Orchard Trench and Orchard Alley. Lieutenant Colonel Storey, Commanding Officer 9/Devons, with his Battalion's reserve of 9 left-out-of-battle officers and 72 NCOs, caught up with his advancing soldiers. This reinforcement of leaders and men hurried the Devons on to their objective, where the companies regrouped to defend their gains against the expected German counter-attack. To the Devons' right, 2/Gordons and their supports from D Company 8/Devons had cleared Mametz, and had linked up with the West Countrymen at the junction of Orchard and Bunny trenches.

In the war diary it is recorded that the Devons had fired very little small arms ammunition during the day. Fighting through trenches, the West Countrymen had been engaged in close-quarter combat, where bomb and bayonet had been the primary weapon of the infantry. Conversely, the German machine guns had fired prodigious amounts of ammunition, which had, in turn, ensured that the British infantry could not attack over the open ground between trench lines, and confined them to 'bombing' along trench lines.

By 18.00 hours, 7th Division's pioneers and sappers were hard at work in the old front lines and No Man's Land, digging communications trenches for 'up and down traffic' as well as repairing roads to ensure that new positions could be held and supported. It was also noted in the Official History that while 7th Division's new front was:

> ... being wired and strong points constructed, the battalions at the front reported that the enemy had cleared off, and that ground further to the front could be made good, but no orders for any further movement were issued by any of the higher staffs.

With 9/Devons, 2/Gordons and 2/Borders all having suffered heavy casualties, it fell to 8/ Devons to hold the Brigade front overnight while the other battalions collected their scattered men and reorganized.

Now that the front had moved on, the Devons had the chance of exploring the strong and elaborate German positions. One Devons soldier wrote:

> We stood gaping with wonder at the long flights of steps banked up with three-inch timber, and at the safe and comfortable bunks within. The ordinary German soldier must have enjoyed a degree of comfort which no one short of a general tasted on our side of the line.

German dugout captured by the Devons at Mametz.

The Devons had been successful, and with 7th Division, they had won a victory though not perhaps as great as the optimists had expected or hoped for, in contrast to absolute failure elsewhere, any success was highly significant.

Why was XV Corps Successful?

Despite heavy casualties and barely reaching the first of their three objectives, XV Corps's attack is considered to be a success when compared with the total failures and token successes north of the Albert–Bapaume Road. At Fricourt, 21st Division had established a significant lodgement in the German line to the north of the village, a thousand yards deep, but the frontal attack on Fricourt had been bloodily repulsed. Meanwhile, south-east of Fricourt, 7th Division had captured the German forward defensive system, including Mametz, on a frontage of a full mile, to a depth of 1,000 yards. In addition, this gain was fully linked up with that of XIII Corps to the right.

As has already been mentioned, the artillery bombardment had been more effective than elsewhere, because of the proximity of the French heavy guns and the good positions available to artillery observers. However, an additional factor was at work. In most other corps, the artillery fire plan worked on timed lifts that took the exploding shells from line to line in an inflexible programme. However, in XV Corps, a portion of the artillery's field guns used an early form of creeping barrage, which gave the infantry much better support and was more flexible. The key passages in XV Corps' Artillery Operation order stated:

> 4. When lifting, 18 pdrs should search back by increasing their range, but howitzers and heavy guns must lift directly on to their next objective.
>
> 5. When barraging, open ground fire should be in bursts, searching back as far as necessary, and not at a continuous rate. Woods and hollows beyond the actual line laid down for the barrage should be searched periodically.

Thus not only were XV Corps's 18-pounders to add range after every round fired rather than jumping a distance to a second line, they were given an unusual degree of latitude to respond to events. The Royal Artillery was able to make use of this flexibility from their excellent OPs, with their dug-in telephone communications back to the batteries. During the course of the Battle of the Somme, the creeping barrage and artillery tactics in general became more sophisticated and better able to support the infantry[10].

The Aftermath of Battle

The 8th Battalion lost fifty-three all ranks killed or missing and 151 men

German prisoners help move a water cart belonging to 21/Field Ambulance, who supported the Devons from the time they joined 7th Division until the end of the war.

wounded. 9/Devons, one of the assault battalions, lost a total of 196 men killed; 55 men were listed as missing and 267 were wounded. This

1 July 1916 a dead soldier photographed in 7th Division's area.

made a total of 463 out of 775 in action. The battle had been equally costly to both sides. *Unteroffizier* Scheyett described the fate of his company of 109 Reserve Regiment:

When our last cartridge had been fired, we withdrew through the enemy barrage to Klein-Bazentin. When the Regiment collected in le Transloy that evening, my kompanie *consisted of twenty men.*

On the battlefield, the dead of both armies were numerous and were only cleared in the days following the battle. Lieutenant Siegfried Sassoon, of 1/Royal Welch Fusiliers, recalled in his *Memoirs of an Infantry Officer* how, on the evening of 2 July, he was moving up with 22 Brigade to dig a new trench beyond Mametz:

> As we went up the lane towards Mametz [from the Halt via the Shrine] I felt that I was leaving all my previous war experience behind me. For the first time I was among the debris of an attack. After going a very short distance we made the first of many halts, and I saw arranged by the roadside, about fifty of the British dead. Many of them were Gordon Highlanders. There were Devons and South Staffordshires among them, but they were beyond regimental rivalry now – their fingers mingled in blood-stained bunches, as though acknowledging the companionship of death. There was much battle gear lying about, and some dead horses. There were rags and shreds of clothing, boots riddled and torn, and when we came to the old German front line, a sour pervasive stench which differed from anything my nostrils had known before.

Another medium, relatively new to war in 1916, has left a visual record of the aftermath of the battle around Mametz. In an attempt to rally workers at home through the example of the troops at the front, cinematograhical officers Geoffrey Mallins and J. McDowell visited the front of 7th Division, filming the battle in the Mametz area. Lieutenant Frank Wollcombe wrote in his diary that the resulting film included his Battalion:

> Two pictures of the Devons. 'Artillery taking up positions east of Mametz, 2 hours after the battle started over ground strewn with the dead of the Devons and Gordons' and 'The Devons

The village of Mametz after its capture.

Begs to forward as requested a Photograph of
the Grave of :—

Name *Adamson.*

Rank and Initials *2/Lt T.*

Regiment *9th Devonshire Regiment*

Position of Grave *Devonshire Cemetery
Mametz .*

*N*earest Railway Station *Albert*

All communications respecting this Photograph should quote
the number 17/2 794.) and be addressed to :—
Director of Graves Registration and Enquiries,
War Office,
Winchester House,
St. James's Square,
London, S.W., 1.

Owing to the circumstances in which the photographic work is carried
on, the Director regrets that in some cases only rough Photographs can
be obtained.

" COPYRIGHT FU

*receive their post'. There was one of the 9th and
the Gordons going over the top. There was a
picture of the Manchesters resting in Danzig
Alley after having captured it. As a matter of
fact Sergeant Melhuish and a few bombers
took it and the Manchesters relieved us
there a day or two after.*

Danzig Alley was the opposite side of Rose
Valley and a considerable distance from the
Manchesters' area and firmly within the
bounds of the ground taken by a mixed group
of 8 and 9/Devons on 1 July 1916. McDowell
was in the area filming on 1 July and Malins
between 2 and 4 July and, therefore, it is
reasonable to assume that the soldiers filmed
could be from either regiment. This demonstrates
that from its early days, film war reporting, in
common with other media, has not always been
accurate and should not necessarily be accepted at
face value.

The third Somme tale connected with the Devons and

Mansel Copse that continues to capture the imagination, is that of Devonshire Cemetery. 8 and 9/Devons, unlike many divisions on the 1 July front, were able to evacuate their wounded and clear the dead from No Man's Land and the captured German trenches. The Devons decided to collect their dead, and they laid them together in their former front line trench in Mansel Copse, overlooking the scene of the attack and their death. At 18.00 hours on the evening of 4 July, 9/Devons, now out of the line, along with a party from the Reserve Company of 8/Devons, paraded for the burial service of 160 of their officers and men. The Battalion's Padre, Reverend E. C. Crosse, led the bare-headed West Countrymen who gathered around the mass grave, in the burial service, which he read from his well used *Field Service Prayer Book*. Afterwards, as the men silently filed away, the Battalion's pioneers filled in the grave and erected a large cross looking out over what had been No Man's Land. On the back of the cross were the words that have continued to resonate over the succeeding decades:

The Devonshires held this trench. The Devonshires hold it still.

1   With two battalions of Devons in 20 Brigade, it was decided that it would be less confusing for commanders and the staff if 8/Devons used the traditional A, B, C and D and 9/Devons adopted 1, 2, 3 and 4 to distinguish their respective companies.
2   Known as 'Smiler Hodgeson' by his fellow officers. P98 Frank Woolocombe's war diary.
3   William Noel Hodgson. *The Gentle Poet. Jack Medomsley*, Mel Publications, Durham, 1989.
4   A full version of Hodgson's poem *Before Action* is to be found at Appendix X.
5   Public Record Office WO 95/163.
6   *The Devonshire Regiment 1914–1918*. C.T. Atkinson, Exeter, 1926.
7   Martin Middlebrook *The First Day on the Somme*. His calculations demonstrate that pro rata commanders suffered higher casualties than their subordinates, with those holding the rank of private having a statistically lower chance of becoming a casualty.
8   Martin Middlebrook believes that 'the marksman was almost certainly a soldier from 8/Devons'.
9   L/Sgt Clay also earned the MM.
10   7th Division's artillery fired 7,000 18-pounder and 900 heavy howitzer rounds during the course of 1 July 1916.

The memorial stone at Devonshire Cemetery that replaces the original wooden cross put up by the Devons' Regimental Pioneers.

Chapter 9

Fricourt and Mametz Wood:
The Second Phase

The decisive issue of the war depends on the victory of the Second Army on the Somme. We must win this battle. Important ground lost in certain places will be recaptured. For the present the chief thing is to hold on to our positions at any cost. I forbid the voluntary evacuation of trenches. The enemy should have to carve his way over heaps of corpses. GENERAL VON BULOW. SPECIAL ORDER OF THE DAY. 3 JULY 1916

It will be no surprise that, following the heavy casualties suffered by four of the five West Country battalions in action on 1 July, the part the Devons and the Dorsets played in the battle over the following days of early July 1916 was a secondary one. 1/Dorsets, as we have seen, held the trenches near Ovillers, while 2/Devons, with the badly shattered 8th Division, left the Somme to be reconstituted. However, the three battalions serving in XV Corps remained in action on the southern portion of the Somme front over the following week. Here the German position had been breached on a six-mile front, to a depth of almost 1,500 yards.

Despite success south of the Albert – Bapaume Road, Field Marshal Haig, who was initially unaware of the scale of the losses, let it be known that he 'wished the assault to be renewed as soon as possible in order to wear down the enemy's resistance and to secure a line from which to attack his second position'[1] on a broad front. Despite the limited success on 1 July 1916, there was a belief that 'the enemy was badly shaken, that his defence was strained nearly to breaking point, and must give way if the pressure upon it was maintained'.[2] In response to Haig's direction, at 22.00 hours on 1 July, General Rawlinson ordered the attack to be 'continued under corps arrangements as early as possible compatible with adequate previous artillery preparations'. XV Corps was directed to complete the capture of Fricourt village and Wood and, with XIII Corps, attack Mametz Wood. However, despite the success in the Mametz/Fricourt area and westwards to the boundary with the French Army, the British main effort lay on the centre around Ovillers and la Boisselle and to the north; the very areas where they had been most bloodily repulsed. With hindsight, many have theorized that with good communications the Fourth Army should have reinforced success and promptly driven XV and XIII Corps forward to the German second position.

In the Fricourt/Mametz area, the night of 1-2 July was quiet. The

137

3 trees x6.c7.2

Oxford Willows

Acid Drop Copse

copse
Bottom Wood
x 28. 6

Quadrangle Alley

Quad Support

Wood Support

Quadrangle Trench

Wood Support

6/Dorsets' area of operations during the first half of Jul

Mametz Wood

Bazentin

Quadrangle
c.1

Stripwood

Acid Drop Copse

Cemetery

Mametz
Wood

Peake Woods

5208

5055
4060
95

22

23

A
24

100

25

C

Tree
d

The
Quadrangle

Stripwood

4686

7870

6466
100

A

34

Crucifix

5910

90

Bottom Wood

3615

The Poodles

31

28

Railway
Copse

29

30

Fricourt Farm

80

enemy, 28th Reserve Division, had been defeated, and patrols sent forward by 7th Division reported that they had been able to enter Fricourt unmolested. Orders were sent to the 7th and 17th Divisions that they were to complete the 'pinching out' of Fricourt 'in the small hours of 2 July'.

The Capture of Fricourt

At Fricourt, Major General Pilcher, of 17th (Northern) Division, was ordered by Lieutenant General Horn to take command of the part of the front that was already held by his own 50 Brigade from 21st Division. Having assumed command, he reviewed the situation before issuing orders to clear the enemy out of Fricourt the next morning. Pilcher decided to replace the depleted 50 Brigade with the fresh battalions of 51 Brigade. His intention was to leave Brigadier Glasgow and his headquarters in command, as they were familiar with the ground. However, on visiting the trenches, he found the Brigadier in his front line command post 'a broken man in a state of mental collapse'. Having been repeatedly ordered, despite his protestations, to send his soldiers forward against the unsupressed defences of Fricourt, even the most determined commander would have been affected by the sight of his brigade lying dead and wounded in No Man's Land. 6/Dorsets, alone spared the carnage, were left holding the trenches and recovering the wounded from No Man's Land. As the casualty system was being overwhelmed, the wounded were 'temporarily placed in sheltered positions in the vaults of the cemetery'. The divisional history explained that the Dorsets' relief was delayed because:

> ... the roads were so encumbered with transport, ambulances and men of [mainly walking wounded] streaming back from the line that progress was slow and when the line was reached the trenches were blocked with wounded, bearer parties and stragglers, and there was a good deal of confusion, so that it was not till broad daylight, about 5.30 a.m. on 2 July that the relief was completed.

As dawn crept across the sky, the exhausted Dorsets made their way back down the communications trench and marched to join the remainder of 50 Brigade in billets at Meaulte.

At 08.50 hours, a strong patrol from the South Staffords crossed No Man's Land and entered Fricourt, to be met by 'a party of twenty-two men of the 111th German Infantry, who came out of the trenches, holding up their hands and bringing with them a couple of men in British khaki ... They said that the enemy was evacuating Fricourt.'[2] Orders were given for 51 Brigade to advance once the bombardment had been cancelled, but stopping the artillery fire took a considerable time and it was not until midday that the British finally cleared Fricourt, taking another 100 prisoners. However, as the Lincolns reached the far edge of the village, they came under fire from Fricourt Wood[3] and were

Transport drivers belonging to either 8/ or 9/Devons resting during operations in early July 1916.

checked. However, this was a delaying position and eventually the three German machine guns withdrew, allowing the advance to continue. The Lincolns, Staffords and Sherwood Foresters took the wood and Fricourt Farm before dark.

7th Division

The main part of 7th Division's operation on 7 July, to capture the western portion of Fricourt, fell to 22 Brigade, with 8/Devons being tasked to provide fire support to the attack from Orchard Trench. It was planned that, once Fricourt Wood had been cleared, the Devons would advance and seize the northern portion of Orchard Trench, where a strong point would be established.

While 22 Brigade were occupying Fricourt, the Devons were waiting in their part of Orchard Alley, where what is described as a 'half-hearted enemy counter-attack' was beaten off by concentrated rifle and Lewis gun-fire, supplemented by a section of Vickers guns from the Brigade Machine Gun Company. With operations in Fricourt reported as going smoothly, 8/Devons were duly ordered to advance north up the extension of Orchard Trench to the Orchard. 20 Brigade's engineers, pioneers and machine gunners joined the West Countrymen in forming a new strong point, in what was now the centre of the XV Corps area.

From here, sensing a lack of coherent enemy opposition, 8/Devons continued the advance and eventually gained touch with 17th Division in Willow Trench, which led to Fricourt Wood. In doing so, they gathered numerous prisoners.

While 8/Devons were advancing into the enemy position, 7th Division's artillery support was limited, as the guns were being moved forward. With the latest advance by the infantry, the 18-pounders were now too far to the rear to cover lateral targets across the divisional front and to engage targets in any depth. Their new gun positions were in the former No Man's Land and Rose Valley, where the Devons were engaged in the grim task of clearing their dead from the battlefield. Over the succeeding days the 8th remained holding the line, but once 17th Division had advanced across their front, they were now holding the second line, and the Devons were able to explore the elaborate positions they had captured on 1 July.

8/Devons remained in the line until relieved on 5 July. However, so heavy were 9/Devons' 1 July casualties, they had already been withdrawn to reorganize and take in a draft of replacements. Once fully relieved, the whole of the 7th Division marched back to the Fourth Army's rear area for a well-earned rest.

6/Dorsets at the Quadrangle

The Dorsets were in reserve, but had spent two exhausting days and nights carrying ammunition and defence stores forward to supply dumps in the new line north of Fricourt. The Battalion history recorded that:

> Fricourt was crowded with troops, the debris was being cleared, and dumps were springing up. The way passed the Crucifix, and men stopped to gaze at the figure that looked silently down upon them in the dark, or rifled German packs for their brown bread, or hailed in, strong language, a great wire-bound mortar of wood, which had sent over many "oil-cans". Other parties had to dig posts on the edge of Fricourt Wood. The work done, the Dorsets returned to Meaulte.

Meanwhile, the two fresh brigades of Major General Pilcher's 17th Division had seized Shelter and Bottom Woods before advancing to take Quadrangle Trench, where they were held up.

At 02.00 hours on 6 July, 50 Brigade received a warning order to move to the front and 'to be ready to co-operate in an attack on Mametz Wood'. Marching from Meaulte at 20.00 hours, the Dorsets completed taking over the front line trenches from 14/Welch (38th Division) at midnight. The front line lay from Fricourt Wood via Railway Alley to Bottom Wood. In their unfamiliar trenches 'heavy guns shelled the area promiscuously' and the Dorsets had an uncomfortable time, suffering casualties, some of whom were barely known or recognized replacements, coming into the line for the first time. Major Hughes-Onslow's Battalion Headquarters was shelled out of the

Major Hughes-Onslow

142

Sunshade Alley Dugouts in Fricourt Wood at midnight, and was forced to move to a large German dugout in Railway Copse. Meanwhile, 52 Brigade failed in their attack on Mametz Wood, being unable to take Quadrangle Support and Quadrangle Alley. 7/E. Yorks were consequently ordered to attack the junction of the two trenches. This they managed to do

> but were unable to maintain themselves there, being forced back by enfilade and cross machine gun fire and bombs to a stop about 50 yards short of the junction. Meanwhile, the 6th Dorsetshire Regiment were waiting to take advantage of any advance by the Division on the right but there was no evidence of any progress in this situation which continued until 6PM.[4]

The German 9th Grenadier Regiment was holding fast.

The following morning, D Company moved forward from Bottom Wood 'up to Quadrangle Trench to support the E. Yorks but as they were not required, they handed over their bombs and returned to Bottom Wood.[5] The war diary goes on:

> 10.00 a.m. The line we were holding was a series of small pits on the north edge of the wood, affording very little protection from shellfire. A very heavy barrage was maintained throughout the whole day just behind this line, but casualties were surprisingly few.

A map from the Dorsets' history showing their area of operations following the initial assault.

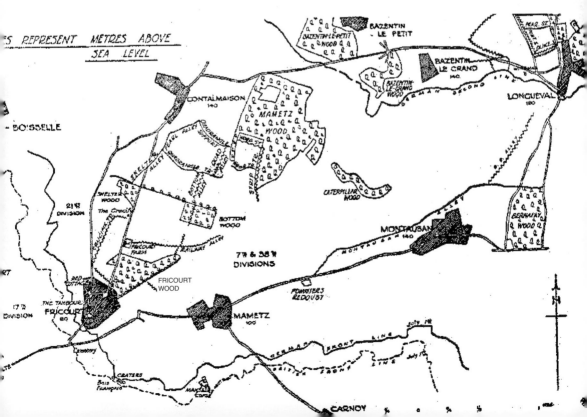

> *7.45 p.m. Orders received to attack Wood Trench at 8 p.m. in conjunction with the 38th Division who were to attack Strip Trench.*

The time of 7.45 p.m. recorded in the Dorsets' war diary is incorrect, as Divisional Operation order No. 61 was issued at 16.40 hours, requiring 50 Brigade to be ready for an on call Zero-Hour from 18.30 hours. 50 Brigade eventually ordered 7/. Yorks and 6/Dorsets to attack at 20.00 hours, after a thirty minute preliminary bombardment. The Dorsets' attack was not to be an advance 'over the top' but an assault by B Company, spearheaded by the Battalion's bombers, who were to fight from traverse to traverse along the trench from Quadrangle Trench into Wood Trench. Brigadier Price-Davies, Commander 113 Brigade, who was at the time of the attack visiting 15/Royal Welch Fusiliers, subsequently wrote:

> *I was visiting my forward posts and looked down on Mametz Wood at a few hundred yards range. I was by a Lewis gun post when I became aware of an attack in progress by what I believe were 6th Dorsets. They were creeping forward and using rifle grenades against the strip wood jutting out towards us. I had never heard of this attack and got covering fire to work as quickly as possible, but the Lewis gun jammed and the attack fizzled out ... We occupied a position from which heavy covering fire could have been brought to bear had this been organized.*

Without suppressive fire support coordinated between the two divisions, the Dorsets, as described in the Battalion's war diary, '... came under very heavy machine gun fire from three different directions and were unable to gain their objective'. 17th Division's war diary recorded a message from 50 Brigade at 21.50 hours, explaining that the E. Yorks' attack over the open had failed due to the wire being uncut and '6th Dorsets still engaged in bombing down Wood Trench and along a strip of wood by the Railway. The situation about the junction of Quadrangle Trench and Quadrangle Alley is uncertain.' Without progress on the left flank, and 15/Royal Welch Fusiliers failing to provide the expected support on the right, B Company and the bombers were forced to withdraw back to their start point. The regimental history describes how 'incendiary bombs from Strip Trench set alight the clothing of the wounded, and only a few struggled back'. Major Johnson was wounded during the withdrawal, but he was eventually brought back to Quadrangle Trench by his soldier servant, Private Cummings. Cummings was himself wounded in three places, but dressed his company commander's wounds and dragged him back, 'having spent three perilous hours in No Man's Land'. For this action, he was awarded the Distinguished Conduct Medal (DCM).

Among others earning awards during the attack was Second Lieutenant D'Albertanson. His Military Cross citation read:

> *... On the night of 7th July, when ordered to attack Wood Trench he led a battle patrol of volunteers he had called together. He got back with three men, having learned that the enemy were in great strength and by his action prevented his men from falling into a trap and saving many lives.*

Private Harris received a Military Medal for heroically rescuing a wounded Royal Welsh Fusilier from No Man's Land, in spite being hit himself no less than five times, while Company Sergeant Major Adams was awarded a DCM. An extract from his citation reads:

> *For splendid devotion to duty, after being buried and rendered unconscious on 7th July, he refused to leave the line until given a direct order, and then returned after two hours, offering a splendid example to his men.*

The Second Attack

At 01.05 hours, under instructions from XV Corps, 17th Division issued a fresh operation order[6] for a renewed attack on Quadrangle Support early on the morning of 8 July. The plan was to attack up a pair of parallel communications trenches. 51 Brigade were to attack up Pearl Alley and 50 Brigade were to attack up Quadrangle Alley[7], with a Zero-Hour of 06.00 hours. The attack was preceded by a bombardment, reinforced by the guns of 21st Division. The fighting went on all day, and repeated attacks foundered in the mud, which was in 'Quadrangle Trench, four feet deep in parts'. The Green Howards only progressed about 100 yards before being halted. Meanwhile, 6/Dorsets had been moved back into close reserve, where the rifle companies, now

British infantry attacking through their own wire entanglement.

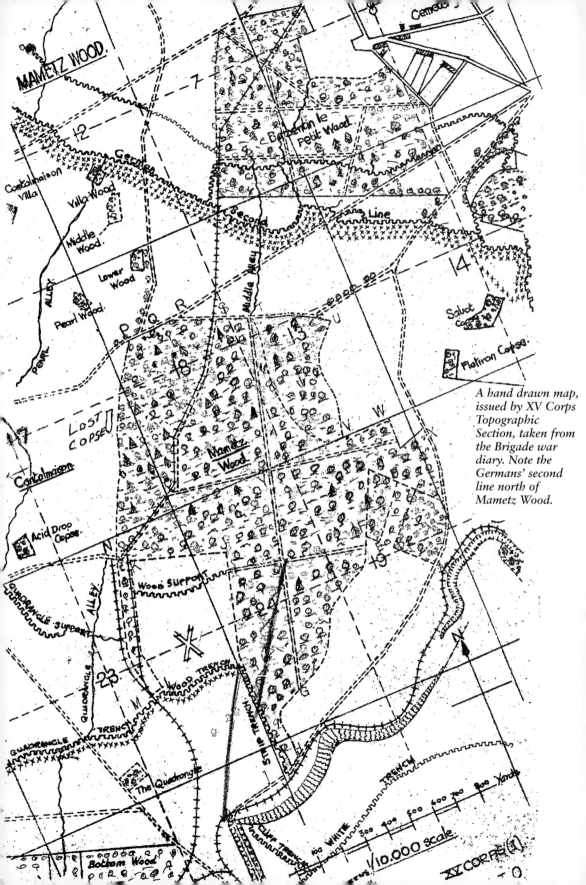

A hand drawn map, issued by XV Corps Topographic Section, taken from the Brigade war diary. Note the Germans' second line north of Mametz Wood.

numbering 60 to 90 men each, rested before resuming operations in the Wood Trench area in support of 38th Welsh Division.

It was considered essential that Wood Trench be taken and linked up by a new trench with Quadrangle Trench before 113 Brigade (38th Division) began its infamous attack on Mametz Wood. Being rested and familiar with the ground, 6/Dorsets were again given the task. The plan was similar to the previous night's attempt: an attack by a single company, C Company on this occasion, supported by the Battalion's bombers. They moved forward to their jumping-off positions in Quadrilateral Trench at 15.00 hours; however, Zero-Hour was delayed until 21.00 hours.

Major Hughes-Onslow decided that the attackers should send a small group of bombers across No Man's Land to Wood Trench before Zero Hour, as 'the desultory bombardment ceased at dusk'. Private Hicks, the leading bayonet man, led Lance Corporal Routliff's bombing squad in a

rush over the open ground between the E. end of Quad Trench and Wood Trench. The objective to make a stop [a defended barricade across the trench] *at the W. end of Wood Trench. At the same time, a patrol under Second Lieutenant Moss advanced into the S. end of the belt of trees.*

The bombing squad meeting with little opposition proceeded up the trench to a point 70 yards from Mametz Wood, where they made their stop.

Private Hicks carried out 'his very nervous work with admirable courage and skill. He was easily first over the parapet and into the German trench and led the way throughout the attack ...'[8] Through their remarkable dash and change of tactics, Captain O'Hanlon's[9] C Company and the Dorsets' bombers had secured Wood Trench by 21.15 hours, with minimal losses, almost five hours ahead of schedule. The war diary recorded: 'During the night the trench was consolidated, one counter-attack was repulsed, and another was dispersed by Lewis gun fire before it had time to develop'. However, a message to Major Hughes-Onslow, at Battalion Headquarters, from Captain O'Hanlon explained:

Last night or rather early this morning some men including my sergeant Major vowed they saw about forty [Germans] *attack from direction of Wood Support against our left. Fire from MG and rifles was opened. My MG Sergeant declared later on he saw them fetching in wounded. For myself I could make out nothing due to trees and thistles.*[10]

Meanwhile, as recorded by the Adjutant in the Dorsets' war diary, 'A Coy had moved up two platoons to dig a trench joining up Quad[rangle] Trench and Wood Trench. This was done. 10 p.m. remaining two platoons of A Coy moved up into the W. end of Quad Trench.'

The Dorsets' success contrasted with the repeated failure by the remainder of 50 and 51 Brigade to capture Quadrilateral Support, and with 38th Division's failure to gain a toehold in Strip Trench along the southern extremity of Mametz Wood. Without Strip Trench in Welsh hands, the planned attack on Mametz Wood failed to take place at 02.00 hours, and was subsequently postponed to the next day. However, at dawn, C Company prepared to complete the clearance of the last seventy yards of Wood Trench to the junction with Strip Trench. At 06.00 hours, bombing platoon commander Lieutenant Davidson led another successful rush over the open ground to a strongly fortified German stop near the junction. In the broad daylight, Lieutenant Davidson was hit twice before falling mortally wounded, and was awarded a posthumous MC for 'performing this very gallant action'. With C Company holding a portion of Strip Trench, the Welshmen of 113 Brigade were able to advance and link up with the Dorsets who had opened the way for the attack on Mametz Wood. Meanwhile, A Company's connecting trench, New Trench, was reported as being five feet deep.

Lieutenant Davidson

Holding the Line

For the remainder of 9 July, the Dorsets had to endure an unpleasant day, that started with C Company being shelled by their own artillery, who had not been told that the junction of Wood and Strip Trenches had been captured. Throughout the day a 'heavy enemy barrage was maintained round battalion HQ and Bottom Wood and Railway Alley, but this did not deter the runners, who did invaluable work, nor the linesmen, who were kept busy practically the whole day and night mending the wires.' Lance Corporal Ennos was awarded an MM:

> For most conspicuous bravery ... He was absolutely indefatigable in his work as a linesman. For four days he went out at least a dozen times a day under terrific fire, mending wires. In particular on the night of July 9th he passed through an extraordinarily heavy barrage seven times to mend the line to a company in front with whom communication was imperative.

During 10 July, 6/Dorsets remained in Wood Trench on the periphery of the awful battle fought by 38th Division in Mametz Wood. Their battered position in a former German trench was repaired, and the soldiers scooped out 'funk holes' in the side of the trench in which they could shelter from enemy airburst shells. During the day, another junior officer, Lieutenant Clarke, was killed in No Man's Land while leading a patrol into Mametz Wood to find out how far 113 Brigade had advanced. However, the chief loss, amongst a steady stream of casualties, was that of the Acting Commanding Officer, Major Hughes-Onslow, 'who had been superintending operations in Wood Trench since the 8th, and was killed by a bullet at 11 a.m.' CSM Franklin located 'Major Onslow's sniper and with a well-aimed shot settled the account'. 17th Division was relieved by 21st Division on the night of 10-11 July, and 6/Dorsets left the Somme having lost a total of four officers killed and eight wounded. Casualties continued to be heavy amongst junior commanders.

The Dorsets had been spared the worst of the fighting on 1 July, and during the period 6-11 July avoided the very heavy casualties suffered by other units. This was largely as a result of the Battalion bombers' audacious dash across No Man's Land to secure Wood Trench. However, it is tempting to wonder how much more quickly operations would have developed in Mametz Wood if the Dorsets' attack on 7 July had been properly coordinated with 113 Brigade. This failure must be regarded more as a lack of training among inexperienced brigade and divisional staffs, in an Army that had expanded beyond its pool of experienced staff officers and commanders.

The battle on 1 July had been a clear success for the Germans but now they were fighting from their defences that were less well prepared, and they were suffering. Without the numerous deep dugouts of their main defensive line, the German casualties from the British artillery bombardments mounted. The most heavily engaged German battalions typically lost 500 men each, with 1/Lehr Regiment losing no less than 613 men during this period. Conditions were now extremely bad for the Germans: 'Reinforcement was difficult under the pitiless fire of the

In the heat of summer, corpses started to decay rapidly. Flies cover these German bodies.

British artillery, the troops were in a miserable state, lying in mud and water with many sick and wounded amongst them'[11]. Reacting to the growing threat posed by the British on the Somme, Falkenhayan halted offensive operations at Verdun on 11 July and put the German Army there on the defensive. This was exactly the effect Joffre wished the British attack to have, and hence forward, German reinforcements were marching in increasing numbers towards the Somme.

The Sacking of General Pilcher

When 17th Northern Division came out of the line, Corps Commander Lieutenant General Horne sent for its commander, Major General Pilcher, and immediately accused him of not driving his division forward regardless of loss. Pilcher was dismissed from his command and sent home. The General subsequently complained that:

> It is very easy to sit a few miles in the rear and get credit for allowing men to be killed in an undertaking foredoomed to failure, but the part did not appeal to me and my protests against these useless attacks were not well received.

Major General Pilcher served for the rest of the war in administrative and training posts in the UK.

1   *Official History, France and Belgium 1916*, Vol 2.
2   *History of the 17th (Northern) Division.* A. Hillard Atteridge.
3   This was in fact the wooded park of Fricourt Château rather than a proper wood as shown on the trench maps.
4   50 Brigade war diary. PRO WO 95/1998.
5   6/Dorsets war diary. PRO WO 95/2000.
6   17th Division war diary. PRO WO 95/1981.
7   On this part of the front, the name 'Alley' was generally used to denote a communication trench rather than a fighting trench.
8   MM citation in 50 Brigade war diary. PRO WO 95/2000.
9   Captain Geoffrey O'Hanlon had served with 6/Dorsets since 1914 and received an MC for capturing and holding Wood Trench.
10   6/Dorsets war diary. PRO WO 95/2000.
11   Quoted in the *British Official History. France and Belgium 1916*, Vol 2.

Chapter 10

The Battle of Bazentin Ridge

They dared: they won.
FRENCH LIAISON OFFICER

The Somme's next phase, the Battle for the Bazentin Ridge[1], is widely acknowledged to be one of the tactical highlights of the summer of 1916, in which the British infantry's success stands in stark contrast with the disasters of 1 July. 8/Devons were to play a significant part in the attack on Bazentin Ridge on 14 July 1916, which was also the high point of the Battalion's six-year existence during the Great War. It is, sad to say however, that the battle as a whole, despite its innovations and brilliant tactical success, proved to be one of the great missed opportunities of the war.

The story of the Battle for Bazentin Ridge began:

> On the 8th July, when the Fourth Army had yet to secure the important preliminary objectives – Trones Wood, Mametz Wood and Contalmaison – General Rawlinson issued a preparatory order for the attack against the German 2nd Position to be launched on the 10th. General preparations behind the Battle front, similar to those which preceded the great assault of the 1st July, were begun without delay, the engineers and pioneers clearing roads and tracks and filling in old trenches, the artillery moving forward guns and ammunition.[2]

The attack was, however, delayed until 14 July. Meanwhile, General Rawlinson's Fourth Army was fighting its way forward to the south of the Albert-Bapaume Road, on a five mile front towards the preliminary objectives listed above. The Fourth Army consisted of, from left to right, III Corps, XV Corps and XIII Corps.

The German Second Position

In the two weeks following 1 July, the Fourth Army had pushed the Germans back some 6,000 yards. With their forward position taken and the British slowly fighting their way through the intermediate lines such as those in the Quadrangle area, the Germans worked at strengthening their second position on the Bazentin Ridge between Pozières and Longueval. This position was not as well developed as the first, but still contained the basic features that had made the British infantry's job so difficult two weeks earlier.

The German defenders on the Somme, however, were now under pressure. Not only were they suffering heavy casualties, but units were also becoming mixed, as reinforcements were sent up to the line to plug gaps created by the flow of casualties suffered during repeated British attacks. Replacements at the

151

rate of approximately 100 men per battalion arrived on the Somme to make good the losses, which were typically in excess of 500 men from every battalion. Fresh German divisions were also arriving to reinforce General Fritz von Bulow's Second Army, and regrouping of German units and formations was taking place when British operations permitted. 20 Brigade's Operation Order[3] summed up the German situation on the southern portion of the Somme front:

> The enemy has been greatly disorganized by our attacks. He has been forced to draw on his reserves from all parts of the front, from the Ypres Salient, from Valenciennes and from Champagne. These troops have been thrown into the line at the shortest notice. ... Numbers of prisoners have been captured from all these units; but so much disorganization has been caused by the hurried arrival of reinforcements, that it cannot be stated with certainty which units will be met with, in or behind the German Second Position.

General Sixt von Armin's IV Corps held the area where the British were about to attack. The point in the German line that 8/Devons (20 Brigade, 7th Division) was preparing to assault proved to be astride the boundary of two of von Armin's divisions; the 183rd Division to the east of Mametz Wood and 3rd Guards Division to the west of the wood. To complicate the picture, one of the German formations arriving at the end of the second week of July 1916 was 7th German Division, who were in the process of relieving 183rd Division in the Mametz / Bazentin area.

The Fourth Army Plan
In planning the attack on the German's second position, the British commanders had to consider the distance between opposing front lines, which was on average 1,000 yards. After experiencing the fire from German machine guns on 1 July, the prospect of crossing that distance of No Man's Land was extremely unattractive. Therefore, as the Official Historian commentated:

> General Rawlinson decided, in agreement with the whole body of infantry opinion, that the main attack should be made at dawn, before there was sufficient light for the enemy machine gunners to see very far.

Furthermore, to reduce the distance that the assaulting troops needed to cover at Zero Hour, they were to form up at night, in the open, well out into No Man's Land.

As the following paragraph indicates, Field Marshal Haig doubted the ability of his troops to conduct such a complicated and risky operation:

> The Commander-in-Chief, however, raised objections to the forming up of divisions in the dark and to the dawn attack. He considered that the troops lacked the necessary training and discipline, and that many of the staff officers were not sufficiently experienced, for such a task; to move ... [two corps] in the dark over a distance of nearly half a mile, form them up, and deliver an attack in good order and in the right direction at dawn, would be very difficult even as a peace time

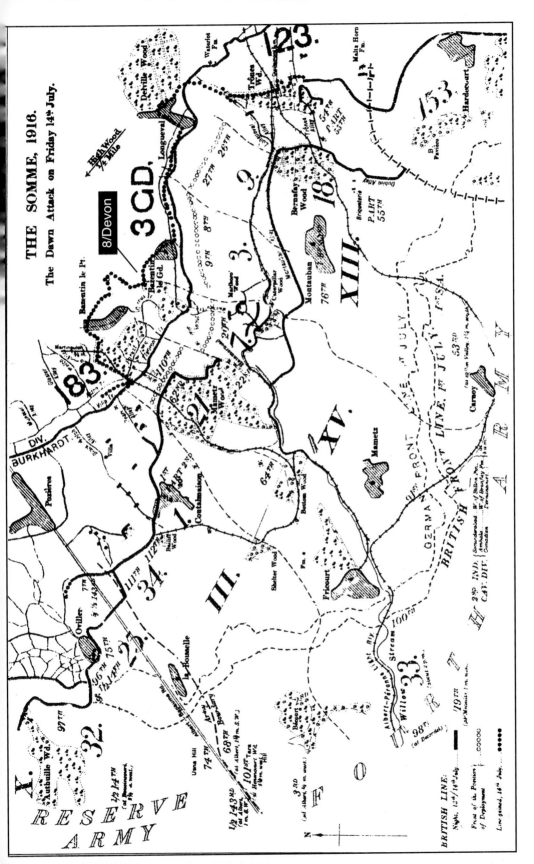

Fourth Army's attack on the German Second position.

manoeuvre.[4]

After much discussion, Field Marshal Haig was persuaded that General Rawlinson's plan for the Fourth Army's attack was viable. It was eventually agreed that XV and XIII Corps were to attack early on 14 July on a front of 6,000 yards, following a short 'hurricane bombardment'. Behind the attacking infantry, three cavalry divisions were ready to exploit a breakthrough. On the left, III Corps was to make a subsidiary attack with one division in order to protect the flank.

General Rawlinson hoped to extend the frontage of the attack by including the French on the right flank. The French, however, on seeing the plan, refused to take part, and sent notes to General Rawlinson imploring him not to take a course of action that they viewed as doomed to failure. They also doubted the ability of the relatively inexperienced British infantry and thought that the bombardment would be far too short to give any chance of success. One French general went so far as to say that he would eat his hat if the attack were to be successful! The French divisions were ordered to stand on the defensive throughout 14 July, but their commanders agreed to provide artillery support, which included their heavy guns and gas shells. While the possibility of a breakthrough on a wide Anglo/French front was gone, the resulting concentration of Allied artillery represented a significant improvement over that available prior to 1 July 1916.

The 7th Division's artillery had been in action since the beginning of the barrage in late June, while the infantry had benefited from five days comparative rest. However, as the date of the attack approached, the divisional Commander Royal Artillery had the use of the guns from those divisions who were out of the line, to boost his strength. Lessons had been learnt from the failure of the bombardment leading up to the attack on 1 July. The increased concentration of heavy guns available to support the assault on a much reduced front offered the prospect of being able to destroy enemy dugouts. The Germans' forward position in the Snout, 8/Devons' first objective, was to receive particular attention. With sufficient heavies, some medium guns could be released to help with tasks such as cutting wire, as the field guns' 18-pounder shrapnel shells could not alone be guaranteed to cut enemy wire. The artillery fire plan was carefully designed not to communicate the imminence of the attack to the enemy. It was to be a steady, calculated affair, slackening at night; but it was, in a surprise 'hurricane bombardment' just before Zero-Hour every gun, howitzer and trench mortar would fire as rapidly as possible for just five minutes.

As the British prepared for the attack, the aircraft of the Royal Flying Corps made use of their air superiority over the battlefield to photograph the enemy's second positions, which they could see were now being improved. On 11 July, the British artillery started the measured process of isolating the battlefield from its reserves by engaging key junctions to prevent supplies, and, above all, defence stores (needed to strengthen the positions) from reaching the German battle area. Light guns started to cut the enemy's wire, and, along with the heavier guns, started to destroy the forward defences. Meanwhile, a counter-battery fire plan targeted emplaced German batteries, along with those arriving on the Somme with reinforcing divisions.

Despite the number of guns available, there were initial concerns about the limited quantity of heavy howitzer ammunition for the British guns when the bombardment began. 2,000 rounds per field gun were eventually brought up, however, and batteries were pushed forward to the slopes behind Montauban. With British aircraft controlling the skies, it was possible to bring ammunition up by day and night. This was just as well, as the 1 July battlefield was so heavily broken that it took ammunition limbers up to six hours to complete a round trip from the ammunition dumps to the new gun positions. Crossing a belt of wrecked land captured at the beginning of an offensive was a perennial problem during the Great War, and was to have a profound effect on the outcome of the battle on 14 July 1916.

Following the salutary experience of 1 July, when the British had relearnt the old lessons of security and surprise, deception plans were carefully laid. In the Mametz/Bazentin area, reconnaissance and other activities that could give away the British intentions were strictly controlled. Meanwhile, the tempo of operations around Ovillers was stepped up, with the aim of disguising the point

Infantrymen sleep in funkholes in the side of a hastily dug trench, while one of their number keeps watch.

of attack. Also among the deception measures was an artillery bombardment on the Reserve Army's front to the north of the Ancre, during the hour before the Fourth Army's attack. Despite German claims that the British did not achieve total surprise, it is clear that they achieved an impressive degree of tactical surprise.

By 1916, signal intelligence was a growing source of information for both sides. On 13 July, it had been discovered that a German patrol had penetrated the British lines and tapped into one of the telephone lines forward from a brigade headquarters. Turning this discovery against the enemy, a message was passed to all companies in the front line at 21.00 hours: 'Operations postponed'. This simple deception measure almost certainly contributed to the success of the attack.

Both XV and XIII Corps were to attack with two divisions: the 7th and 21st on the left, and 3rd and 9th on the right. Their first objectives were the enemy's front and second positions, which stretched from Delville Wood to Bazentin le Petit Wood. Their second objectives included the whole of Delville Wood the Bazentin woods and villages. In protecting the left flank of Lieutenant General Horne's XV Corps, III Corps was to attack the area of Contalmaison Villa. 18th Division (XII Corps) was to attack Trones Wood, thus protecting the right flank, exposed by the French refusal to take part in the attack. Of the three cavalry divisions allocated to the attack, 2nd Indian Cavalry Division was under direct command of XV Corps, whose objective was High Wood, lying on the crest of the ridge beyond the Bazentin woods. Retained under command of the Fourth Army were 1st Cavalry Division, whose objective was Leutze Wood, and 3rd Cavalry Division, which were to take Martinpuich. With these divisions under his direct command, General Rawlinson had to rely heavily on accurate and timely information from the two assaulting corps to cue the cavalry into action.

Corps and Divisional Plans

Aiming to make a significant advance, Lieutenant General Horne's plan for XV Corps was that both of his two divisions should attack on a single brigade frontage. These brigades were to seize initial objectives, after which fresh infantry brigades and cavalry would cross the newly captured ground to resume the advance deep into enemy territory. On the left, 21st Division was to attack, with 110 Brigade, from positions forward of Mametz Wood. 7th Division, whose front line lay some way up the Montauban Ridge, was to assault on the Corps' right, with 20 Brigade. As an insurance policy against the disaster envisaged by the French, the Commander-in-Chief had insisted that the strong points be constructed across the front of XV Corps.

Orders for the attack arrived at 7th Division's Headquarters on 11 July, the day that the divisional artillery began the deliberately desultory process of cutting the wire in front of the second position. It was also that evening that 7th Division returned to the line, in the form of 9/Devons, who took over the new front line. Meanwhile, the staff officers planned the coming battle and issued the divisional operation order the following morning. Having extracted his tasks from

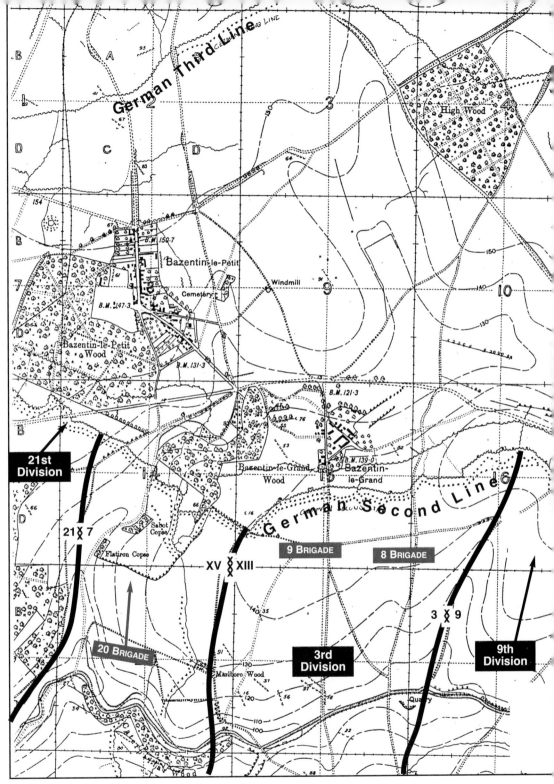

XV Corps plan for 14 July 1916.

the Corps orders, Major General Watts elected to attack with 20 Brigade. They were to clear the 'Snout', a salient at Bazentin Wood's southerly extremity, and the flanking German trenches, and then advance through Bazentin Wood to its northern limit with two battalions. 22 Brigade was then advance through the assault brigade and take the village of Bazentin le Petit and its cemetery. 91 Brigade, south of Mametz, was to remain in reserve, while the Indian Cavalry Division took over the advance.

One of the preliminary tasks detailed in the divisional operation order was the formation of advanced dumps of trench stores and infantry ammunition in what was still No Man's Land. This led to sleepless nights for the Devons, with the 9th deploying strong patrols in No Man's Land to cover the exhausted men of the 8th Battalion who, among others, were carrying forward trench stores and ammunition.

Brigadier Deverell, Commander 20 Brigade, had little planning to do other than nominate his battalions to given tasks, as the general plan had been laid down by Major General Watts. The Brigadier selected 2/Borders, the only Regular Army unit among the fourteen battalions chosen to lead the Fourth Army's assault, to attack on the left. 8/Devons who amongst the Brigade's New Army battalions, had lost the fewest men on 1 July, were chosen to assault on the right. 2/Gordons, who had suffered grievously on 1 July, were to be the brigade supports, occupying positions in the Hammerhead, at the tactically important junction of Caterpillar and Flatiron Valleys. Once the assault had begun, 9/Devons were to leave their strong points and concentrate in Caterpillar Wood where they would become 20 Brigade's reserve.

20 Brigade's initial objective was the front trench of the German's second position, Flatiron Trench[5], which ran across the open ground in front of Bazentin le Grand Wood and around the Snout. Having taken the enemy's front line, the Brigade was to advance and take its second objective, Circus Trench, which cut through the centre of Bazentin-le-Grand Wood. 20 Brigade's final objective lay along the northern edge of Bazentin-le-Grand Wood.

In contrast to the orders issued for 1 July, those for 14 July were daring and encouraged risk taking:

... deployment is to be completed one hour before the Zero Hour. During this hour, both battalions will advance forward by crouching and crawling to a position as close to the barrage limit as they possibly can do, so they enter the German front line immediately the barrage lifts, when they will go forward at once in the same advance and occupy the second objective of the Brigade, and will at once consolidate the first two objectives.

There was to be no repetition of the pause that allowed the German machine gunners to set their guns up and open fire at the steadily advancing khaki ranks. However, the orders concluded with what proved to be tragic inflexibility; 'The 20th Brigade *will not* advance beyond their 3rd Objective.' They were to await the arrival of the cavalry, who would then advance to the ridge's crest line in the area of High and Delville Woods.

Preparations for Battle

158

9/Devons had been out of the line since 2 July, and had received drafts totalling 486 men, to replace the heavy casualties suffered during its successful attack on Mametz. Of these replacements, only forty-six were from the Devonshires' regimental reserve, 3/Devons. For the second time in a year[6] the complexion of the Battalion had changed and further diluted its West Country character. In contrast to the experience of the Devons, 2/Gordons received a draft almost exclusively of Highlanders. Also, all the Irish soldiers arriving amongst the various drafts were extracted and directed to 2/R. Irish in 22 Brigade. Meanwhile, the newly arrived 'Devonians' had little time to get accustomed to their new companies, as 9/Devons, during the afternoon of 11 July, marched to take over the front line from 38th Division. The positions occupied by the Battalion were a series of outposts about 1,000 yards from the enemy, the chief of which was located in Marlboro Wood[7]. Here a 'stop' and a strongpoint were formed at the point where Marlboro Trench cut across No Man's Land towards the Snout. The construction of this position was one of Field Marshal Haig's stipulated insurance policies, designed to provide a firm line for troops to fall back on, in case of disaster. According to 7th Division's history, the Battalion's new position:

> *... ran from East of Mametz Wood in front of Caterpillar Wood with outposts in Marlboro Wood. Caterpillar Wood was itself untenable owing to shell fire, so a line was taken up at the foot of the rise towards the next ridge where good cover could be obtained, and though the enemy fired away steadily during the next two days, casualties were remarkably low.*

While 9/Devons held the line, the remainder of 20 Brigade spent the days before the attack occupied with reconnaissance patrols and with rehearsals for the coming battle. Meanwhile, the British artillery continued its measured bombardment of the enemy's wire and the trenches.

During the afternoon of 13 July, 8/Devons and 2/Borders concentrated at Minden Post. Major Dawes, who had taken over command of the battalion, wrote in his post-operational report:[8]

The Battalion marched

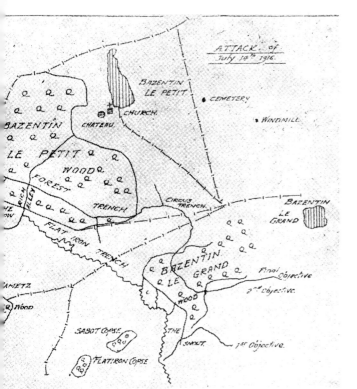

Map from Devons' regimental history.

159

from Minden Post at 10.25 p.m. Owing to the necessity of crossing trenches by bridges, the Battalion moved in single file. Several obstacles, wire and open trenches were encountered which greatly delayed the troops. Only one casualty occurred before the companies deployed, which was caused by a [falling shell[9]] fuse from our own guns.

While 20 Brigade's assault troops were covering the four miles to their assembly area, 9/Devons and the other front line battalions were dominating No Man's Land with fighting patrols. The Germans had deployed very few patrols however, and those that were active were driven back to their own lines or, in one case, according to German accounts, simply disappeared. At 11.30 hours, 9/Devons reported that there was no enemy activity on the 20 Brigade front.

When German prisoners were subsequently interrogated about their lack of patrol activity on the evening of 13 July, their answer was that there were not enough reliable NCOs to mount patrols. The Official History scathingly commented that apparently patrolling 'in the German Army was not officers' work'.

Having reached their assembly area in Caterpillar Wood, the two assault battalions paused, while a screen of scouts was sent forward into No Man's Land as a further precaution to prevent German patrols from interfering with their deployment. Once the screen was deployed, Brigade staff officers, who had made a thorough reconnaissance of the route, led 8/Devons forward in single file. This route took them along the Marlboro trench and then across the shell-marked fields of No Man's Land up the slope towards the brooding silence of the Snout.

The Brigade staff officers and attached Royal Engineers had laid out a start line using rolls of white cloth 'mine tape' on which the Devons and 2/Borders were to form up. According to the Official History, there had been anxious moments while GHQ's logistic staff tried to locate the several miles of two-inch white tape required to mark out the forming-up points. This vital night assault item had been misplaced in one of the

A heavy shell bursting on the German lines.

hundreds of supply dumps between Rouen and the front. The tape was eventually located in good time for it to be laid out by the much maligned staff officers. Start lines marked with tape ensured that the attackers, on unfamiliar ground, started the operation in the correct formation and heading in the right direction.

2/Borders were deployed to the right of the track that ran along the bottom of Flatiron Valley, which was the Division's left boundary, and up onto the hillside. Beyond them, eighteen officers and 637 other ranks of 8/Devons deployed in the open, with the forward assault platoons along a low bank, with scrubby trees growing along its length. Major Dawes wrote:

> At 2.25 a.m., the companies reported that they were in position. The Battalion was then deployed as follows: 2 companies formed the assaulting line in column of half companies, with the leading platoons of each extended at three paces, the remaining two platoons of each in a second line, 100 yards in rear, similarly extended. [A Company was right forward and D Company was on the left]. One Company [C Company] in small column 150 yards in rear again. One company [B Company] was in Battalion Reserve close to Marlboro Wood. The left of the leading Company was in touch with 2/Border; the right on a track in touch with 3rd Division (West Yorks).

8/Devons' Bombing Platoon had made their way up Marlboro Trench and were positioned forward of the Battalion's start line. Also deployed with the two assault battalions were the engineers of 95th Field Company and two Companies of the divisional Pioneer Battalion, 24/Manchesters. The task of these two units was to put the German trenches into a state of defence and to construct strong points, which were to be occupied by the Brigade's Machine Gun Company before the Germans could counter-attack.

Confounding the expectations of Field Marshal Haig and the French, 20 Brigade and the rest of the assaulting troops had successfully formed up in the open, within 500 yards of the enemy position, without confusion or being detected. This was the first major achievement of the Battle of Bazentin Ridge.

The Attack

The night was overcast with little ambient light but direction could be more or less kept, as the outline of the woods behind the Snout was silhouetted on the horizon above and in front of the infantry. The Devons started moving forward shortly after 02.30 hours.

> ... covered by scouts in front the battalions got level with the Southern edge of Flatiron Copse undetected. Here they halted for a few minutes and then started off again crawling up the slope. They moved steadily with incredible silence, gradually getting nearer the German line without any indication that their advance had been discovered. An occasional shell from the German guns burst over them, but it was nothing more than the usual intermittent firing ...[10]

Tension rose at the various headquarters, as every minute that passed improved the chance of success. Captain Bellwood, commanding D Company, wrote:

> Could the silence last till the hurricane bombardment of five minutes was due to start? 3.0 am, all quiet; 3.5, all quiet; 3.10 only a few of our MGs doing overhead fire in a casual way; 3.15, a few stray shells, but nothing to denote an alarm; 3.18; 3.19; 3.20! Then every gun for

miles around gave tongue as the shells hurled overhead. The surprise had succeeded.

The regimental history continues,

> shortly before 03.20 hours, *there had been some crowding in this stealthy advance; companies had got mixed, men were in their wrong lines. Still, when the barrage burst out, the battalion was in a line of sorts and under 100 yards from the enemy's line.*

The British bombardment was tremendous; it lit the sky behind the crawling infantry, and the ground heaved beneath the men as the hurricane of exploding shells struck the enemy positions. The gunners behind the Montaban/Mametz Ridge sweated, despite the cold of dawn, as they loaded and fired their pre-prepared shells as fast as they could. According to Major Dawes, 'during the intense bombardment the leading line crept further forward and at Zero Hour was within 25 yards of the enemy's line'. The regimental historian continued that, despite some casualties from their own artillery, 'directly the guns lifted [their fire], the men leapt up, and a wild rush carried them up to the trenches, almost before any German could put up any fight'. So heavy and accurate had been the fire of F and T Batteries Royal Horse Artillery (both affiliated to the Devons) that Flatiron Trench on either side of the Snout was almost totally wrecked. The German wire was in front of D Company on the left was only cut in patches but on the right, A Company found plenty of gaps. A Company's commander, Lieutenant Lewis,[11] led his men into the German trenches on the eastern face of the Snout as planned. 8/Devons' after action report recorded that:

> *At 3.26 a.m., the Battalion entered the enemy lines. The right company met very little resistance in the front line. They cleared it easily and bombed a few dug-outs. They remained in it for 10 minutes and reached the second line [Circus Trench] at 3.45 am, which appeared unheld.*

However, during the consolidation, Lieutenant Lewis was killed by a belated enemy artillery barrage. Despite his loss, the company, along with its engineer and pioneer support, formed two strong points, while the West Countrymen pushed patrols forward into Bazentin Wood.

On the western part of the Snout, the barrage did not lift until 03.30 hours. During D Company's crawl forward from the start line, they and the right flank company of 2/Borders veered in to each other's area, and the poorly cut wire worsened the mixing. Major Dawes recorded that this:

> *... allowed some enemy to man trenches and get an automatic rifle into action which caused casualties. This party was soon accounted for by bombers. Dug-outs were bombed as the enemy in several cases would not surrender and fired from the dugouts. One bomber and a Lewis Gun team co-operated with great success. A long tunnel dug-out contained many of the enemy. The bomber threw in at one entrance, while the Lewis Gun accounted for the enemy attempting to retire from the far entrance. Very little remained of the trench, which formed the 2 objective. The Company finally advanced to the north edge of*

The attack of 8/Devons and 20 Brigade on Bazentin-le-Grand Wood.

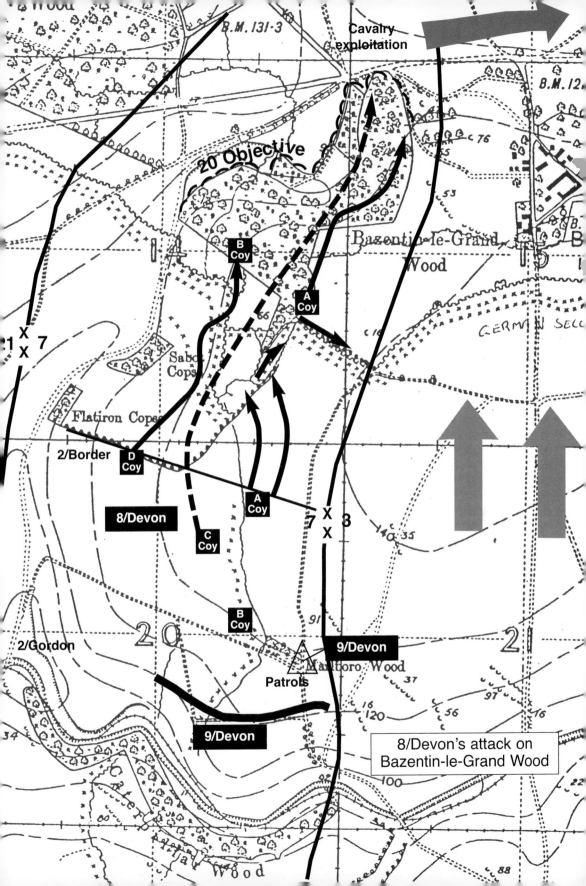

8/Devon's attack on
Bazentin-le-Grand Wood

the Wood and dug in. At 4.10 am a message was sent to Brigade Headquarters that this Company had reached its final objective. This Company only took a very few prisoners.

The combination of resistance with the salutary experience on 1 July, of active German infantry appearing behind the advancing Devons, led D Company to clear the dugouts thoroughly and not to take risks – or many prisoners.

The two assault companies sent forward patrols from their positions along Circus Trench into the flanks of Bazentin Wood, which was being raked by a British artillery and machine-gun barrage. A Company patrols returned with about sixty prisoners. Equally successful were 2/Borders on the left and 3rd Division's 12/West Yorks on the right, but the bulk of Bazentin-le-Grand Wood was still to be captured. However, 8/Devons' A and D Companies had diverged to left and right as they cleared the Snout. C Company, in support 450 yards to the rear, was summoned forward to plug the gap in the centre of the Battalion's area. Led forward by Lieutenant Savill, C Company entered the Snout at 03.34 hours. C Company's leading platoons swept across the captured ground and on towards the wood, despite a 'light enemy barrage'. However, they were attacked in the rear by a group of twenty Germans who appeared from a dugout. With C Company's support and reserve platoons following, the Germans found themselves surrounded, and surrendered. Other groups of less determined Germans were hurried on their way by,

> Corporal Selby, [who] *handled his Lewis Gun most skilfully, got it into action directly the trench was rushed and knocked over many Germans who were trying to retire through the wood.*[12]

As the Devons continued their advance into the wood, Lieutenant Savill took the surrender of the German regimental commander, who 'was disconcerted at having to surrender to such a junior officer'. Having filled the vacuum between the A and D Companies, C Company supported by the flanking patrols, advanced into the depth of the enemy position and on towards the Battalion's final objective. So successful had they been that, having got into the wood, the Devons had to wait to advance while the timed barrage ran its course on the 'One Hour Line'. The advance to the northern end of the wood resumed at 04.25 hours, once the British artillery lifted. The advance was helped by:

> *Second Lieutenant Joseph bringing up reinforcements to help the leading lines of C to clear the wood. When it reached the crest in the middle of the wood, C found two companies of enemy sheltering at the bottom of the slope beyond. C at once opened fire, on which the Germans promptly bolted and made up the opposite slope towards the windmill, affording a magnificent target, of which C took full advantage. Sergeant Potter got his Lewis Gun team promptly into position, and hardly any Germans escaped.*

In revenge for 1 July, the boot was now on the other foot: the Devons glared north over the green slope towards Bazentin-le-Petit which was covered in crumpled field grey bodies, victims of their concentrated fire power. It is worthy of note that the Official Historian complained of the attack as a whole that:

> *In many units, the men, owing to lack of training, could not be depended upon to hit anything even at 300 yards; in despair, officers took up rifles and picked off fleeing Germans until the machine guns could be brought forward.*

Prisoners alone exceeded the Devons' total casualties, and an 8-inch howitzer and its crew was captured in the wood. As was often the case, the reserve, B Company, suffered the majority of the casualties, having been caught by a German barrage while crossing the former No Man's Land.

At 05.45 hours, 20 Brigade was informed that 8/Devons controlled the whole of Bazentin Wood and that the battalion had seized its third objective on the northern edge of the wood. The attack had been successful virtually all along the front, but nowhere was the success so rapidly achieved as in Bazentin Wood. 2/Borders also successfully cleared Sabot Copse and the valley between Bazentin and Mametz Woods. The divisional historian commented:

> *The Seventh Division's rapid success had certainly opened up possibilities which, if promptly turned to account, might have been of the utmost importance. ... The country ahead was a refreshing sight,*

The German gun captured in Bazentin Wood by 8/Devons.

green pastureland unscarred by shell-holes and broken by an occasional hedge, while High Wood itself was in full leaf, not a tree as yet damaged by shell fire.

2/Warwicks and 2/Royal Irish Regiment (RIR), both of 22 Brigade, advanced through the Devons and the Borders towards Bazentin le Petit. Meanwhile, at 06.45 hours, 20 Brigade was reporting that it was 'consolidated', in good order, with virtually no opposition in front of it. The Brigade also had uncommitted reserves, in the form of both 2/Gordons and 9/Devons, of whom the latter 'were cooling their heels in Caterpillar Wood'. However, the order that 'The 20th

A German observation platform and sniping position in Bazentin le Petit Wood.

Brigade will not advance beyond its 3rd Objective' held them back, despite officers from the Devons and Brigade Headquarters walking up the hillside towards High Wood. At 07.40 hours, word came that 22 Brigade had taken the Bazentin le Petit area. Runners bore the news back to the two brigade headquarters, and telephone requests were passed back to Division and Corps to be allowed to continue the advance. These 'increasingly exasperated requests' from 3rd and 7th Divisions were repeatedly rejected, with the 7th being told to wait for the cavalry. In Atkinson's words, to those at the front:

> ... it really seemed as if prompt exploitation of this opening might lead to great results. High Wood, at least, was to be had for the asking, and had another division been put in at once High Wood and the ground on either side of it, much of which was not to pass into British keeping until the tank attack two months later, might have been secured.

The Official Historian was more direct in his criticism of 'higher authority'. 'It was in the highest degree unfortunate that at a moment when fresh troops were at hand to maintain the impetus of the advance, such a delay should have been imposed. ... Every hour was precious.'

General Sixt von Armin who took personal command of the crumbling German front at 09.00 hours to find that 'there were no rear positions, no switches, no communication trenches and the artillery had suffered severely.'[13] General von Armin ordered all forward troops to hold where they were, while he set about organizing the scant reserves into depth positions. He was aided by the fact that troops from the 7th German Division arriving on the Somme were available, to be fed into battle piecemeal, or halted to cover important pieces of ground. This process took most of the day and his efforts were successful, thanks largely to the British failing to immediately press home their advantage.

The window of opportunity offered by the breaching of the German line was short, and before long, the volume of artillery fire on the Devons, who were digging in along the northern edge of the wood, increased. Between 10.00 and 11.00 hours the Germans heavily bombarded the wood and mounted their first counter-attack, which was beaten off. However, pressure mounted as troops from the German 7th Division were rushed forward to support the desperate 183rd Division, 'whose front had been broken'. Major Dawes wrote:

> During this time an urgent request for support came from [2/RIR at] the Cemetery. The OC Support Company [C Company] in position on the left, sent forward an officer [Second Lieutenant Joseph] and a platoon. It was reported that this party gave valuable assistance during the enemy's counter-attack.

8/Devons remained in position on the northern edge of the wood until the following night, witnessing the advance of the cavalry. During the attack and the thirty-six hours spent holding positions at the edge of the wood, 8/Devons lost three officers killed in action and five wounded. The other ranks suffered nineteen killed, 123 wounded and twenty-one men listed as missing in action. Though bad enough, the casualties were relatively light when considering the fact that the Devons had pushed the enemy front line back by almost a mile. This was one of the Regiment's most significant achievements of the war, and it is a tragedy that 9/Devons were not brought forward with the Gordons to exploit the success.

The Attack on High Wood

After a considerable delay, the Secunderabad Cavalry Brigade arrived at the front. They had started moving forward from their assembly area four miles south of Albert at 08.20 hours 'but its progress across slippery ground cut up by trenches and pitted with shell-holes proved very slow'. It was well past midday when the advance guard arrived in the Montauban area. British infantry and German counter-attacks delayed the cavalry's deployment. At 17.40 hours, Brigadier Gregory received orders issued by XV Corps to take his Brigade to Sabot Copse, where it arrived to support a coordinated attack by 91 Brigade (7th Division) and troops from 33rd Division. However, by late afternoon, the enemy had recovered from the surprise attack and were completing the process of plugging the gap that had been torn in their line. Never had the German genius for improvisation been tested so thoroughly. The divisional history described the attack:

> The belated effort to utilize the chance of capturing High Wood was made by the South Staffords and the Queens, who were to be supported on their right by the advance of the Secunderabad Cavalry Brigade ... and on their left by the leading brigade of the Thirty Third Division, who were to come through the Twenty First. The Queens and South Staffords had moved up earlier in the morning to a position East of Mametz Wood, where they dug in under heavy shell fire, disposed in artillery formation. Here they remained for over six hours...
>
> It was well after 5 o'clock when at last the orders reached them: the South Staffords were to lead and to deploy with their left on the Bazentin le Petit cemetery; the Queens were to form on the South Staffords' right, their right flank being approximately North of Bazentin le Grand village. The barrage was to lift at 6.15 p.m. ... There was no chance of reaching the position of deployment before the barrage lifted, but the two battalions pushed ahead and about 6.45 p.m. deployed ... with about a mile to cover to reach the wood. Nothing was to be seen of Thirty Third Division ... By 7 p.m. however, all was ready and the advance started.

The Devons were 'thrilled' by the rare and unfamiliar sight of cavalry advancing past them into action. Armed with lances, the squadrons of the 7th Dragoon Guards and the Decan Horse, tack and accoutrements jangling, formed up on the open ground in front of the West Countrymen who looked on from their newly dug trench. The two regiments set off up the hill, at the trot, towards High Wood in open column of squadrons. Meanwhile, the supporting infantry of 91 Brigade

> at once came under machine-gun fire from the high ground just West of High Wood, which enfiladed it and caused the South Staffords several casualties, while there was some fire from Germans in shell-

Indian cavalrymen photographed on 14 July 1916 during one of their many delays on their move forward.

holes straight ahead. However, orders were issued to the Queens to push on hard for High Wood, hoping that they would be able to get into the wood and outflank the troublesome machine-guns.... As they came on, they dislodged the Germans in the shell-holes, a few of whom stopped to surrender or be bayoneted; the majority bolted....

It took the two battalions half an hour to reach High Wood. The process of clearing German infantry from defended shell holes was 'hampered and delayed by the persistent machine-guns on their flanks'. The Queens and the Staffords plunged into the wood together. 'It was thick with dense undergrowth, in which it was hard to see twenty yards ahead, so direction was difficult to keep.'

To the infantry's right, the Secunderabad Cavalry Brigade, benefiting from the cover of the low ground and the fact that it was crossing 3rd Division's front, advanced up the slope towards Longueval village and Delville and High Woods. There was some 'sniping' from infantry concealed in the standing crops, but one of the machine guns brought up during the day opened fire as the horsemen trotted up onto the ridge between the two woods. A British airman spotted the enemy position in Delville Wood, and in a strafing attack, successfully engaged the enemy gun. The advance continued into the gap between Delville and High Woods. Here, with a misplaced German bombardment falling behind them, the,

7th Dragoon Guards charged some infantry and machine gunners in the crops, killed a number with the lance and captured 32, whilst a German machine gun near Longueval was silenced by the cavalry machine guns before it had done much damage.

By 21.30 hours, it was too dark for further mounted action. Cavalry could not advance across unreconnoitered ground and retain speed necessary for protection in the modern age.

Despite the delay, the cavalry, supported by their mounted machine-gun sections, artillery and aircraft had, in fact, fared better against the improvised German positions than many commentators have given them credit for. They had suffered casualties, but these were not disproportionate in either men or

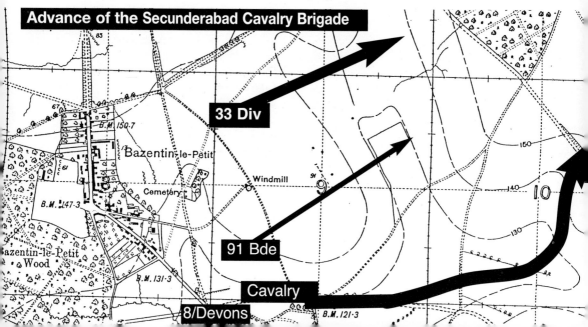

Advance of the Secunderabad Cavalry Brigade

horses, when compared with those of the supporting infantry advancing on High Wood. However, as recorded in the regimental history, 'before long, the Devons saw, to their great disappointment, the cavalry coming back'. It is probably the infantry's lack of understanding of the characteristics and abilities of the cavalry that led to the legend of failure.

Regarding the Secunderabad Brigade's advance, the German Official History recorded that:

> The appearance of cavalry near High Wood gave rise to alarmist reports at Corps and Army Headquarters that the British had broken through northwards between Longueval and Pozieres and by 9.40 P.M. had reached the line Flers – High Wood – Martinpuich and were still advancing.

Overnight, German reserves, no less than four divisions, were rushed to reinforce the Longueval High Wood area and to occupy the Switch Line, which was now their new second line. The number of reinforcements is an indication of how seriously the German commanders considered the possibility of a breakthrough in case of a renewed British attack. The battle continued over the following days against stiffening German opposition. However, having suffered significant losses during the attack and in defence, 8/Devons remained in position on the edges of Bazentin-le-Grand Wood until relieved at 13.00 hours on 15 July.

The 9th Battalion remained in reserve in Caterpillar Wood, where they suffered no less than ninety casualties in two days, despite the fact that they were now almost a mile behind the front line. It was not without reason that over the coming two months of fighting for High Wood, the route forward to the front became known as 'Death Valley'.

Missed Opportunity

It is worth looking more closely at the failure to take High Wood on the morning of 14 July, that condemned the British Army to two months of some of the most desperate fighting of the whole battle. It was not until the middle of September that the wood was finally captured at a terrible cost, including the lives of hundreds of West Country soldiers. The 7th Division History analyses at some length the failure to exploit their success:

> ...about 9 a.m. on July 14th, a rapid advance, either of a fresh Division or of all the reserves of the Seventh, might have led to the capture of High Wood. Only four battalions had been employed to secure the Division's objectives, and General Watts with two-thirds of his infantry in hand had been most anxious to be allowed to exploit the opening which his leading battalions had so brilliantly made. The artillery, as already mentioned, had pushed forward and taken up new positions in Flatiron Valley and Caterpillar Valley and could have supported a further advance. Two hours passed before the Germans ventured on a counter-attack, and though later in the morning they had counter-attacked with vigour and persistence, these efforts

apparently exhausted all their immediately available reserves... An advance at 9 a.m. therefore might not have met more opposition than the Division could deal with successfully. It might of course have been difficult to get the reserves forward or to move up the guns in time for an advance as early as 9 a.m., but if the whole 91st Brigade had gone forward ... instead of being kept back by orders to let the cavalry advance, there would still have been a chance of a considerable success. General Watts had had the 91st Brigade ready soon after 11 a.m., and had it advanced about 3 p.m. the cavalry might have achieved more by following it up than was actually done.

It is one of the drawbacks of attacks with strictly limited objectives that complete and rapid success may sometimes not be fully exploited just because it has exceeded expectations. The Seventh Division had done its task so quickly and so cheaply that the limitation of its objectives was for once a handicap. It is easy to be wise after the event, but had General Watts had a freer hand it does look as if High Wood might have been secured; and High Wood, as events showed only too clearly, was the key to much. Its capture would have, for example, outflanked Switch Trench and the other defences between it and Longueval, doubtless with very salutary results on the struggle for Delville Wood. The opening was not fully improved, but the Seventh Division deserves all the credit for having made it.

Nonetheless, 8/Devons could relish the letter of praise borne by one of Field Marshal Haig's aide-de-camps to 20 Brigade, conveying his personal congratulations on their performance on 14 July 1916. Despite the senior commanders' failure to exploit the unexpectedly complete success, this was indeed the apogee of the 8th's existence during the First World War.

1   So named by the Battlefield Nomenclature Committee to cover the fighting on the Fourth Army front between 14 and 17 July 1916.
2   *Official History. France and Belgium 1916.* Vol 2.
3   20 Brigade Op. Order No. 74. PRO WO 95/1653
4   Ibid.
5   A corruption of the name of a nearby copse – Flatrion Copse taken from the original French base map.
6   The Battalion had suffered 476 casualties at Loos in September 1915.
7   There are several different spellings used in the various accounts. The spelling used throughout this chapter is that found on the 2 June 1916 Montauban map sheet.
8   Contained in 20 Brigade's war diary. PRO WO 95/1653.
9   Up to 25% of some natures of artillery shell, particularly the heavy ones, failed to detonate. The manufacturing problems that caused this failure were not resolved until late on in the war.
10 *The Seventh Division 1914 – 1918.* C.T. Atkinson, John Murray, London, 1927.
11 In the peacetime British Army and during the Devons' early battles, majors had commanded the rifle companies.
12 *The Devonshire Regiment 1914 – 1918.* C.T. Atkinson, Exeter, 1926.
13 Quoted in the British Official History.

Chapter 11

The High Wood Attack and Veale VC

Dear Louise and Children – my darlings
The gods only know if I am writing for the last time. We have now
been two days in the front trenches. We get nothing to eat or drink and
life is almost unendurable. Here I have given up hope of life and there
really is no hope that we will see each other again

GERMAN SOLDIER. THE SOMME, JULY 1916

One of the Devonshire Regiment's two Victoria Crosses earned during the Great War was won on the slopes south-east of High Wood during the fighting there in July 1916. It is appropriate that following the Regiment's success at Mametz and at Bazentin Wood the highest award went to a soldier who fought in both of these actions with 8/Devons. The two Devon battalions serving in 7th Division remained on the Somme following the 14 July attack, and 8/Devons had the distinction of taking part in three major attacks, within three weeks. In the third attack, the objective was the ridge that lay between High Wood and Delville Wood: the same ridge that had been held briefly by the Secunderbad Cavalry Brigade on the evening of 14 July 1916.

In the six days between the dawn attack on Bazentin Wood and the Devons' next attack, the fighting had been heavy. The German reserves, sucked into battle with the Fourth Army by the threatened breakout, had restored the situation, and were resisting every attempt by the British to advance. The fighting was particularly severe in the Longueval and Delville Wood area, where 9th Scottish Division, along with their attached South African Brigade, fought themselves and the Germans to a standstill. On XV Corps' front, it became clear that High Wood and the ridge to the west were heavily defended, and would need to be attacked by the Fourth Army in a properly prepared and mounted general attack. However, the attack was delayed and the plans changed several times before it could be delivered.

After an absence from the Somme of six months, 5th Division, along with 1/Devons (95 Brigade), returned to Picardy and joined XV Corps, alongside 8/ and 9/Devons in 7th Division. The rate of casualties amongst the infantry meant that divisions were sent to the Somme, rested, trained, and took in casualty replacements, but after a week or so in battle they left again, exhausted and depleted in numbers. 1/Devons, however, were not to play a significant part in the next operation, as they were 95 Brigade's reserve located near Montauban, over a mile behind the battle. Despite their distance from the front, the battalion suffered twenty casualties from intermittent enemy counter-battery artillery fire that was searching out the British gun positions that surrounded them.

The Germans

Following 14 July, the Germans had regrouped their forces, and recognizing the severity of the threat posed by the British offensive, had not only called off offensive action at Verdun but were now diverting troops, key commanders and staff officers to the Somme. As a part of the reorganization of their front, the German First Army was now facing the British Fourth Army, under the overall direction of Army Group commander, 'fire eater' General von Gallwitz. He immediately proposed to launch a counter-offensive south of the Somme. However, Falkenhayn's broader perspective led him to respond that 'to hold on is all that matters'.

As a result of adopting a defensive posture, the Germans were making strenuous efforts to improve their third position or Switch Line, which lay beyond High Wood: Longueval and Delville Wood. Not only was this line improved but it was also manned by 72 Regiment of 8th Division. Consequently, unlike the position that the Germans held on 14 July, the line now to be attacked on 20 July 1916 had significant operational depth. This meant that British attacks would have to return to the step-by-step approach, as the immediate possibility of a breakthrough had passed.

7th Division's Plans

Eventually, orders for the attack were issued. 20 Brigade's Operation Order[1] summarized the British plan and its strictly limited aim of taking the crest of the ridge that extended from Pozières to High Wood to Delville Wood and on to Ginchy:

(a) *The Fourth Army will continue the attack tomorrow.*

(b) *The XIII Corps will be attacking Guillemont and Ginchey. The objective of the III Corps will be the Switch Line west of the Railway (area Pozières Village).*

(c) *The XV Corps will capture High Wood and the German Switch Line between High Wood and the Railway, 7 Division being on the right, 33 Division on the left.*

The 7th Division was ordered to capture the south-eastern edge of High Wood and the portion of the Switch Trench west of High Wood. 33rd Division was to attack the wood itself, while 5th Division (XIII Corps) on the right were to attack on a similarly narrow front between 7th Division and Longueval. The 7th Division's attack was again to be delivered by 20 Brigade, who had been out of the line in bivouacs[2] since 16 July. Brigadier Deverell's plan was for his brigade to assault on an 800 yard frontage, with 8/Devons on the right and with 2/Gordons on the left. 2/Borders and a company of 9/Devons were in support, located at Caterpillar Wood. 1/Royal Welch Fusiliers (1/RWF), who were to be Brigade Reserve, reinforced 20 Brigade. The remainder of 9/Devons had stayed in the rear, absorbing replacements for casualties suffered on 1 July and while the Battalion had been holding the line after 14 July.

Private Oatley, along with a draft of Gloucester Regiment soldiers, was taken from a 'cushy week's duty guarding Rouen railway station, in the rear area ... to

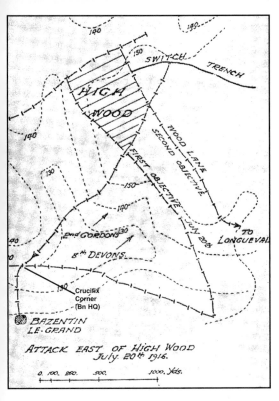

A map from the Devons' regimental history.

join a battered battalion of Devonshires who were somewhere on the Albert [Somme] front'. Joining the 9th Battalion, they arrived:

... outside one of the cottages the Devons were using as stores, where we left our caps with the Gloucester badges and were issued with our new 'tin hats', a bully beef stew awaited us after we had refreshed ourselves with a lathering of soap under the village pump.

Then, continuing our way towards the firing line, we saw overhead, intrepid airmen were fighting their battle like knights of old in modern armour. Fascinated, we watched them as they manoeuvred their planes between puffs of smoke from bursting [anti-aircraft] shells. Behind us, mounted on a railway track, a gun of ours was hurling its shell to land on German strongpoints to the east.

Batches of prisoners under escort passed us on their way to the cages at the rear. Some sullen, some arrogant when returning our scrutiny. All of them weary. Dirty with the grime of shell ploughed earth.

The men of 9/Devons were further up the valley, entrenched in what they called Death Gully[3]. The Devons were resting there stunned it seemed by the losses they had sustained.[4]

Assembly

The Devons' regimental historian described the ground and the German position.

The map shows two roads running S.E. from High Wood to Longueval, parallel and about 300 yards apart. These ran along the top of a ridge covered with standing corn. It was over this ground that the Secunderbad Cavalry Brigade had tried to advance on the 14th, and the many dead horses lying about testified to the efficiency of the machine gun against cavalry.

Beyond this crest line 'lay Switch Trench, which ran east and west through the northern part of High Wood and was full of machine guns'.

The Gordons and the Devons led the Brigade forward from the concentration area at White trench at 21.00 hours on 19 July. Their route forward took them via Caterpillar Valley.

By this time the Germans had developed the habit of shelling the valley south of Mametz Wood, where some of the supporting artillery were

8/Devons' Lewis Gunners sleep by their carts on the afternoon before the attack.

> *in position, with systematic frequency; and they also barraged the depression north of Bazentin Wood persistently, and to reduce casualties the supports had to be scattered about and well dug in. The attacking battalions, however reached their positions with but little loss.[5]*

Private Oatley had been allocated to Number 1 Company's single surviving Lewis gun crew, as an ammunition carrier. He and his new comrades joined 20 Brigade's column of men moving up to the front:

> *With the fading light of the evening of 19 July, we moved into Bazentin Wood. Each of us digging our own protecting trench[6] at an interval of several yards apart, the Lewis-gunners on the right with myself at the end. That Bazentin Wood had been the scene of bitter fighting not long before was evident by the number of German and Scottish soldiers lying dead on the ground beneath the trees. Two Germans and a kilted Scot immediately in front of me kept me company all through that night.*

Meanwhile, by 22.50 hours, 20 Brigade's attacking troops were forming up in a position familiar to 8/Devons, in the open, to the north-west of Bazentin-le-Grand Wood. To the right of the Devons, 5th Division was similarly deploying into its assault position. News of progress was brought to Major Dawes at Battalion Headquarters, located at 'Crucifix Corner'.[7] 'At 2.30 a.m. the two assaulting companies deployed and moved forward and extended [into line formation] under a bank.' Again under the cover of darkness, the Devons' two assault companies moved out into No Man's Land towards the start line, which lay along a bank 600 yards from the first objective along Black Road.

The Attack

Zero Hour for the attack was 03.35 hours, and in a repeat of the formula that led to surprise being gained on 14 July, at 'about 3.14 a.m., 20 minutes before Zero, twenty officers and 564 other ranks of 8/Devons, began crawling forward up the slope'. With only the normal desultory night-time artillery and machine-gun fire breaking the silence, the coarse grass and standing corn cloaking the slope up towards High Wood, covered 20 Brigade's advance. The plan initially worked extremely well. However, the Germans were not to be shocked and confused again and, to a certain extent, the first British blow punched into thin air. It had been established by patrols that the positions that were the first objective along Black Road were 'unoccupied by the enemy'. In the event, 'The leading lines were quite close to the Black Road when the barrage opened, and rushed it without meeting any serious resistance'. The Black Road 'trenches' were probably a rudimentary protective outpost line dug by the Germans, who realized the vulnerability of a front line system to surprise attack. It appears that it was intended to absorb the first blow of an attack. Alternatively, the Germans had abandoned these trenches in favour of better and less exposed positions along Wood Lane on the crest of the ridge. Whatever the case, the hammer blow of the hurricane artillery bombardment fell on largely unoccupied trenches, which the two leading platoons of each assault company wastefully attacked. Consequently, the German defenders of the Wood Lane trenches were fully prepared and alert.

Major Dawes wrote in his after action report that:

> The two platoons in support [of each assault company] occupied Black Road Trenches, while the leading platoons then pushed forward to the second road [Wood Lane]. During the advance to the second road, our artillery caused many [own] casualties, as our barrage was falling short of the road. The enemy were found to be holding the second road and opened a heavy fire from machine guns and rifles. The two platoons suffered very heavy casualties and started to dig in 25 yards from the road. They stayed there for about an hour. Green flares were used freely but our guns did not lift and continued to fire short. Finding they were not in touch on either flank they then commenced to crawl back in twos to the first road [Black Road]. Here they dug in.

Both of the leading companies lost their commanders during this attack. The regimental history records that: 'Captain Heyward of A Company was killed, the other commander, Lieutenant Savill, of C, was badly wounded and two of the four Devons platoon commanders in the first wave were killed. During the withdrawal, the redoubtable Company Sergeant Major Melhuish, 'led A Company magnificently under specially difficult conditions and by Corporal Jordan, whose wonderful coolness steadied the survivors of his platoon and

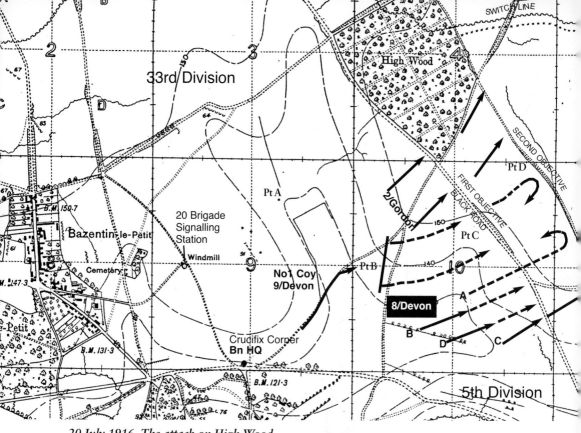

20 July 1916. The attack on High Wood.

helped greatly to rally them at the first objective'.

Meanwhile, as his next record makes plain, Major Dawes, back with his tactical headquarters at Crucifix Corner, was working with a general lack of information, while the information that did reach him was incomplete and largely incorrect.

> At 4.30 a.m. no information had reached Battalion Headquarters and an officer was sent forward to report on the situation. A message reached Battalion Headquarters at 7.00 a.m. timed 5.00 a.m., [incorrectly] reporting that we had gained both objectives but that our artillery were shelling both roads.

On the Devons' left, 2/Gordons had fared little better. They too captured their part of Black Road, but advancing to the second objective they also suffered heavily. However, a single platoon of highlanders did establish a lodgement in the Wood Lane trenches. Unfortunately, it was 'destroyed by fire from the High Wood and Switch Trench, directly ahead and only the platoon commander and five men escaped'.[8] Further to the left, 33rd Division had gained some ground in the increasingly hellish High Wood but insufficient to clear the German machine guns from the edge of the wood. Consequently, from these positions, the enemy could continue to pour enfilading fire into the flank of the unfortunate 20 Brigade.

Number 1 Company, 9/Devons, under the command of Second Lieutenant

Cary, was summoned forward from the supports to fill a gap in the front that had been produced by the Gordons concentrating on the edge of High Wood. Private Oatley described the move up from Bazentin Wood:

> With the dawn coming up in the sky, we moved out from the wood, emerging into the open ... Then forming up, well spaced out, in a single line abreast, we moved off. Each man was carrying an extra bandoleer of ammunition [100 rounds in clips of 5] over his leather equipment, Lewis gun ammunition over mine as well, two hand grenades one each in our lower tunic pockets, our water bottles filled and iron rations in our haversacks. Our rifles and bayonets held ready for the task in hand.

At 05.20 hours, Number 1 Company came under command of 2/Gordons. Second Lieutenant Green described the action in his after-action report. Lieutenant Cary moved his company forward by half companies

> ... Nos. 1 and 2 Platoons under 2/Lt Cary and Nos. 3 and 4 2/Lt Green. The Coy moved from Bazentin le Grand Wood along the sunken road to point S.9.d.2.0 [point A on the map opposite]. At this point, the coy was extended, advanced and took up positions on the road from S.10.a.3.3 to s.10.c.2.7 [point B]. Nos. 1 and 2 Platoons then advanced followed 15 minutes later by Nos. 3 and 4 platoons in file. When Point S.10B.2.6 [point C] was reached, a message was received from 2/lt Cary that he had gone on with Nos. 1 and 2 Platoons and that the remainder of the Coy was to follow. I again extended Nos. 3 and 4 Platoons and advanced keeping well down under cover of the corn until we came in contact with the enemy who were holding a position about 20 yards in front of the road [point D]. Machine gun and rifle fire was opened on us and what cover available was taken in shell holes. I sent out a Cpl and two men to find out if I was in touch with our own troops on the flanks. One man got back and reported that he was unable to see anyone on my right. I then saw a man of the 1st half Coy, who told me that 2/Lt Cary was killed.
>
> Seeing that it was useless to go on owing to lack of support and equally useless to stay where I was, I retired to the road and took up a position S.10.b.2.6. to S.10.b.7.0. and ordered the men to dig in as rapidly as possible.[9]

At 07.00 hours, the remains of the leading wave of 20 Brigade's assault companies had all returned to their first objective, having crawled back to Black Road through the standing corn. Private Oatley with the Lewis gun section moved up to join the company and records in his personal account that:

> We had reached our objective without a casualty. And there, with scarlet poppies amid the field of ripening corn in front of us, the Germans somewhere beyond the corn, their snipers in the High Wood trees, we started to dig in by the roadside. Barbed wire thrown across the road along towards the wood. A lone dead horse on the road beneath a tree about half way along from us.

Firing a Lewis gun. This type of light machine gun was issued following the formation of brigade machine-gun companies, with the infantry battalions original Vickers machine guns.

> *Up on the top there were no other men in sight, British or German. Shells, gas and shrapnel, were bursting in the cornfield in front of us, as we went on with our digging. There was no sound of any rifle fire.*

Having set Number 1 Company digging, Second Lieutenant Green coordinated the layout of his defences with flanking units. He wrote, 'I was now in touch with the Gordons on the right and the 8th Devons on the left. I sent forward two patrols to enable me to have timely warning of any counter-attack'. However, when the inevitable counter-attack came, it fell on the right flank of 8/Devons. Private Oatley, digging in the corn during his first battle, recorded:

> *A spotting plane flew over us in the direction of High Wood and then came back with its klaxon giving a warning. "Stand by! Get ready! They're coming!" our company commander called out. We dropped our entrenching tools and grabbed our rifles. This was it!*

Fortunately, two 8/Devons Lewis gun sections under Sergeant Potter (who had distinguished himself on 14 July) and Lance Corporal Forrester:

> *... remained out in advance after the rest had withdrawn, and not only covered the withdrawal but prevented the Germans from following it up. Sergeant Potter's team dug in on the left, within forty yards of the enemy, and brought most effective fire to bear on Germans coming down the hill in front from Switch Trench, checking their advance. A little later, as the Germans were pressing on the right, the team moved across towards that flank and established themselves in a shell hole.*

Almost immediately German bombers attacked them, but Private Clarke switched the gun round and shot them down, and the attempt was not repeated. A German officer then came forward and called to the team to surrender, but Sergeant Potter would not hear of it, and shot the officer.

Eventually, Sergeant Potter went back to get reinforcements but was wounded, leaving Privates Bates, Jones and Dalby to man the gun. Private Bates recounted that, 'Parties of the enemy were coming over the hill in front of us. We kept up fire on them, and a number of them were driven back by it. I have never seen so many Germans as I saw that day, and our gun caused them many casualties.' Out of ammunition, Bates and his two fellow gun crew crawled back with their gun. Meanwhile, Lance Corporal Forrester's party remained out in No Man's Land until evening, though one man was killed and three others wounded. The regimental history recorded that:

Forrester refused to retire: he had a good position, could bring effective fire to bear on the enemy near Delville Wood, and meant to bring his gun and his wounded in. This he eventually accomplished, he and his remaining effective men, Privates Budd and Tout, getting back after dark with their gun, their three wounded comrades, and another wounded man, whom they had picked up on the way.

Both Private Forrester and Sergeant Potter were cited for the VC following 'their splendid and resourceful gallantry during the attack on 20 July 1916'. However, they were downgraded, with Sergeant Potter being awarded a DCM, while Lance Corporal Forrester received the MM. Private Oately wrote of the attack's aftermath:

When the German attack had petered out, we went on with our digging. I was waist deep in my trench, as were the others. While stretching up to ease my aching back, a shrapnel bullet the size of a marble smashed into my face and embedded itself in my lower jaw. A young Lieutenant of the Devons took my rifle and bayonet and my bandoleer of ammunition and slipped into my place by the side of the Lewis gunner.

Behind the assaulting troops were the stretcher-bearers: a group of three stretchers sheltering under a bank was led by Padre Crosse, who wrote:

We knew nothing of the situation and the fighting was pretty heavy, then I met an 8/Devon runner who told me. Whereupon I set out with my squad in open order. I reached the nearer road where I found only one officer. He was quite dazed and could hardly answer my questions as to whether there were any wounded and, if so, where they were. At first, he said there was no one left. Eventually I found one wounded Devon on the road. I gathered that he had tried to advance to the second road and found it too strongly defended. Another Devon crawled back through the corn as I was there. I still had one empty stretcher, so I went to the Gordons and took down a wounded Jock.

This was about 8 a.m.

Private Oately was, however, one of the walking wounded:

As soon as he had dressed my wounded face, our Medical Officer suggested, 'If you think you can get down to the dressing station on your own, you'd better go now.' He added, 'We can't spare anyone to go with you, but if you can do it, it's up to you to do so.' I got up to cross the road, not thinking of the target I was presenting. 'Keep down! D'you want to live or don't you', a voice called out behind me. A smoke haze was clinging to the ridge and helped me to get away. On reaching the edge of the ridge, I moved down the slope. I was very much alone.

A near miss from a shell must have knocked me out. When I recovered consciousness I was sitting on a road with a severed leg of a soldier lying on my own leg, complete with its boot and puttee.

Private Oately was found and evacuated. He had served with 9/Devons at the front for less than twenty-four hours.

Back at the front, the Devons' Lewis gunners were still dominating No Man's Land, allowing 20 Brigade to dig in along Black Road. Without overhead protection from airburst shells, casualties mounted as they dug. Among the casualties in the A and C Companies were the last of the officers. However, Second Lieutenant Renton who had been detailed to coordinate the evacuation of the 8/Devons' wounded 'removed his Red Cross brassard and took over command'. According to the regimental history, he did 'splendid work, organizing the men, directing their effort and steadying and encouraging them under heavy shellfire'. Supported by Sergeant Smith who was 'conspicuous in reorganizing the men and superintending consolidation, Lieutenant Renton sent situation reports back to Battalion Headquarters'. Consequently, Major Dawes recorded that: 'At 11.30 a.m., strong posts were being made on the right and left of the line held by the Battalion'. By midday, a combination of casualties from the assault and a steady stream of losses to enemy artillery fire had thinned the ranks of the forward companies. The after action report recorded that:

At 12.15 p.m. orders were issued to the support company to reinforce the front line. To move in small groups and to keep out of view as much as possible. Orders were then issued to the reserve company to occupy the line previously held by the support company with two platoons.

Though ground had been gained and the width of No Man's Land reduced, the attack had not succeeded, despite its promising beginning. Not only were the Germans more numerous and better prepared than they had been before the 14 July attack, but also British planning was not as thorough as it had been on that earlier occasion. There had been several changes of plan, and the shape of the ground was such that British commanders and artillery observers could not get a good view of the enemy positions. A few patrols had been out, and maps and air photos were available, but these were poor substitutes for commanders being able to familiarize themselves with the ground and its landmarks from a good observation post. Also, because of the lack of good observation posts, the accuracy of the artillery fire support before and during the attack was poor. In fact, the main German position proved to be on a reverse slope almost totally out of view from the British lines. A certain amount of the shelling of the forward elements of 20 Brigade and 5th Division on the right was friendly fire. This was partly the result of the lack of good OPs overlooking the ridge but also because artillery observers were dependent on their telephones and could not get forward quickly. Laying wire across open ground to forward positions near the infantry was slow, and the resulting connection subject to repeated cutting by enemy shellfire.

An example of the difficulty in communicating experienced by 20 Brigade is afforded by Lieutenant Frank Richards of the Royal Welch Fusiliers (the Brigade's reserve battalion). He was detailed to establish a Brigade visual-signalling station at the site of the windmill, east of Bazentin-le-Petit. Here, with a signalling corporal from Brigade Headquarters, 'a veteran Cameronian soldier, and an escort of five RWF soldiers, he was to relay messages from 8/Devons and 2/Gordons by semaphore signal flags or by heliograph to Brigade Headquarters.' However, the remains of a large mill and the necessity of standing up to signal made them an obvious target.

Crucifix still standing today and marks the location of 8/Devons' Battalion HQ.

10 a.m. 12-inch, 8-inch, whizbangs ... were bursting around us continually and this lasted during the whole day. When receiving a message the smoke, bursting shells, the earth and dust ... constantly obscured our vision and we could only receive a word now and then. The five men were sheltering in a large shell hole; they were absolutely useless and terror stricken.[10]

This was understandable, as the Welshmen had seen both the Signal corporal and the Cameronian being killed in the execution of their dangerously exposed duties. Lieutenant Richards gave up his signalling and detailed his five men as runners. 1/Royal Welch Fusiliers lost ten out of their eighteen signallers on 20 July, with Brigade Headquarter's signallers adding to the total. Casualties among the Brigade's runners were, as usual, heavy.

Relying on information being passed back by runners, 8/Devons' Battalion Headquarters at Crucifix Corner, probably because they were located at an obvious cross roads, were also severely shelled by the German artillery throughout the day. The 8th Battalion's Regimental Sergeant Major, Tyrrell, was badly wounded and a shell fell on the Regimental Aid Post scattering medical equipment everywhere. Amid the chaos, there was laughter at a ridiculous but dangerous incident. An unknown officer wrote:

No one who saw it will forget the sight of Lieutenant Duff climbing a small tree near Headquarters, to rescue some of the MO's bandages, which had been blown up into the tree by a shell, and were said to be drawing fire.

Much of the information coming back was borne by the walking wounded, and as ever, it tended to be pessimistic, seemingly in order to justify their return from the front. Lieutenant Richards recalled:

A number of lightly wounded [a relative term during the Great War] Devons and Gordons from the wood passed by us on their way to the dressing station, which was in the valley below. We enquired how things were going. Most of them said half the Brigade had been wiped out and that Jerry was counter-attacking.

So heavy were casualties in the attack as a whole that the CO of a Middlesex battalion fighting alongside 20 Brigade in High Wood sent the Devons parcels intended for his soldiers who had been killed in action. In these circumstances, the redistribution of parcels from home was a normal and practical part of the routine of trench warfare.

Private Veale VC

The soldiers consolidating 20 Brigade's positions knew that in the 500 yards of corn covered No Man's Land there lay wounded men, many of whom would die for the lack of first aid treatment. However, a few brave men went out to bring them in. On 9/Devons' front, Lance Corporal Goddard was commended by Second Lieutenant Green for 'volunteering to bring in wounded under heavy fire and making a valuable reconnaissance, finding out the exact position of enfilading machine guns' [in High Wood]. On 8/Devons' front, Private Theodore Veale displayed 'conduct beyond the call of duty'.

Private Veale went out into No Man's Land to help the stretcher-bearers, having been told by a corporal that someone was lying in the corn wounded and waving his arm for help. Armed with rifle and bombs and under enemy fire, he approached to within twenty-five yards of the enemy position. In a letter to his mother, Veale described his action:

I flopped down on the ground, but got up again and ran on till I got to the spot where the man had been waving. To my surprise, it was one of our wounded officers [Lieutenant Savill]. I laid down and did all I could for him, and I was well fired at while I was there. He had been [hit] so close to the Germans, I pulled him back about 15 yards, for I found to my surprise that I was only about ten yards from the Germans. I pulled him back, thinking they were going to pull him in. I went back to get some water, and I

Private Theodore Veale VC. Photographed in 1917 after receiving his medal from the King and his promotion to corporal.

took it out to him. They fired at me again, and it was surprising how it was that I was not hit. But I meant to save him at all costs; so off I crawled back again, because it was all open, and I got two more men and a Corporal to come out with a waterproof sheet, which we put him on.[11]

With Corporal Allen, Private Lord and another soldier helping, Veale crawled dragging Lieutenant Savill back another eighty yards, before having to rest 'for you know how one's back aches after stooping'. Private Veale continued his account:

Well, the Corporal stood up like on his knees, and we saw five Germans pop up out of the grass about 100 yards away. We had to go over a bit of a [trench] bridge and they shot the Corporal through the head. That made the other two with me nervous, and they wanted to get back. So I said, 'Get back, and I'll manage'. So they went, and I pulled the wounded officer into a hole, and left him comfortable, and went back. Then I sent a team out to cover any of them that might try to fire at him, and tracked out to him myself with water.

[*Lieutenant Savill had to be left in a shell hole till dusk, when Veale then took out another party, among them Mr Crosse, the Battalion's chaplain, who was up in front as usual, helping the stretcher-bearers with conspicuous courage and self-devotion.*]

In the last light of the day, a German patrol was seen approaching Veale's small group of West Countrymen through the corn. Private Veale returned once more to Black Road in order to fetch a Lewis gun and returned to find that Lieutenant Duff, who had joined the party in No Man's Land, had kept the patrol off with his revolver. Then Private Veale and Lieutenant Duff gave covering fire, while Padre Crosse, Sergeant Smith and a stretcher-bearer carried Lieutenant Savill back across the remaining yards to Black Road and relative safety.

8/Devons' commanding officer, Major Dawes, submitted a list of nominations for awards, which included three Victoria Crosses, and the citations for Private Forrester and Sergeant Potter that have already been mentioned above. In highly irregular circumstances, Private Veale discovered that he had been awarded the VC when he read about it some months later in a newspaper during a quiet moment in the trenches! Veale received a VC ahead of other worthy nominations, as not only was his 'courage and determination of the highest order' but also his conduct, example and leadership had been consistently above that expected of a soldier of his age, rank and experience. Private Veale eventually received his well deserved medal from the King at Buckingham Palace on 5 February 1917.

Relief of 20 Brigade

During the afternoon, 20 Brigade's reserve, 2/Royal Welch Fusiliers, was called up to reinforce 33rd Division in High Wood, having bravely set off into a maelstrom of exploding shells, and were virtually destroyed. They suffered almost 200 casualties in moving up to the wood. Among the wounded was the poet Captain Robert Graves[12]. At about 22.20 hours, 20 Brigade received orders that they were to be relieved by battalions from 13 Brigade, 5th Division. There was also the welcome news that the whole Division was to move back for a long rest at Ailly-sur-Somme, near Amiens. Number 1 Company 9/Devons, under command of 2/Gordons, were relieved by a battalion of Royal West Kents fairly quickly, and once out of the trenches marched back to the sound of bagpipes. 8/Devons, however, had a little longer to wait before 14/Warwicks started to arrive and take over the improved trenches.

The day's fighting had principally fallen to A and C Companies 8/Devons, and consequently the bulk of the seven officers and 153 other rank casualties were suffered by the 300 men of these companies who went into action that morning. These two companies would again be rebuilt with new soldiers, who were already on their way to meet their new battalion in the 7th Division's rest area. Meanwhile, after a sleepless night and a day spent in action, the battalion did not to get any rest until dawn, and that was only after a ten mile night march to billets in the rear area.

The poet and writer, Second Lieutenant Siegfried Sassoon, who had been among 1/Royal Welch Fusiliers 'left out of battle' detail, described the return of 7th Division to the rear area after its relief in the line.[13]

The distant gun-fire had crashed and rumbled all night, muffled and terrific with immense flashes, like waves of some tumult of water

After the battle, salvage and reclamation platoons scoured the field for reusable equipment.

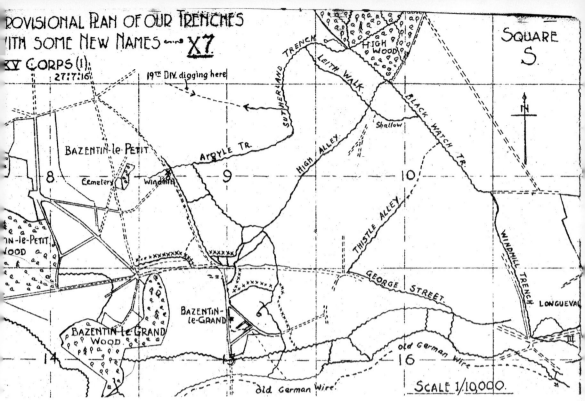

A hand drawn trench map dating from a week after the attack. Note that communications trenches had been dug and that the trench begun by the Devons was officially named Black Watch Trench.

rolling along the horizon. Now there came an interval of silence in which I heard a horse neigh, shrill and scared and lonely. Then, the procession of the returning troops began. The camp-fires were burning low when the grinding jolting column lumbered back. The field guns came first, with nodding men sitting stiffly on weary horses, followed by wagons and limbers and field-kitchens. After this rumble of wheels came the infantry, shambling, limping, straggling and out of step. If anyone spoke it was only a muttered word, and the mounted officers rode as if asleep. The men had carried their emergency water in petrol-cans, against which bayonets made a hollow clink; except for the shuffling of feet, this was the only sound. Thus, with an almost spectral appearance, the lurching brown figures flitted past with slung rifles and heads bent forward under basin-helmets. Moonlight and dawn began to mingle, and I could see the barley swaying indolently against the sky. A train groaned along the riverside, sending up a cloud of whitish fiery smoke against the gloom of the trees. The Flintshire Fusiliers[14] were a long time arriving. ... Then, as if answering our expectancy, a remote skirling of bagpipes began, and the Gordon Highlanders hobbled in [accompanied by Number 1 Company 9/Devons].

I had seen something that night which overawed me. It was all in the

187

Highlanders of 2/Gordons march to the rear, while infantry stretcher bearers, possibly Devons, evacuate a wounded German POW.

> *day's work – an exhausted Division returning from the Somme Offensive – but for me it was as though I had watched an army of ghosts. It was as though I had seen the War as it might be envisioned by the mind of some epic poet a hundred years hence.*

1 20 Infantry Brigade Op. Order No. 75 dated 18 July 1916. PRO WO/ 95/1653.
2 Also in 7th Division's bivouacs at this time were 1/RWF. Second Lieutenant Siegfried Sassoon records in *Memoirs of an Infantry Officer* that the infantry bivouacs were huts largely constructed from the wood from shell boxes.
3 This branch of Happy Valley was more commonly known as Death Valley.
4 Personal account. Archive RHQ Devon and Dorset Regiment.
5 *The Seventh Division 1914 – 1918*, C.T. Atkinson, John Murray, 1927.
6 A 'shell scrape'. A trench about eighteen-inches deep in which infantrymen can lie in to shelter from surface bursting enemy shells; but such shell scrapes offered little cover from air or tree bursts.
7 Many wayside Calvaries were known as 'Crucifix Corner'. The one at the junction with the track up to High Wood and the Bazentin – Longueval Road marks a particularly notorious site.
8 *The Gordon Highlanders in the First World War Vol IV*, Cyril Falls, Aberdeen, 1958.
9 Pages from 2Lt Green's field message pad included in 9/Devons' war diary. PRO WO 95/1653.
10 *Old Soldiers Never Die*. Frank Richards, Faber and Faber, 1933.
11 Archive copy RHQ Devon and Dorset Regiment.
12 Author of *Goodbye to All That.*
13 *Memoirs of an Infantry Officer.* Faber and Faber, 1930.
14 Sassoon's name for 1/RWF in his memoirs.

Chapter 12

Holding the Line

The decisive battle of the war is now being fought on the fields of the Somme. It must be impressed on every officer and man in the front line that the fate of our country is at stake in this battle. By ceaseless vigilance self sacrifice and courage the enemy must be prevented from gaining another centimetre of ground. His attacks must break against a wall of German breasts.

GENERAL VON GARLOWITZ, SPECIAL ORDER OF THE DAY, AUGUST 1916

1/Devon at Longueval

As already noted in the previous chapter, 1/Devons had returned to the Somme with 5th Division in time for the 20 July attack, but had been held as 95 Brigade's reserve. Their turn in the front line was, however, not long in coming. The West Countrymen were to go up to the Longueval / Delville Wood area where the fighting had continued unabated since 14 July. According to the divisional historian, 'Longueval will always be remembered by those who were there, as the place where there was a more intense and continuous shellfire than any other in the whole course of the war'.[1]

On the night of 22-23 July, 13 and 95 Brigades attacked Switch Trench and the northern end of Longueval, as a part of another general Fourth Army attack 'but nowhere ... were very satisfactory results achieved'.[2] The Devons had moved forward from reserve to be Brigade supports for this attack, while the attack on Longueval village was delivered by 1/East Surreys and 1/Duke of

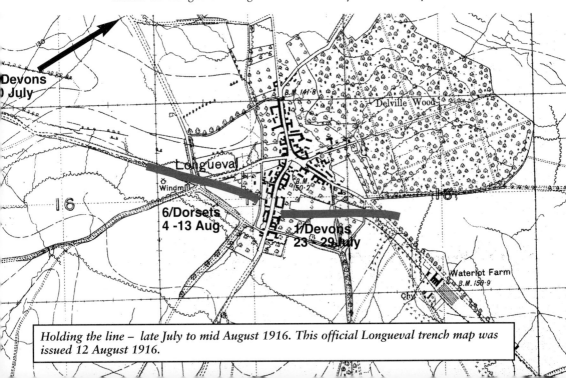

Holding the line – late July to mid August 1916. This official Longueval trench map was issued 12 August 1916.

German infantry sheltering in a front line 'funk hole'.

Cornwall's Light Infantry (DCLI). The attack had started well, overrunning several German machine guns, but the cost was heavy and the shattered battalions were pushed back by 'violent counter-attacks almost to their starting-point, Pont Street, a trench just west of Longueval'. The Devons were summoned forward to take over the front line from 1/DCLI on the evening of 23 July.

Lt Wells was sent off to command another company, which left me, [twenty-year-old] 2nd Lieutenant Westropp, in charge of the company.

At about mid-day we were ordered to move up to the trenches facing Longueval and Delville Wood. My company was to face Delville Wood. We moved up the road by platoon in fours with one hundred yards distance between them. We used this formation to avoid, as far as possible, casualties from shelling. We had not gone far when the enemy began to shell the road with high explosive shrapnel. This type of shell burst in the air with a loud crash and emitted a large quantity of black smoke. Hence the name of "coal box", which the troops gave it. It was not nearly so effective against troops in the open as our shrapnel.

They did not cause my company any casualties on this occasion but they caused some to other companies. We passed an officer lying on the ground being attended to; it was our acting adjutant Lt Tomlinson who had just been hit and was already dying. At last, we reached the shelter of the support trenches. I was quite pleased to enter them.

These support trenches were old German trenches captured in the middle of July. They were of course facing the wrong way but were good

German occupants of a trench lie dead in front of Longueval. A British soldier can be seen in the next bay.

and deep trenches, with deep dugouts. The front line trench turned out to be a narrow one but not very deep and running along the edge of the track. It had not been planned and had little in the way of traverses but it marked the place where our forward troops had reached some days previously and dug-in under fire.

Three of my platoons were strung along it and were overcrowded. The fourth platoon was in support to the rear in a temporary trench.[3]

Second Lieutenant Monty Westropp, despite his lack of practical experience, was not impressed with the defensive qualities of the front line trenches, when compared with the neat theory that he had learnt during officer training. 'There was no fire step as the trench was too shallow to permit one being built. It was so narrow that it was difficult for me to pass when I went to walk down it and there was little or no wire in front of it.' About 300 yards ahead of him lay the blasted ruins of Delville Wood, which 'was a mass of tree stumps of varying height'. Closer to the West Countrymen's position lay the dead and wounded of the DCLI, who had been hit during the previous evening's attack, who needed rescuing. A divisional historian commented on the plight of the wounded out in No Man's Land:

It was one of the horrors of trench warfare that the firing was practically continuous, and it was rare that there was even a local informal truce to clear the battlefield. The dead lay unburied in No Man's Land or tangled in the wire; the wounded were often left without help. Rarely British and Germans worked together at succouring the wounded and getting them back into their own lines. But this was an irregular proceeding and higher authority of both armies had a dread of anything like 'fraternization'.[4]

Westropp commented that 'During the afternoon it was quiet, for the Somme'.

The remains of a German trench in Delville Wood.

24 August was 'relatively quiet' with the war diary recording only 'intermittent shelling'. Making the most of the enemy's relative quiescence, the West Countrymen of Number 1 and 2 Companies worked on improving the front line trenches. However, the unaccustomed quietness was not to last. At 20.00 hours, the Germans started shelling the Devons' trenches and according to Lieutenant Westropp, 'after a quarter of an hour, it was clear that this bombardment was no ordinary strafe. It certainly heralded a counter attack.' Westropp commented that the enemy barrage was nothing like as heavy as that from the British artillery, and that the German gunners had not properly located his company's trench, as most of the shells fell behind them.

> Looking through my periscope at the edge of Delville Wood, I could see movement through the smoke. I had difficulty in stopping my troops firing at nothing. They were induced to do it by imagination and even more so by the company on the left getting the 'wind up' and firing into the cornfield in front of them. However, with the help of my stick, another young officer and my NCO's we between us managed to stop it. Orders could not be heard except by a man standing close to one and only then if one shouted loudly enough.

What Monty Westropp does not explain is that he was faced with a 'Major from an adjacent unit who was fleeing, terrified, from the trenches causing general panic [amongst his company]. Westropp drew his pistol and brought the officer down with an aimed shot to his posterior.'[5] In his own words, the very young temporary company commander continues, '... then with the aid of my stick and my good Sergeant Major, I readdressed the Company's attention towards the enemy'. Order restored and confidence reinforced by force of Westropp's personality and the leadership of his Senior NCOs, the Devons were about to be tested by the enemy attacking in two strong columns.

> At about 10 p.m. or when it was just getting dark the barrage intensified. Now was the probable time I ceased to look through the periscope and looked over the top to the edge of Delville Wood. Sure enough within five minutes or so, lines of men appeared in front of the edge of the wood and advanced towards us. The whole of the company lined the trench and poured rapid rifle fire into them, as did also our Lewis guns. The density of men in the trench, which would have caused unnecessary casualties if any shells had fallen in it, was now an asset. The crackle, roar and flash of over a hundred rifles firing rapidly was inspiring and a relief, as action always is after sitting powerless under heavy shell fire, as we had, for two hours.
>
> I could not resist firing a rifle myself. I took one from a man who was firing with his head below the parapet from where he could see nothing. I expect his bullets must have been passing over the top of Delville Wood.
>
> Our rapid fire was devastating, the attackers were swept away as if by a scythe. The attack had failed and the enemy made no further efforts to leave the wood. Suddenly the enemy bombardment ceased and an astonishing quiet reigned. I looked about in the smoke, saw that the moon

was well up and that it was most unlikely the enemy would make another attempt that night.

I was thinking that we should have to do something about the DCLI, stretching and congratulating myself that we had beaten them off without casualties, when what appeared like a black cloud burst on the parapet and blew me sideways down the trench. A lance corporal and three men on my left were killed instantly and partly buried. It was a 5.9-inch howitzer shell. I had heard no whistle of its approach. This bore out the theory that one does not hear the approach of a shell that is going to hit one.

As I lay on the floor of the trench I thought at first that my left eye and ear had gone so I put my hand over my right eye and found that I could see out of my left. I also found that my ear was there but an enormous lump like a pigeon's egg on my cheek was in front of it. The left of my face felt as if it had number of small pieces of stone or metal in it. I then discovered that my left trouser leg was in rags and that there were a number of wounds in my thigh but apparently no bones broken. At that time I did not know that I had been hit in the back of the head as well.

After recovering from his wounds and a period of convalescence with the 3rd Reserve Battalion in Plymouth, Lieutenant Westropp was posted back to 1/Devons in time for the Battle of Arras in 1917.

1/Devons remained in the line. But with, for example, British aircraft reporting that the Germans were massing for an attack, nervous infantry commanders signalled for emergency artillery fire support. The divisional history records that from across the Division:

...the usual 'SOS Longueval' was received during the evening and night. This message was regularly received by the artillery every night of our stay in this area, often four or five times ... any of which may

The predominent motive power at the heart of the logistics system was four legged. Horses drew all kinds of vehicles, but mules brought stores as far forward as possible. From this point it was men who carried the stores forward.

have heralded an attack. How many times the prompt and effective reply of our guns prevented such an attack, there is no means of knowing, but for the support thus given, the Gunners earned the heartfelt gratitude of the sorely-tried infantry.

The Devons' war diary entry recorded, in an entry typical of the period, that:
The Battalion remained in trenches. Front and support trenches intermittently shelled during day. During the night Nos. 3 & 4 Coys were relieved from front line trenches by 2 coys 1/Cheshire and occupied support trenches with Nos. 1 & 2 Coys. Killed 1 other rank, wounded 17.[6]

On 26 July, 1/Devons remained in the Brigade support line, 'a little distance to the rear', where, spared only the tension of holding the line, conditions were scarcely less dangerous. 'Killed in action ORs 5, Wounded 2Lt Gilliland, 2Lt Davies, and ORs 8.' The following day, 'Number 1 and 2 Companies were called on to support operations at the front' and in this case they moved up to a sector at the southern end of the pulverized village of Longueval and 'had merely to sit tight and be shelled'. These two companies returned to join Numbers 3 and 4 Companies in the support trenches that night (27-28 July). 15/Warwicks finally relieved the Devons on the evening of 29 July.

During their three days in the front line and four days in support, one officer, the adjutant, and eleven men were killed, while nine officers, including Westropp, and ninety-six men were wounded. This was a very heavy casualty rate for defensive operations, especially where they did not directly come into close contact with the enemy. Compared with the attacks of 22-23 July, the casualties among the East Surreys and the DCLI, which both exceeded 300, the Devons were lucky. The divisional history records that 5th Division's Medical Services '... cleared the wounded expeditiously and gallantly, but casualties amongst the bearers were heavy. On one day alone, over 600 lying cases and 2,000 walking cases were passed through the Advanced Dressing Station [15/Field Ambulance].' Waiting for the Devons at Pommiers Redoubt were twenty-eight reinforcements from 1/Hampshires, who were mainly Devonians or soldiers previously badged Devonshire Regiment. A further forty-eight men arrived from an infantry holding unit at Etaples the following day.

The 5th Division as a whole, having suffered heavy casualties in almost two weeks in action, was relieved by 17th Division during the course of 1 and 2 August and moved to a rest area at Abbeville. However, the Division's artillery remained behind to support the 17th. Consequently, it is not without some justification that the German historians refer to this phase of the battle as the beginning of *die material-schlacht*, as the industrial might of the British Empire was applied on the Western Front.

6/Dorsets at Longueval

In the first days of August 1916, the West Countrymen of 6/Dorsets were back at the front, with 17th Division, after two weeks' in the Abbeville area. Although they were rested, the demand for infantry replacements was heavy, and despite receiving 3,366 all ranks, the battalions of 17th Division was still 1,400 men below strength when they returned to the Somme.

52 Brigade was the first to take over the line from 5th Division, with 51 Brigade in support; 50 Brigade, along with 6/Dorsets, were divisional reserve. However, the Dorsets did not have long to wait before they were on their way forward, as three days was all a Brigade could manage in the front in the prevailing conditions.

How things had changed, from the time when the Dorsets had left the Fricourt/Mametz Wood area. Gone were the green fields, battered farms and leafy woods. The 17th Division's historian described the new scene around Longueval:

> Countryside where every marked feature by which a map can be set has been beaten flat and the outlook is of shattered woods and orchards, and of ground churned by weeks of shell fire into a stretch of craters, with trench lines hardly distinguishable from the chaos around them, – this forms a prospect very different from the trim legibility of neatly squared maps, full of clearly shown detail, some of which has ceased to exist in reality. These were the conditions in August 1916 at the corner of Delville Wood and among the devastated orchards, at the end of the ruined village.

The scene was a profound shock for many of the Dorsets' new officers and men, who had only seen the training trenches, and had no experience of trench warfare in a quiet sector before being thrown into conditions of full battle. Rather than the neat lines of the theoretical trenches found at the depots and in the rear area, the new men faced 'trench positions that had all but disappeared in a wild confusion of shell craters and heaps of debris'.

52 Brigade mounted a limited but failed attack to improve positions on the night of 3 August, 6/Dorsets, in reserve at Pommiers Redoubt, were subject to an enemy bombardment which included phosgene gas. The almost odourless gas attacked lungs, causing its victims to drown in their own body fluids. 52 Brigade's failure added to the number of 'bloated and putrefying corpses' lying out in No Man's Land. A Dorset commented that, 'The smell of the front line where there had been battle and little movement was unspeakably awful'.

On the afternoon of 4 August, General Robertson met his three brigadiers at Pommiers Redoubt, and when arrangements for the reorganization of the line had been agreed, orders were given. A part of this reorganization was an extension of the 17th Division's front by taking over a part of Delville Wood from another division. As this extended the front needed two brigades to hold it, the remainder of 50 Brigade was concentrated at Pommiers Redoubt alongside 6/Dorsets, before moving to the front. Meanwhile, 51 Brigade prepared to take over the unenviable trenches to their right in Delville Wood.

On the night of Friday 4 August, 6/Dorsets relieved 9/Northumberland Fusiliers (51 Brigade). They took over trenches near those that 1/Devons had held a few days earlier. 6/Dorsets' historian wrote of the line west of Longueval and Delville Wood:

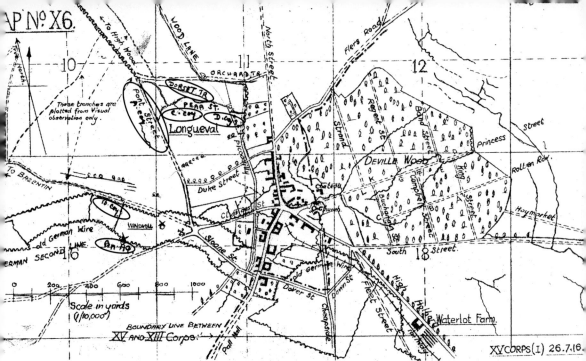

A map taken from the Dorsets' war diary showing company positions. This hand drawn map formed the basis of the official trench map issued later in August. The Dorsets' positions have been indicated.

Headquarters were in a dugout on the high ground, which had been captured on 14 July. All round lay the debris of the struggle. One company remained round headquarters; the rest were in Pear and Pont Street, unaware of the horrors being suffered in Delville Wood, that cost the Division 1,500 more casualties.[7]

Conditions were now much quieter in the Pont and Pear Street trenches than they had been when the Devons had held the line. This represented an opportunity to dominate No Man's Land with patrols, as well as maintain 'an offensive attitude' in the Battalion. The patrols tasked were of three types. The first was the reconnaissance patrol, sent out to check the enemy defences, while the second, the fighting patrol, was strong enough to take on a body of enemy encountered in No Man's Land or in a forward enemy position. The third was the raiding patrol, designed to gain information. However, with the recent attacks by 5th Division and now with a greater level of British patrol activity, 'The Germans were very nervous at night, sending up quantities of brilliant light [shells and flares]'. Consequently, the Dorsets found operating beyond their trenches difficult, and although they made No Man's Land their own during the hours of darkness, few patrols were fully successful. A contributory factor was that many of the Dorsets lacked training and practical expertise of patrolling.

The Dorsets' war diary entry for 7 August records at length the first of the day's patrols in the afternoon:

After an artillery bombardment, two battle patrols were sent out. One to reconnoitre the junction of Wood Lane and Orchard Trench and to occupy it if it was found not to be held. This patrol was met by very

197

heavy MG fire from three directions and from rifle fire from Orchard Trench. Seeing that the trench was strongly held, the patrol was withdrawn having accomplished its primary object.

Private Morgan accompanied the patrol. His Military Medal citation throws light on the cost of this daylight expedition into No Man's Land.

During an attack on the junction of Wood Lane and Orchard Trench three men were badly wounded 100 yards from our lines.

Pte Morgan (Stretcher Bearer) bandaged their wounds and carried them one after another back to our trench. This was done in broad daylight, under very heavy machine gun and rifle fire from three different directions.[8]

A second stronger patrol under the command of Lieutenant D'Albertanson which went out at the same time, no doubt benefited from the enemy attention focussed on the first patrol and the broken ground in their area, and had better luck. Its mission was to 'join up the trench SW of Pear Street with a trench shown on the map as running through the Orchard'. Having captured their objective, and established themselves, the patrol dug their trench during the night and produced a tactically important forward strong point to the north-west of Longueval. However, while moving around encouraging his men, Lieutenant D'Albertanson was mortally wounded, and was awarded a posthumous MC 'for his brave and cool work.' Private Morgan was again out in No Man's Land:

In the evening of the same day another man was wounded 70 yards away from the trench and fell in a shell hole. Pte Morgan calmly went over to him, bandaged his wound and carried him back safely

An infantry section 'stand-to' on the fire step in their narrow newly-dug trench.

although the enemy were sniping hard the whole time.

This was the third time that Lieutenant Colonel Rowley had recommended Private Morgan for an award since 1 July. On this occasion, he received his well deserved Military Medal. However, another man, Private Matthews, was recommended at the same time but was unsuccessful, despite a citation describing how he bravely brought back casualties through an enemy artillery barrage from Orchard Trench.

Lieutenant Max Plowman of 10/West Yorks, also of 50 Brigade, had cause to reflect on the inadequacy of words written after battle. After reading a newspaper report of an action some time between 4 and 10 August, he recorded how difficult it was to write a true history of the war:

> The report says that on one of the nights when we happened to be in the line at St George's Hill, the Germans were seen to leave their trenches but were driven back by Allied barrage fire before they could reach our line.
>
> Now the true history of that little episode is this. There were strict orders at the time that SOS signals were only to be used in extreme urgency. A certain company commander (close to us but not of our battalion) became unnecessarily alarmed and sent up his SOS rockets. The concentrated fire was given, and the Germans, apparently thinking that we were going to attack, replied in kind just in front of the British trenches. Absolutely nothing happened. On neither side did men attempt to leave the trenches. But the company commander had to save his face. Hence the report; received no doubt with enormous armchair satisfaction. Probably the German version was precisely similar.

Insufficient information is available that could determine if this incident refers to 6/Dorsets or another infantry battalion of 17th Division. However, an examination of 17th Division's artillery war diaries reveals that, during this period, all battalions holding the front (including 10/West Yorks), called for SOS artillery fire missions on a regular basis. In some cases, with very junior officers acting as company commanders, it is hardly surprising that, with experience measured in just months rather than years, this kind of incident happened in the tense hours of darkness.

After the dusk stand-to,[9] pairs of sentries were posted in each traverse or bay along the line, while the remaining soldier or two dozed, fully dressed and equipped, at the sentries' side. Night was the most active time for infantry in the trenches, and the only opportunity to go out into No Man's Land to repair wire and occupy forward listening posts. After the dawn stand-to, sentries were reduced to one man, and with the danger of being seen moving in daylight, most of the day was spent resting.

The Dorsets' main night-time achievement during this tour of duty in the line was in pushing the line forward with the spade! On 5 August, 6/Dorsets were ordered forward to dig a new line across the existing L-shaped line from the extremities of Pear and Pont Streets, thus making use of some slightly higher ground. With a company deployed in No Man's Land and artillery and machine-

gun fire covering the sound of digging, three companies laboured throughout the night. The resulting trench was known as 'Dorset Trench' and was proudly marked up as such, with painted ration box lids fixed at every junction. Before dawn, the majority of the battalion retired to what was now the support line, leaving a single company of Dorsets to finish the work on the new trench.

At the end of the Dorsets' six day tour in the front line, 7/Lincolns, 51 Brigade, were to take over the front line, while the West Countrymen were to become brigade reserve; but, as recorded by the regimental historian,

> *The relieving troops, instead of filing along the trench* [from Pont and Pear Street trenches], *ran across the open in line, and the Germans, imagining an attack, sent up an array of lights and opened fire with machine guns and rifles. The Dorsets held up their shovels and stopped many bullets before the Lincolns jumped in.*
>
> *A digging party lost their way coming out, for certain landmarks, a phosphorescent* [rotting cavalry] *horse included, had disappeared since coming in, and they miserably ended up in High Wood of all places, and after a night spent with a Scots company came out next day.*

Hebuterne: a Quiet Sector

41 Brigade took over 50 Brigade's trenches to the west of Delville Wood on 13 August. The 50th went back to Bellevue Farm, 'where it deloused with the aid of hot flat irons' killing the loathsome insects that had taken up residence in the seams of their uniform. The battalion then spent two days as Corps reserve at Buire. After this, the Dorsets enjoyed a rare twenty-four hours' of complete rest, without labouring or carrying parties in Bernaville, before five days' easy march to the trenches at Hebuterne. This was a quiet sector, where the Dorsets,

> *... remained till September 18th, enjoying the orchard fruits and thoroughly appreciating the quiet of the trenches and the ridiculous freedom of No Man's Land; but working hard to prepare the ground for an assault intended to reach Serre, and rectify the failure in the attack here on 1st July.'*[10]

'Quiet' and 'safe' were, of course, relative terms. The battalion history records that Second Lieutenant Fleming was killed only two days after joining the battalion. Men were also killed and wounded during the routine exchanges of fire in trench warfare. The level of activity represented the minimum accepted by commanders on both side of No Man's Land, which was wide at this point.

In the village of Sailly, just behind the line, where the Battalion was billeted,

> *There was fruit to be picked and honey could be rifled by men in gas masks. This was against orders; and the Adjutant, Lieutenant Barber, came up to stop it. An infuriated bee chased him to the orderly room, and for all his innocence stung him there.*

In the frontline, in contrast to Longueval, conditions were 'pleasant'. The trenches could be relieved by daylight and the Quartermaster's cookers brought up to the reserve line. Consequently, the West Countrymen enjoyed the luxury of warm food in the trenches. However, even though 'the line was almost

A sentry keeps watch through a loop hole in a former German communication trench blocked with sandbags.

luxurious', the job of holding these trenches and preparing for a renewed battle had its grim aspect.

> *The main task was to clean out the unoccupied starting line of July 1st; a melancholy business, as there were many dead bodies and quantities of abandoned material. This was preparatory to a renewed attack. Imitation trenches were dug behind the lines, studied in detail and attacked but somehow with no great faith.*

Commanders too had little faith, and the idea of attacking Serre was abandoned. Consequently, the Dorsets spent the remainder of August and the whole of September in the routine of defence in a quiet sector, only ten miles from some of the grimmest fighting of the Great War.

1 *The 5th Division in the Great War*, Hussey and Inman, Nisbet and Co. London, 1927.
2 *Official History, France and Flanders 1916*, Vol 2.
3 *The Memoirs of Colonel Westropp*. Privately published 1970, RHQ D and D archive.
4 *History of the 17th (Northern) Division*. A. Hillard Atteridge, Glasgow 1929.
5 Regimental biography, RHQ D and D archive.
6 1/Devons war diary. PRO WO 95/1579.
7 *A Plain History of the Sixth (Service) Battalion, The Dorsetshire Regiment 1914-1919*. Capt G. O'Hanlon.
8 50 Brigade war diary PRO 95/1998.
9 The British Army in defensive positions customarily 'stands to arms' for the hours astride dawn and dusk. Not only are these the most likely times for the enemy to attack, but stand-to also marks the transition between day and night routine in defence.
10 *History of the 50th Infantry Brigade 1914-1919*, Anon, Privately printed in 1919.

The war of 1914 – 1915! Private Williams of 1/Dorsets photographed during the summer of 1916.

Chapter 13

Guillemont and Leuze Wood

The C in C has decided that the attack projected for the middle of September must be a decisive operation and all preparations made accordingly.

HAIG'S ORDERS TO THE ARMY COMMANDER, AUGUST 1916

By the end of August 1916, General von Falkenhayn's strategy of attrition that he had launched at Verdun was now wearing down the remains of what had been his own admirable Field Army. Now, poorly trained Germans were replacing his experienced soldiers, who had attempted to execute the inconceivably demanding Schlieffen Plan in 1914. Meanwhile, on the other side of No Man's Land, to maintain the battle, fresh troops were arriving on the Somme. In the Allies' case, these included the Australia and New Zealand Army Corps (ANZAC), who were to establish a reputation as a part of the BEF's elite. Under command of General Gough's Reserve Army, the ANZAC fought for the

A typical daytime trench scene during the battle; infantry rest in funk holes dug into the side of some rudimentary trenches.

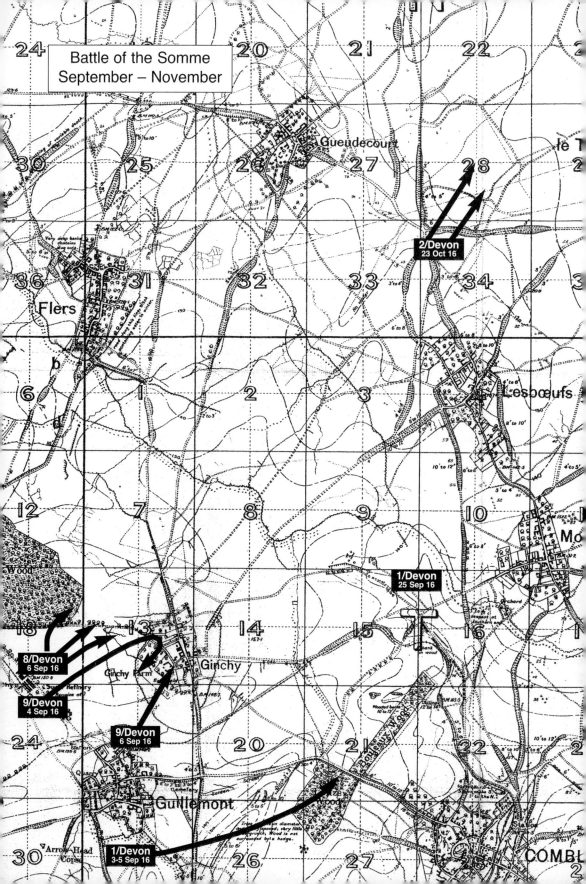

Battle of the Somme
September – November

2/Devon
23 Oct 16

Gueudecourt

Flers

Lesbœufs

1/Devon
25 Sep 16

8/Devon
6 Sep 16

9/Devon
4 Sep 16

9/Devon
6 Sep 16

Ginchy

Guillemont

1/Devon
3-5 Sep 16

COMBL

ruins of Pozières and the redoubt-crowned ridges beyond. Meanwhile, to their right, General Rawlinson's Fourth Army was continuing the offensive to the south of the Albert / Bapaume Road. However, after the success of 14 July, in almost six weeks of fighting, the front remained virtually stalled on a line between High Wood and Delville Wood, while further to the east, the British line crept forward towards Guillemont. The official historian summarized this part of the battle:

> It was a period of bitter fighting when hardly any ground was gained and the struggle became, more than ever, a grim test of endurance. There was little to encourage or inspire the troops of all arms who fought on the Somme in August: subjected to heavy losses, great hardships, and tremendous moral strain, they had only their own dogged spirit to maintain them.

This was the battle that the West Countrymen of 1/Devons were to join on their return with 5th Division to the Somme for their second tour at the front.

In memoranda dated 16 and 19 August, General Rawlinson outlined his 'plan for a big offensive, tentatively fixed for the middle of September'. He also told the Commander of the Fourth Army 'of the arrival of a new offensive weapon – the armoured fighting vehicle known as the 'Tank'.'[1] However, before the new weapon could be unleashed, Rawlinson was to capture the ground from which Field Marshal Haig intended to mount the attack. There were three weeks in

Battle of the Somme September – November 1916. Quartermaster preparing equipment and ammunition to be collected by the incoming unit on their way up to the trenches.

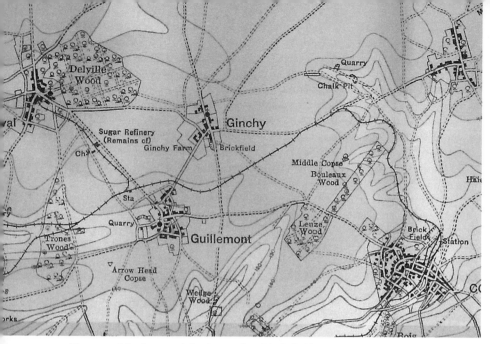

Topographical map of the September battlefields.

which to secure the line Leuze/Bouleaux Wood, Ginchy and High Wood. Troops to capture this line were in short supply, as the Commander-in-Chief wished to retain six fresh divisions for the September offensive. Haig's concept for this phase of the battle was that 'relentless pressure is to be maintained along the whole Army front, every opportunity being used to gain ground in small enterprises, especially surprise attacks by night'.[2]

Following attacks that made little progress over the period 23-24 August, General Rawlinson decided to bring 5th Division (1/Devons) into the line, under XIV Corps, with orders to take Guillemont. To the north, 7th Division (8 and 9/Devons) returned to the front to attack Ginchy (see Chapter 14).

During the night of 26 August, two brigades of 5th Division relieved the soldiers of 35th (Bantam) Division[3] on the eastern slopes of Maltz Horn Ridge. To the Division's immediate left was 20th (Light) Division and to the right were the French, with the Inter Army Boundary bisecting Angle Wood.

Devon Trench

1/Devons, holding the line in front of Guillemont, were quickly at work preparing for an attack, which was to be mounted by 5th Division on 3 September 1916. During the battalion's four-day tour in the line, all four companies took their turn as Battalion reserve and as supports and worked at the backbreaking task of digging advanced depots and carrying up combat supplies for the attack. All the while, the growing number of enemy guns regularly bombarded the Devons' position, bringing sudden death to the soldiers labouring in the battered trenches. With active British operations being conducted on a front of only seven miles, the Germans could concentrate their artillery fire at threatened points. To make matters worse, the rain fell heavily and incessantly.

However, the Battalion's main task during this 'stint' in the line was to dig an assembly trench for the coming attack across a reentrant between Lonely and Bantam Trenches, under the noses of the alert Germans. The process started with patrols going out into No Man's Land to check for German activity. They were followed by a company who deployed into shell holes forward of the new trench line's position in order to protect the working parties. While a protective screen was being established, officers with guides and men with white canvas tapes left the trenches to mark out the course of the new line. Only then did the diggers creep out of their trenches and, lying down or at the very most crouching, start digging as quickly and silently as possible. Silence was essential until they were twelve to eighteen inches down, as they had little cover from shellfire or machine-gun fire, should the Germans be alerted by the clink of steel on flint. An assembly trench had to be neither as deep nor as well developed as a proper defensive trench, but even so, for protective purposes, it needed traverses and in this case it was barely completed by dawn. First light brought shells, as the Germans ranged their guns on the new trench that had appeared in front of them. The new trench was, with little ceremony, named Devon Trench.

The West Countrymen were relieved by 1/East Surreys between 21.30 hours and 04.00 hours on 31 August, and went back for two days' rest in the 'huts' at Billon Wood. The sun shone, and while the Devons

A British infantryman killed during the attack. Note that he still has the breech cover on his his rifle.

scraped mud from their sodden greatcoats, groundsheets and web equipment were laid out to dry.

Guillemont

The attack on 3 September was to be a major joint attack with the French and with XV and III Corps, on a front that stretched as far west as High Wood. The aim was to 'reach a more favourable position from which to launch the mid-September offensive' by taking Guillemont, Ginchy and Leuze Wood. 20th Division was to take Guillemont itself, while 5th Division was to take the enemy trenches in the area south-west of Guillemont and advance to Leuze Wood. The 5th Division's assault was to be preceded by an attack on Falfemont Farm[4], from which position the main attack on Guillemont could be enfiladed by German machine guns. The divisional historian described the farm as 'one of the strongest redoubts ever made by the engineering skill of the Germans'. The main attack, which was to be delivered by 95 Brigade on the left and by 13 Brigade on the right, was to begin at midday.

Facing the British in the Guillemont area, in trenches that were originally the German second position, was the 111th Division. This division had deployed 73 Fusilier Regiment in Guillemont and 164 Regiment in Wedge Wood and Falfemont Farm. The lightly held gap between the two regiments was covered by interlocking arcs of machine-gun fire.

At 21.00 hours on 2 September, 1/Devons left Billon Wood[5]. They occupied the front or 'firing line', which was now several hundred yards behind the assembly trench that they dug some days earlier. 95 Brigade's part in 5th Division's plan was to attack from the forward assembly trench, at 12.15 hours, with two battalions; 1/Duke of Cornwall's (left assault) and 12/Gloucesters (right assault). 1/Devons, who were to be in support of the attack, were behind the Gloucesters, and 1/E. Surreys were behind 1/DCLI.

At 08.50 hours, 13 Brigade began the operation with the preliminary attack by 2/Kings Own Scottish Borders (KOSB), who advanced on Falfemont Farm. The attempt was an utter disaster, as the Jocks were unable to advance across the 400 yards of open ground, swept by machine guns, without heavy artillery support. The French artillery fire support had been cancelled when the guns were needed to halt a German counter-attack in their own area. The message sent by a British liaison officer at the French headquarters failed to get through in time for alternative arrangements to be made. Making the KOSB even more exposed, the French 127 Regiment, who were to attack on their right, were pinned down in their own trenches. The Borderers lost nearly 300 men 'in a very gallant attempt to carry out its impossible task'.

Despite this reverse, the main attack started punctually at 12.15 hours. The Cornwalls and 12/Gloucesters followed

> the rolling or creeping barrage which was to cover the advance of the infantry. This was now an established practice and the troops were becoming accustomed to keeping as close as possible to it.[6]

5th Division's operation order gave explicit instructions for the assault troops 'to

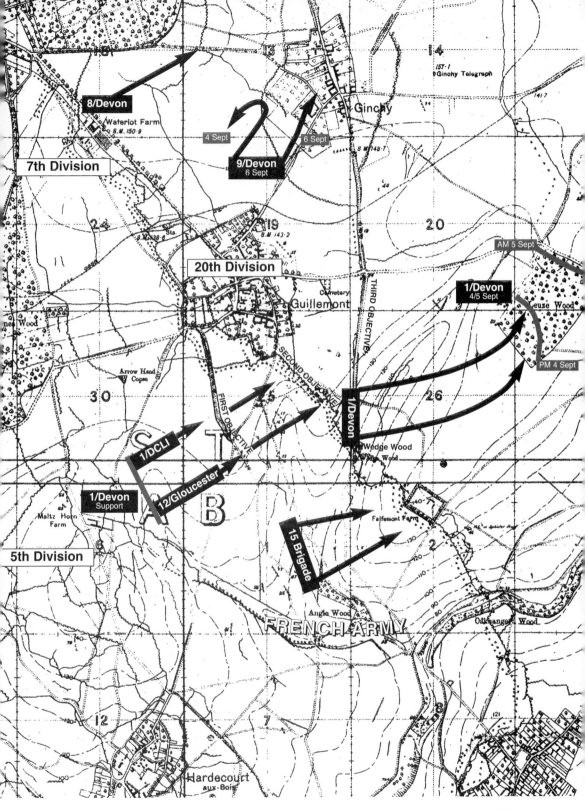

8/Devon

7th Division

Waterlot Farm
B.M. 150·9

4 Sept

9/Devon
6 Sept

6 Sept

Ginchy

Ginchy Telegraph

20th Division

Guillemont

AM 5 Sept

1/Devon
4/5 Sept

Leuze Wood

PM 4 Sept

1/DCLI

1/Devon

Wedge Wood

1/Devon
Support

12/Gloucester

5th Division

Maltz Horn
Farm

15 Brigade

Falfemont Farm

Angle Wood

FRENCH ARMY

Oakhanger Wood

Hardecourt
aux-Bois

keep about 25 yards behind the barrage, which was to move at the rate of 50 yards per minute'. Keeping well up behind the barrage, the Cornwalls and the Gloucesters advanced according to the timings detailed in their orders. Meanwhile, Numbers 1 and 2 Companies 1/Devons had moved forward to Devon Trench with their place being taken by Numbers 3 and 4 Companies. As 12/Gloucesters were approaching the first objective, the Devons left the assembly trench. A little while later, a runner was sent back across No Man's Land, with a message to Battalion Headquarters from the Devons' forward company timed at 13.25 hours. 'The Devons were consolidating the first objective and the Gloucesters were continuing towards the second objective.' From Battalion Headquarters, the message was telephoned to Brigadier Lord Gordon-Lennox who anxiously paced in his HQ dugout.

On this occasion, the process, of the assault troops seizing the enemy position and the supports clearing the enemy trenches in detail and dealing with prisoners of war, worked as intended. It is recorded that, 'about a hundred and fifty prisoners were sent back, chiefly from the 73rd Fusiliers and 164th Regiment and that I/73, holding the trenches south of Guillemont, was surprised and almost annihilated'. Once the objective was clear of the enemy, the leading Devon companies (Numbers 1 and 2) started the work of putting the trenches into a state of defence. Fire steps to the rear of the captured trench (now the front) were dug, and detachments of 15 Brigade Machine Gun and Trench Mortar Companies came forward. Even if the Germans counter-attacked and drove the Gloucesters back, at least the Devons would hold the Brigade's first objective.

Despite heavy casualties from machine guns in Falfemont Farm, the Gloucesters' signal flares were soon seen rising over the second objective. Numbers 1 and 2 Companies 1/Devons then moved on again, their place being taken in the consolidated first objective by Numbers 3 and 4 Companies. Again, a message reached Brigade Headquarters via a runner who had to brave the enemy barrage falling in the former No Man's Land. At 15.55 hours, the Brigade war diary recorded that '1/Devon consolidating second objective'. However, one of 1/Devons' forward companies was summoned to assist the Gloucesters, who were in trouble at their final objective, having again suffered from the fire of the machine guns in Falfemont Farm. Overnight, Numbers 1 and 2 Companies moved forward and relieved the depleted 12/Gloucesters in the front line between Wedge Wood and the Ginchy Road at 03.10 hours.

In summarizing the attack on 3 September, the divisional historian recorded that:

> ... two hours after zero, 95 Brigade had gained their final objective and had dug in along the line of the road from Ginchy to Maurepas, north of Wedge Wood. Their advance was magnificently executed, and, in spite of a withering machine gun fire, the line never wavered for an instant.

With 95 Brigade's attack going well, 20th Division fighting through the rubble of Guillemont and with few enemy in sight, it is tempting to speculate about the results of an immediate further advance. However, such an advance by 95 Brigade would have formed an extremely vulnerable salient. 20th Division on the left was exhausted and 13 and 15 Brigades on the right had again failed to secure Falfemont Farm.

The Advance to Leuze Wood

4 September proved to be a windy day with heavy showers and bright intervals, conditions which persisted on the morrow.

The Germans in Falfemont Farm were still holding out against 15 Brigade and despite repeated attacks, the strong point remained unsubdued, although the British were closing in on the German garrison. The history of the German 73 Fusilier Regiment makes it plain that they appreciated the advantageous position 95 Brigade had gained and records that a counter-attack was broken up by British artillery before it came to grips with the enemy. At 14.00 hours, Field Marshal Haig arrived at Headquarters Fourth Army. He emphasized that the capture of the high ground between Leuze Wood and the site of the telegraph Station north-east of Ginchy 'was of the first importance'. Consequently, 95 Brigade prepared an attack, with its first objective being Valley Trench and its second objective Leuze Wood up on the spur beyond. Orders were given that the assault was to be on a single battalion front, led by two companies of 1/East Surreys, with 1/Devons in support.

The remains of Leuze Wood at the end of the battle.

Such was the ferocity of the fighting at Falfemont that German attention and reserves were 'fixed' on holding the Farm, and the Surreys took 'Valley Trench without trouble, the battalion reporting that "Our own shrapnel caused the only casualty"'. The remnants of the German II and III Battalions, 73 Fusilier Regiment withdrew north-east up the valley and rallied in Leuze Wood. While the Devons were coming forward to take over leading the advance, the German 111th Division rushed forward an ad-hoc force to hold the line. Advancing from the north-east they were halted by combined rifle and Lewis-gun fire from the East Surreys and the Devons. The Germans withdrew in disorder.

Two companies of Devons took up the advance at about 18.30 hours. They deployed strong patrols closely following the creeping artillery barrage, while the main body of Numbers 1 and 2 Companies were further back, advancing in open order. The Devons adopted a deep formation in order to minimize casualties from enemy counter bombardment and to present as small a target as possible to any surviving enemy machine gunners. This is an example of a tactical development, where having been identified by advanced patrols, enemy positions would be bombarded and attacked in detail. Gone were the simplistic linear wave tactics of eight weeks earlier.

Advancing under the darkening skies of an early dusk, the two companies pressed on, suffering 'numerous casualties' but despite this,

> What resistance was offered lacked determination and was easily and cheaply overcome, and by 7.30 the two companies were consolidating a line just inside Leuze Wood.[7]

However, having reached the edge of the wood at 18.55 hours, according to the official historian:

> Here the British barrage prevented further progress; but after a message had been sent back to the artillery by a Forward Observation Officer, the Devonshire were able to enter the wood and begin to consolidate a line inside it.

The West Countrymen had advanced a mile across the open shell-pitted landscape, up out of the valley, on to the spur and into the wood. This disciplined advance to Leuze Wood on 4 September 1916 was the longest single advance made by any battalion on the Somme in over two months of battle since 1 July.

The two companies of Devons, lacking combat power to continue the advance further into the wood, were very exposed at the end of a pronounced salient. 20th Division on the left was still held up east of Guillemont, and 15 Brigade was now 600 yards further back on the right, presenting a gap in the British line. Consequently, the Devons wisely chose to hold their gains rather than being sucked deeper into the wood where, overextended, they would have been extremely vulnerable to counter-attack.

During the course of the evening, the arrival of reinforcements from Number 3 Company on the left flank and sections of 95 Brigade's machine guns and trench mortars improved the Devons' situation in the wood. Number 4 Company remained in the trenches along the Ginchy road, as a reserve. On the

Battalion's left, the advance of a battalion of Royal West Kents further improved matters, but the Leuze Wood Salient was still marked and highly vulnerable. For the second night running, the Devons laboured hard to strengthen their new position against the inevitable German counter-attacks, but patrols sent further into the wood, according to the Battalion's war diary, 'came across none of the enemy'.

Even though 15 Brigade had eventually captured Falfemont Farm after dark, at dawn on the morning of 5 September, 1/Devons remained in an exposed position. 20th Division was still to their left rear and the gap on their right between Leuze Wood and 15 Brigade at the Farm was yet to be closed. Consequently, the three companies holding their trenches just inside the wood remained in cover. However, by afternoon, 15 Brigade had filled this gap by clearing Germans and machine guns from shell holes on the ridge between Falfemont Farm and Leuze Wood and 'with its right flank thus secured the Battalion could advance again'. Numbers 1, 2 and 3 Companies advanced 500

The gruesome task of sorting through equipment and personal effects of those who had become casualties had to be faced after every attack.

yards through the tangle of splintered tree stumps, blown down branches and shell holes, and rushed a German trench running through the northern part of the wood. The war diary records 'By 4.15 p.m. the trench was in our hands and consolidation was commenced'. Against light resistance, the Devons sent patrols forward towards the northern edge of the wood.

Having been in action since leaving their bivouacs on the evening of 2 September, the 5th Division were relieved by the 16th Irish Division. Two companies of 7/Royal Irish Fusiliers relieved the Devons in the trench, while guides led two further companies of Irishmen forward to the patrol line, where they occupied positions just before dawn on 6 September. The West Countrymen, weary but flushed with success, marched back to Billon Farm. Letters and messages praising the troops' 'dash and vigour' were not long in coming to 5th Division, to 95 Brigade and 1/Devons in particular. However, the battle had inevitably cost the Battalion further casualties. In their time on the Guillemont / Leuze Wood front, the Devons suffered what were considered to be comparatively few casualties. The Battalion's killed and missing totalled just 36 men, while the list of those soldiers wounded contained 159 names. The relatively low proportion of killed to the number of wounded was the result of sound, well-practised, casualty evacuation arrangements and, of course, of a highly successful advance. The war diary recorded that:

However, the gilt of success quickly faded, as we were not to go back to rest with the rest of the Brigade but were to immediately return to hold the line as a part of a composite brigade. This was a cruel blow to the Battalion.

1   *Military Operations, France and Belgium 1916*, Vol 2.
2   Ibid.
3   A division raised in 1915, after the relaxation of recruiting standards. It largely consisted of men shorter than five feet three inches, who had previously been considered 'under height'.
4   As spelt on the 5 August 1916 edition of the composite Guillemont map. The modern replacement farm is *Faffemont Ferme*.
5   1/Devons' War Diary PRO WO 95/1579.
6   Quoted in *Military Operations, France and Belgium 1916*, Vol 2.
7   *The Devonshire Regiment 1914 – 1918*, C. T. Atkinson, Exeter, 1926.

Chapter 14

Ginchy

The loss of ground was of no strategic importance and the course of the fighting must not be measured by this. However, the loss of men and the heavy expenditure of material ate heavily into the strength of the German Army. The mighty material strength of the enemy did not fail to have its psychological effects on the German soldier.

GERMAN OFFICIAL HISTORY

In early September, while 1/Devons were fighting to the south of Guillemont, 8 and 9/Devons were back in action with 7th Division just a mile to the north at Ginchy. To have returned to an active battlefront for a fourth time during just over two months of a major offensive was exceptional. However, the Devons along with the rest of the Division had been out of the line for almost a month since 22 July 1916. During this time, further drafts arrived from the rear area to 'fatten up' battalions for their next attack. Ready to return to the front, 8/Devons numbered 964 all ranks, while 9/Devons were over 800 strong. The divisional historian wrote:

... there was some general dissatisfaction over the physique and general quality of some of the drafts which poured in. One battalion received about 25 men who were physically and generally quite useless, another had 40 men too undersized to march in full marching order, and the musketry and marching capabilities of the new hands provoked some severe criticisms.

The hitherto unprecedented level of casualties placed enormous pressure on the recruiting and training organization. Quality inevitably suffered, as even imperfectly trained men were urgently needed at the front. The situation regarding officers was little better. Twenty officers or about fifty per cent of the 8th Battalions' officer corps were replacements. Some, such as Lieutenant Frank Wollocombe, were returning to duty having recovered from wounds, but the majority were young officers, joining to feed battle's insatiable appetite for the blood of junior commanders[1]. However, with the battalions at rest, the newly arrived officers had an opportunity to get to know their men during sports competitions and during the more serious business of training. To address the infantry's increasing reliance on the grenade or bomb, emphasis was on marksmanship at 100 and 200 yards and bayonet fighting. However, unharvested crops on the training areas were noted as 'impeding field training'.

In late August 1916, as a successful assault division, the 7th was to have been saved to take part in Field Marshal Haig's attack with the tanks in mid-September. However, the need to replace one of XIII Corp's shattered divisions brought a call for their return to the front on 26 August. The 7th Division,

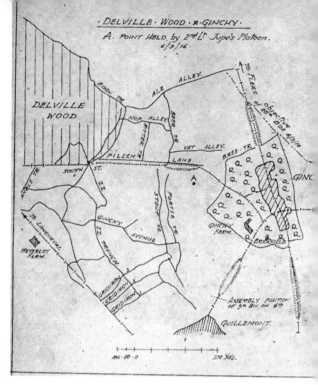

however, was not to be deployed as a whole, but would be fed into battle piecemeal, from Corps Reserve, in order to take increasingly important preliminary objectives before the coming offensive. First up to the front, on the eastern edge of Delville Wood, was 22 Brigade, taking over a portion of the line from 14th and 20th Divisions facing Ginchy. Next into the line was 91 Brigade, who took over a sector to the right, as successive battalions were ground down by costly attacks on Ginchy and relentless enemy artillery fire. These two brigades, with 20 Brigade carrying up their ammunition, trench stores and food, made steady progress forward, and 1/Royal Welch Fusiliers established a toehold in Ginchy. However, they were ejected by a vigorous counter-attack, and despite new assaults by the depleted and disorganized Royal Irish and

A map from the Devons' regimental history.

The perennial problem was bringing the guns forward across the wrecked battle area to support troops who had made a successful advance.

Manchesters, it proved to be impossible to retake the village.

On 3 September, 22 Brigade had been fought to a standstill, and 20 Brigade was ordered forward to attack Ginchy. Atkinson wrote:

The 9th [Devon] led the way. It was about 7 p.m. when they left Buire, by 8.30[2] they were debussing [from trucks] at Mametz, there to draw rations and bombs, and then to proceed [on foot] to Montauban. The situation, when the 20th Brigade reached the front, was that ... the remnants of 22 Brigade were holding on to Porter [and Stout[3]] Trench, just west of Ginchy, and some were even believed to be in the village itself. This, however, was uncertain and if anything, rather a disadvantage, as it prevented a proper artillery preparation. The chances of success were further prejudiced by the inevitable delays over getting from Mametz to Ginchy. It was a long way over much broken ground, the night was dark, halts had to be made at Bernafay Wood to draw picks and shovels and water, and again at the Quarry, north of Benafay Wood, to draw detonated [primed] bombs, there had been none at Mametz, and by the time they were crossing the high ground south of Delville Wood it was getting light.

The communication trench, Ginchy Avenue, though exposed in full daylight to carefully positioned German observers, gave limited protection from sniper, machine-gun and artillery fire. The Brigade report explains that '9/Devon however were directed to continue their advance, as it was considered that Ginchy might be entered without serious opposition and under cover of the morning mist. The mist cleared however before the attack could develop'.

The German Defenders

Ginchy, a small straggling set of pulverized ruins surrounded by the shell-blasted remains of fruit trees, was a strong point in depth, behind the German second position. It was held by 35 Fusilier Regiment reinforced by 88 Regiment, while the trenches in the remains of Delville Wood were held by 118 Regiment. These three regiments all belonging to 56th Division, who had been one of ten German formations rushed to the Somme during August 1916. While 56th Division had originally been a well-founded regular formation, after a month in battle it was much reduced in strength. Prince Rupprecht also expressed his reservations over the quality of battle-casualty replacements directed to his army on the Somme. He recorded that in August, German Division '... received drafts of *Landsturm* – men over 38 years of age who had never seen action before – and these had to be sent back, "as they were merely a danger"'.[4] The pressure of feeding both the battles at Verdun and the Somme was now telling on the German Army. However, despite the reducing quality of its soldiers, 56th Division had held Ginchy and on several occasions restored their positions by counter-attack. However, within 56th Division, 88 Regiment could still be regarded as powerful opponents, having savagely counter-attacked 22 Brigade and driven them back in a close combat, armed with spades and axes.

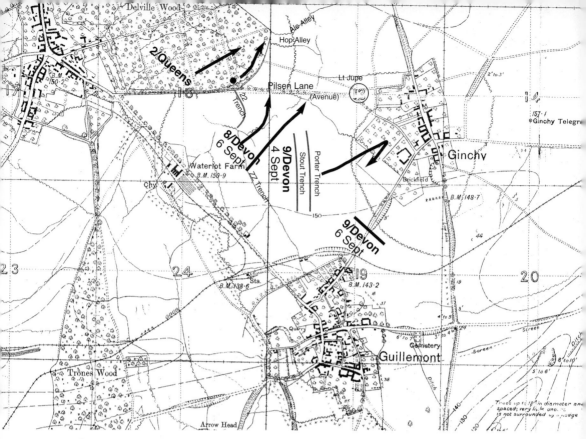

The Devons' part in the attack on Ginchy.

The Attack of 9/Devons: 4 September 1916

Despite suffering casualties in their daylight move through the inadequate communication trench, Numbers 1 and 2 Companies reached the front line. Here there was confusion, as noted in the Brigade report, '... owing to a mistake in the position of Stout and Porter Trenches on the map'. This is understandable as there was plenty of scope for error, because the location of newly-dug trenches was reported by inexperienced junior officers who had few landmarks to use on the desolate Somme battlefield. Even today, it is hard to make sense of reports and sketches contained in war diaries. An officer standing up to work out his exact position was inviting a sniper's bullet. In addition, as officers updated their maps in red chinograph pencil, further errors crept in during the process of copying from map to map. Consequently, Numbers 1 and 2 occupied ZZ Trench, not the forward assembly line Porter Trench, while Numbers 3 and 4 Companies, who were planned to deploy as supports in Stout Trench, were about 100 yards behind them.

The plan was for the leading West Countrymen to advance behind the by now well-practised creeping barrage. When the forward companies had broken through the German front line trenches and advanced east through Ginchy, Number 3 Company was to fight through the northern part of the village. Number 4 Company at the rear was to mop up and form a defensive flank facing north. It will be recalled that both 5th and 20th Divisions were attacking to the right at Guillemont and Falfemont Farm, at approximately the same time. 2/Borders were to occupy the assault trenches once vacated, and 8/Devons were Brigade's reserve at Montauban.

9/Devons left ZZ trench at about 08.00 hours. 'The attack was gallantly launched and, despite all disadvantages, at first seemed to be going well.' Three of the leading platoons were quickly in Ginchy, and were being followed by the remainder of their companies. By 09.15 hours, Major Green received an encouraging message at Battalion Headquarters, located at the telephone cable head at the junction of Longueval and York Alleys, where he learned that the attack was going well. Second Lieutenant Lillicrap reported that Numbers 1 and 2 Companies were into the ruins of Ginchy and 'were making good progress, but were losing heavily'. However, while this message was being delivered, the attack lost its momentum, '... the advance had been held up by machine gun and rifle fire, and reinforcements were needed'. With the Germans sheltering in concealed positions amongst the rubble, advancing and clearing through the ruins of Ginchy was a costly business, with casualties particularly heavy amongst commanders, who were forced to lead by example, exposing themselves to danger in order to keep their soldiers moving.

88 Regiment recorded in their history that the Devons' attack was eventually beaten off by infantry fire. They also complained that their supporting batteries had not replied to the signal rockets sent up from the front line, calling for emergency artillery fire against the advancing British. However, 20 Brigade reported that eventually 'the enemy had placed a heavy artillery barrage on 9/Devon [support and reserve companies] and the area Stout, Porter and ZZ Trenches'. It is reasonable to presume that, realizing 88 Regiment were being attacked on a narrow frontage and seeing that the communication trenches were full of reinforcements (2/Borders), the German artillery commander decided to concentrate on preventing the reserves moving forward, leaving the infantry in Ginchy to deal with the immediate problem.

The bombardment of Ginchy.

Infantry advancing into No Man's Land during the attack on Ginchy.

Later in the morning, lacking information, Major Green dispatched Second Lieutenant Lillicrap back across No Man's Land to find out what was happening. Amongst the rubble of Ginchy, he found the almost leaderless remnants of 9/Devons, and returning to Battalion Headquarters, reported at 12.35 hours that the attack had failed and that the companies were digging in where they could. Three company commanders were casualties, and those men still on their feet were exhausted. It was largely because of the persistent German barrage that 'an attempt to reinforce the 9th Devons by one company of 2nd Border Regiment did not relieve the situation'. With the British reinforcements halted, the enemy artillery concentrated on Ginchy, and a counter-attack drove the increasingly thin ranks of West Countrymen back. By midday, they were gathered in ZZ Trench.

Ginchy had been too strongly held for a single battalion to overcome. It is likely that, had the German artillery promptly responded to the SOS rockets, 9/Devons' attack would have been halted in No Man's Land before it entered the village. However, they gained the eastern part of Ginchy, but the Germans were in strength, in strong positions and deployed in significant depth. The cost to the 700 officers and men of 9/Devons who left Porter and Stout Trenches that

The leading wave of a reserve platoon moves up to Ginchy under artillery fire.

morning was high. The regimental historian wrote:

> *Little more than half remained to be relieved after dark by 2/Gordons and drag themselves back to Montauban ... It had been a disastrous business for the 9th.*

5 September 1916

Major General Watts persuaded a reluctant Corps Headquarters that the attack on Ginchy should not be renewed until dawn on 5 September. Faced with the continuing stiff resistance by 88 Regiment, he planned to attack with both 2/Gordons Highlanders and 8/Devons. 20 Brigade's new commander, Brigadier Green, ordered 2/Borders to hold the trenches close to Delville Wood. In Phase One of the attack, 8/Devons' mission was to take the maze of enemy trenches in the gap between Ginchy and Delville Wood and form a defensive flank. According to 21/Manchesters, whose attack had failed in this area the previous afternoon,

> *The enemy are reported to have been seen holding a trench just clear of the edge of Delville Wood between Ale Alley and Hop Alley.*

Once this area was secured, in Phase Two, the Gordons were to attack the virtually obliterated village of Ginchy and 'establish a line north east and east, on the slope looking down into the shallow valley towards Flers'.

After dark on 4 September 1916, the rain swept across the exposed uplands of the Somme in cold heavy curtains and the night was pitch black. No lights could be allowed and there were no guides available to help the West Countrymen of 8/Devons move up from Montauban to resume the attack. B Company led the march to the front:

> *The ground was slippery, and there was much mud and many delays. It was already daylight when the leading company, B, filed into ZZ Trench and the attack, which should have started at 3.30 a.m. (September 5th), had to be postponed.*[5]

Although 8/Devons had reached the front line around dawn, it took them until almost 08.00 hours to relieve 21/Manchesters in ZZ Trench. The Battalion's post-operational report[6] explained the difficulties of taking over one strong point: 'Two guides from the Warwicks took a party to relieve a detachment at T13 Central. This party returned after dawn, the guides having lost their way.'

The remainder of 20 Brigade, following 8/Devons, took even longer to get forward:

> *At 2.20 a.m. on the 5th, the 20th Brigade reported to the 7th Division that the 2/Gordon Highlanders could not be in position to attack for three hours, and that even then, owing to the bad state of the ground, nothing more than reorganization of the front positions would be possible.*

So bad were the weather conditions in the trenches and so active were the enemy that eventually the attack proved impossible to mount and had again to be rescheduled.

Major General Watts [probably mindful of the fate of 9/Devons' daylight attack] *consented to this course, and subsequently agreed that the attack should be postponed until 3.30 a.m. next morning. Officers ... who had withdrawn their isolated parties from the edge of Ginchy and ... reported that the village was held principally by machine gunners and that a night attack seemed to offer every prospect of success.*

9/Devons spent the day improving their trenches. One company commander, writing on pages from his field notebook, reported 'The company [B] at once got to work cleaning and deepening the trench which was in a bad condition. Intermittent artillery fire all day.'

Delville Wood

During the morning, 2/Queens, who were temparily under command of 20 Brigade, came into the line to the left of 8/Devons, who received the following warning order from Brigade Headquarters:

2nd Queens will attack and seize the eastern corner of Delville Wood this afternoon covered by a bombardment of Stokes Mortars and medium mortars. The medium mortar bombardment will commence at 3.30 p.m. and continue till 5.30 p.m. at which hour the 2nd Queens will advance to the assault. No advance will be made beyond the edge of the Wood but the line will be strongly consolidated at once and blocks made up Hop and Ale Alleys. The 8th Devons will be prepared to assist the attack with bombers.

In support of this attack, Major Green dispatched Number One Platoon from A Company (battalion reserve located in Longueval Alley) 'to their assistance in a bombing attack on Ale Ally, to keep in touch with the right of the Queens and to guard their right flank'. The first time 8/Devons had seen Delville Wood had been on 14 July, when it was green and leafy; now it was an unspeakable wilderness of splintered tree stumps and shell-churned mud. Number One Platoon worked its way forward into a gap between the two battalions. From this position, they were able to give fire support to help two companies of 2/Queens and their bombers take Ale Alley trench, along the edge of the wood. After dark, 8/Devons were required to send further help to 2/Queens. This time, D Company sent two platoons forward to assist in holding

... the part of Diagonal trench in Delville Wood ... Finding the south east corner of the wood unoccupied, these two platoons dug in ten yards from the south east edge of the wood and got in touch with B Company in ZZ Trench.

Overnight, these two platoons held the South Street and Pilsen Lane trenches.

Meanwhile, under cover of darkness, 'C Company and the remaining two platoons of D Company were ordered to move out into No Man's Land and start digging in on the defensive flank'. Despite persistent enemy shelling, casualties had been relatively light during the day, but during the night, orders came confirming that 8/Devons were to take part in the delayed attack on Ginchy the following morning.

The Devons' Second Attack – 6 September 1916

The 20 Brigade Operation Order that arrived at the battalions' headquarters described the overall situation:

> *The French north of the Somme are advancing with great speed on the line Peron – Bapaume Road along which the enemy is trying to withdraw his guns, and have captured a battery of 420 mm howitzer and a balloon on the ground. The Corps on our right [1/Devon] have seized Leuze Wood and are advancing...*

To expand the front on which the Allied advance was being made and in order to prevent a vulnerable salient being formed, it was important that Ginchy was taken. Commander 20 Brigade needed all his available combat power for attack and the expected advance. Consequently, the shattered 9th Battalion was needed back at the front.

Having lost half their strength, the shocked young soldiers of 9/Devons, many having been in action for the first time, had precious little rest before being summoned from Montauban, back to the battle. Lieutenant Wollocombe and about fifty men of the Battalion's 'left out of battle' details had rejoined the battalion, boosting its strength to a mere 400 all ranks, or approximately forty per cent of its full wartime establishment. Those who have not lived through such experiences can only guess the feelings of the young West Countrymen: fear, resignation and a numbing exhaustion, as they again followed their officers towards their nemesis at Ginchy. Now familiar with the route forward, the battalion was in position at 03.30 hours on 6 September. Located in the south-

Delville Wood at the end of the battle.

eastern extension of ZZ Trench, 9/Devons were behind 2/Gordons, who were in the Porter and Stout trenches ready for a dawn attack now fixed for 05.00 hours. The idea of a phased attack was abandoned. However, the essentials of the plan were the same; the Gordons, supported by 9/Devons' were to take Ginchy, and 8/Devons were to secure the remaining enemy trenches between Delville Wood and Ginchy and form a further defensive flank.

Major General Watt's plans were, however, circumscribed by numerous reports that various remnants of 22 Brigade and 9/Devons were still holding out in Ginchy. Consequently, he was unable to bombard the village before the attack. This, of course, left the Germans able to man their defences with impunity rather than being driven into cover, with the attackers arriving as the barrage crept forward through the ruins. Without a bombardment, the plan was for the Gordons to rush Ginchy before dawn. However, this straightforward task 'looked less easy on a dark morning with two rather weak companies in the lead, spread over a frontage of some 750 yards'.[7] To make matters worse, the 20 Brigade signal log recorded that:

> Lieutenant Colonel Seymour reports that 2nd Gordon Highlanders and 8th Devon Regt unable to issue orders to their companies with regard to advancing onto the barrage line at 3.30 a.m., but that he was making arrangements so the line would be led forward at 6 a.m..

The Gordons had moved forward under the cover of darkness but their two leading companies became lost in the darkness. As a result, the attack was delayed until 06.30 hours, with the artillery continuing to bombard the enemy position except for Ginchy itself. The Gordons' regimental history describes how, having been repulsed,

> Major Oxley had to take them back to their starting point for a fresh effort; this went much better, but came under a heavy fire and was brought to a standstill about 100 yards short of Ginchy.

This was 'heavy fire' of small arms from the unsupressed German infantry. A message, timed at 06.25 hours in 20 Brigade's war diary, records that 'Lieutenant Colonel James 8th Devon Regt reports "Situation very unusual from point of view of attack – there is no reply from German artillery"'. A further message timed 06.37, as the Gordons' attack was going in, recorded 'No enemy artillery fire'. Despite the lack of a German bombardment, the Gordons' second attack had come to a halt and a message reached 20 Brigade '2/Gordons digging-in on west of Ginchy. Attack requires impetus'. Brigadier Green gave firm instructions to 'get the attack moving again'.

Meanwhile, 9/Devons' leading companies, Numbers 3 and 4, had moved up in support behind the Gordons. However, despite 'impetus being given to the attack' by their reinforcement, soldiers of the two battalions made little progress. The following situation report was passed by 20 Brigade to 7th Division:

> Present line is 40 – 100 yards in front of village. Major Oxley, 2/Gordons killed[8]. Suggest that 2/Gordons attack at 12 noon. Barrage to be put back, and lift at 12 noon. Howitzers to fire on Waterlot

Farm. Barrage east of Ginchy to remain on trench till 12.20 p.m.

8/Devons at Delville Wood

While the Gordons, supported by 9/Devons, had been attacking Ginchy as 20 Brigade's main effort, 8/Devons were to secure and dig new trenches in the yard gap between Delville Wood and the village. Advancing in two waves to the immediate left of 2/Gordons was C Company 8/Devons. Starting from the northern portion of ZZ trench, the leading platoon, under Second Lieutenants Field and Jupe, quickly reached Point 13 on the Longueval/Ginchy Road. Here they found themselves isolated and unsupported. The platoons that were following them had got lost at dawn in the wilderness of shell holes and partly dug trenches. Those following an advance are often less diligent in their navigation, and when they become separated can be easily 'geographically embarrassed'. However, a series of messages from Lieutenant Lock, a Battalion Headquarters liaison officer, to Lieutenant Colonel James gives an impression of the difficulties in exercising effective command and control during this phase of battle. The first timed at 06.50 hours, explained:

> *I find the majority of C Company, with Second Lieutenant Old did not get further than the right of B Company in ZZ Trench.*
>
> *I am now just going to lead B Company up and have directed Old to follow and keep in touch with me. As far as I can make out the Gordons have not yet been successful in the village.*

Another message from Lieutenant Lock, written twenty-five minutes later, briefed the Commanding Officer on his progress:

British infantry working to improve trenches among the shattered remains of trees at the edge of Delville Wood.

Have moved along ZZ Trench to junction with Delville Wood and started along Pilsen Avenue. At present have seen no sign of Capt Hole [C Company] and that part of his company not with me. Have come back to Diagonal Trench and find D Company has not moved up, so, except for Captain Hole's small party, which no one knows of, there can be no digging party out.

Am I to move on along Pilsen Avenue under these conditions?

Clearly, a combination of inexperience with difficulties in disseminating orders and map reading had produced a confused situation. Even though he was a junior officer, armed with the Commanding Officer's confirmation of his intent, Lieutenant Lock did extraordinary work to overcome the inherent chaos of battle, and earned a well-deserved Military Cross. Lock's final message of the day, preserved in the Battalion war diary, reads:

C and B Companies digging in from Delville Wood [south-east corner] and thence along Pilsen Lane. I am sending for D Company to work further along Pilsen Lane to the east and will send bombers ahead. There is considerable sniping and the guns are trying to range in on the new work [trench], assisted by Huns firing [Verey] lights [as a known reference point] probably from Hop Alley.

Captain Hole is there and from what I can make out Field and Jupe are down towards Ginchy with the Gordons. Old is wounded.

Thanks to Lieutenant Lock, the Devons were successfully re-organized on their objectives, and digging their defensive flank by linking up the remains of the German Pilsen Lane trenches and some of the abundant shell holes, when at 09.30 hours, 'the enemy's guns suddenly woke up'. The ranging shots reported by Lieutenant Lock, were the foretaste of a barrage that 'plastered' the Devons' positions at 'the eastern edge of Delville Wood, ZZ Trench, and Pilsen Lane, with every variety of shell'. Meanwhile, the platoon of C Company isolated at Point 13 were in a very exposed position, as the Gordons on their right had failed to clear Ginchy. The regimental history records that:

... a strong party of Germans advanced from the village to cut it off. But the platoon [Jupe's] held firm, received the Germans with a steady fire, and drove them back with many casualties. However, later on, heavy shelling forced this platoon to evacuate its position for a less exposed spot.

The Battalion's after-action report explained that:

Knowing both their flanks were not supported and fearing the enemy might work round them in shell holes, they retired by twos to a position at T.13.c.1.5 [see map], facing NE. Here they remained until 4.30 p.m.. Finding themselves out of communication, they then reported to battalion headquarters. The platoon was kept in battalion reserve and the officers rejoined the remainder of the company and assisted in extending and consolidating Pilsen Trench.

Throughout the day and into the evening 8/Devons 'hung onto their new line, though severely punished by shelling, against which the shallow trenches gave

One of the German positions cleared by the Devons at the edge of Delville Wood. Note the featureless country beyond the 'wood' that 8/Devons had to find their way across.

but indifferent protection'. Casualties mounted, and for the remaining Devons, matters were made worse by the loss of their ration and water parties to enemy shelling. One officer commented that their plight was emphasized by 'some humorist having called our trenches Beer Alley and Stout Alley'.

9/Devons at Ginchy

With the Gordons checked just outside Ginchy and digging shallow scrapes, the 400 strong 9/Devons had to endure a bombardment in Stout and Porter Trenches. However, despite the noise and concussion of exploding shells, these trenches were reasonably well made, and therefore casualties were relatively light.

At 11.45 hours, Major C.C. Foss, Brigade Major of 20 Brigade, signed written orders for a renewed attack on Ginchy, to be coordinated with that of 24th Division on Guillemont. Following a general description of the situation, including 8/Devons' successful formation of the defensive flank, the orders gave the following instructions:

> *2nd Gordon Highlanders will renew the attack at 2.00 p.m. assisted by two companies of 9th Devon Regt who will attack from the SW on the line of the Ginchy – Guillemont road. OC 9th Devon Regt will place at the disposal of 2nd Gordon Highlanders such men as OC 2nd Gordon Highlanders requires as mopping up party. Ginchy village will*

227

*be bombarded until 2.00 p.m. when the barrage will lift on to trench
E of Ginchy where it will remain until 3.00 p.m. Lifts of heavy
artillery will be by 50 yard bounds, and lifts of Divisional artillery by
bounds of 25 yards. Pint Trench, Ale Trench, Lager Lane, will be kept
under heavy artillery fire until further orders.*

These orders were later amended, cancelling 9/Devons' mopping up role and
tasking their two remaining companies to be prepared to move up to 'Stout
Trench in close support of the attack'. Behind the Devons, 22 Manchesters were
to occupy ZZ Trench as brigade reserve.

Captain Hearse was to lead the two companies in a right flanking attack,
approaching Ginchy via the light railway cutting and the sunken Guillemont -
Ginchy Road. By 14.00 hours, he was in position, and this time with a proper
barrage on the village, the remains of 2/Gordons and the two weak companies
of 9/Devons swept forward to the village. Having benefited from his covered
approach, Captain Hearse's West Countrymen surprised the German defenders
and quickly fought through the village. It seems that mingled with the Gordons,
they cleared the orchards to the northern end of the village but, 'All the officers
of these companies became casualties and accurate information was never
forthcoming'.

What is known is that, at 14.45 hours, Forward Observation Officers (FOO)
from T Battery Royal Horse Artillery reported heavy rifle fire in the northern
part of Ginchy. Consequently, at 14.56 hours, Brigadier Green ordered one of
9/Devons' two remaining companies forward to Stout Trench. They were to be
'ready to slip in on top of 2/Gordon Highlanders' or to enter the village and
attack through the Gordons' foothold in Ginchy. At 15.10 hours, positive
information was received when the first twenty-five to thirty prisoners of the
German 35th Regiment passed Battalion HQ. Escort states that 2/Gordons and
9/Devons were well into the village.

At 15.55 hours, the watchkeeper at Brigade Headquarters recorded that
'9/Devon asks for reinforcements. Lieutenant Colonel Seymour suggests two
machine guns be sent up'. These guns eventually arrived in Ginchy. However, the
Devons were in trouble. At 16.40 hours, it is recorded that 'Last Company
9/Devon shelled out of southern part of Ginchy and returned to Stout Trench'.
The Brigade Commander sent Major Green forward to bolster his companies
and the Gordons, but he was too late, as the depleted battalions were unable to
hold their gains in the face of growing enemy artillery fire. Lieutenant
Morshead, a Royal Engineer officer, accompanying the Devons, wrote of the
attack on 6 September:

*It was an afternoon assault. They got right into the village, but were
badly knocked about by our big guns, which were dropping short. A
considerable number were forced to retire, and a German counter-
attack cleared the remainder out of the village towards 5 p.m.*[9]

By 17.27 hours, a message was received at Brigade Headquarters via 2/Borders
that they 'can see Gordons and Devons retiring out of Ginchy'. A little later, a
report from an FOO timed 17.15 hours, reached Brigade Headquarters with the

news that a 'German counter-attack captured Ginchy'. This typically violent German response added to the total of 100 other ranks and eight officer casualties suffered by 9/Devons.

Among the wounded was Lieutenant Wollocombe. In a postscript to his diary, his grandson wrote; 'On the evening of the 5th he was called up and took part in the engagement on the 6th. He was seen to fall and was thought to be killed.' However, Wollocombe was not killed and told the Padre of 21 Casualty Clearing Station, who recounted, in a letter to his parents details of his wound:

> It is in his leg and is aggravated by the fact that he was left lying out for some time. His own description is: "I couldn't get out of a shell hole when the Regiment was advancing, and I was left behind for 2 or 3 days when they retired".

Lieutenant Woolcombe died suddenly and unexpectedly of his wounds and from the effects of exposure during his time left out in No Man's Land. The Adjutant,

After a few weeks of fighting, Delville Wood was a shattered wasteland.

Captain G. E. Morrison, wrote in a letter similar to countless others:

It is needless for me to say what a top-hole fellow he was, for you must have known it. I cannot but feel pleased at being one of his friends, but unfortunately, I am about the only one left in the battalion who knew him. I can remember telling him (in fun) as he passed me that morning going into action that he had forgotten to shave, and being told to go to blazes...

The next of kin of many other soldiers received an official postcard regretting the death of a loved one, which was normally followed up by letters from friends and officers. However, in conditions of full battle, many parents of young men barely known to their officers received almost a standard letter containing typical phrases; 'died quickly; he felt no pain; bravely doing his duty; respected and liked by his fellow soldiers'. On occasions, casualties were so heavy that even this convention could not be observed.

After the hard pounding at Ginchy, instead of sharing the debut of the tank on 15 September, the 7th Division left the Somme for a quiet sector in Flanders. As they marched north, the Division's commanders rued the fact that they had been unable to sustain their successful record, due to being committed to battle piecemeal. The divisional historian felt that although they had successfully attracted and fixed many German reinforcements at Ginchy, 'a combined effort on a broader front might have fared better'. He went on to say:

The failure to retain the ground gained had been largely due to the lack of training of the recent drafts who formed so high a proportion of the battalions and to the inexperience of most of its officers and NCOs. The men had too often not known what to do and the heavy casualties among the officers left them with no one to show them.

The regimental historian wrote in summary of the September days that 8/ and 9/Devons spent at the fulcrum of battle:

Ginchy was still untaken, though it was in fact the fruit of the Seventh Division's efforts which was reaped when the next assault, that of September 9th, at last secured the long-contested ruins, while the pressure exerted against Ginchy had occupied no inconsiderable force of Germans. But even so, Ginchy was a bitter memory for the 8th and 9th Devons.

1   *In the Trenches. Frank Wollocombe's War Diary.* Privately published 1994.
2   Other sources record 9/Devons' arrival at Mametz as 21.15 hours. This is a more realistic time given the further delay in their move forward.
3   20 Brigade Report on Operations in the Vicinity of Ginchy. PRO WO 95/1656.
4   Quoted in *Official History, Military Operation, France and Belgium 1916*, Vol 2, Ch VII, Notes.
5   *The Devonshire Regiment 1914 – 1918*, Atkinson, Exeter, 1926.
6   8/Devons' war diary. PRO WO 95/1579.
7   *The History of the Gordon Highlanders* Vol IV 1914 – 1919. C. Falls, Aberdeen, 1958.
8   Their fourth commanding officer to be killed in action.
9   *In the Trenches. Frank Wollocombe's War Diary*, Privately published 1994.

Chapter 15

Mouquet Farm

I send you my greetings from my grave in the earth. We shall soon become mad in this awful artillery fire. Never has it been so bad as this before.

GERMAN SOLDIER'S LETTER HOME

Before recounting 5/Dorsets' operations in the area of Mouquet Farm, it is necessary to mention the activities of General Gough's Reserve Army on the Pozières Ridge, and the arrival of the battalion from Gallipoli.

It will be recalled that following the almost total failure on 1 July of the assault north of the Albert-Bapaume Road, the British main effort was focused on the southern battle area, centred on Mametz. Meanwhile, General Gough and his Reserve Army staff took over responsibility for the northern flank. According to General Gough his '...first task was no enviable one - the reorganization of the defeated and shattered left wing of the Fourth Army'. He went on to say, recalling the situation on the evening of 1 July,

> *The general instructions which I now received verbally from Sir Douglas Haig were: that the Reserve Army would not carry out any grand operations, but that we were to make every effort to progress by "sapping", as he termed it, on the left of the Fourth Army, and gradually enlarge the breach in the enemy's front which had already been created.*
>
> *My conception of carrying out these orders was to endeavour first of all, to establish a broad enough front, facing north and on the left of Fourth Army. From this point I planned to attack always northwards, by which means we could roll up from the flank all the long prepared and very strong German system of entrenchments from which the Fourth Army had just been so heavily repulsed, and thus have to deal with a line which could only be more or less extemporised.[1]*

Once the new command team was in place on the northern flank, although there was heavy shelling of the German positions and a considerable number of minor bombing attacks on the enemy line, the Reserve Army adopted a policy of active defence. This was designed to prevent the Germans from redeploying to the south. However, on 14 July, Gough received instructions from Field Marshal Haig to take over command of operations against Ovillers from the Fourth Army. The resulting Reserve Army attacks around Ovillers made slow progress in heavy rain, which continued for the next few weeks. At this time, the Germans were reported to be still fighting 'desperately and bravely', and inflicted heavy losses on the assaulting troops. While Gough was making steady

Moquet Farm photographed before 1 July 1916. By September it was a ruin.

progress on the Ovillers front, Haig ordered his Army to take over responsibility for the attack on Pozières, in order to relieve General Rawlinson of the distraction of fighting a serious action on his left flank. At this point, 1st Australian Division was allocated to the Reserve Army. According to Gough,

It was immediately evident, owing to the successes of the Fourth Army, that we could now deploy on a sufficiently broad front, facing due north, and attack Pozières in flank from the south, as we had already done at Ovillers.

On 22 July, while the Fourth Army was mounting its attacks on the High Wood/Delville Wood front, the Reserve Army assaulted Pozières and its labyrinth of trenches, which stretched westwards to Ovillers. The Australians launched the main attack at night, assaulting the village itself, while the 48th Division pushed forward on their left between Pozières and Ovillers. The attack successfully carried the village of Pozières in spite of a desperate resistance by the Germans.

The enemy now brought up his heavy artillery, and for several weeks, the Reserve Army's gains were exposed to a terrific bombardment by day and by night. Casualties were very heavy, 'but our troops hung on, repulsed many counter-attacks, and secured and retained this valuable ground round Pozières'. In summary, Gough was successfully fixing enemy forces on his front who could otherwise be employed against the Fourth Army, and 'at the same time, by counter-battery work, bombardments and digging, we were making all the necessary preparations for our own future operations'.

By the end of August, the line had been carried north towards Mouquet Farm, though this strong point still held out. From here, the front ran to the left to the Leipzig Salient, captured on 1 July. From here, as Gough wrote, 'our operations northwards were aimed at the isolation of the fortress of Thiepval. By a series of minor operations, we succeeded in securing ground to facilitate the advance, which would eventually encircle it.' However, the rain fell in torrents and greatly hampered operations, as it will be recalled it was doing in the Ginchy/Leuze Wood area, five miles to the south. During this time, the Reserve Army casualties varied from 1,000 to 6,000 a week. However, 'as the time passed, German resistance weakened and our successes became more pronounced'.

On 3 September, a general Reserve Army attack, in cooperation with the

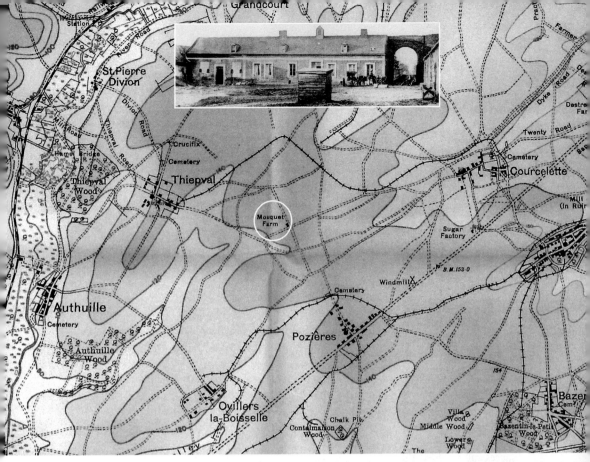

The Thiepval-Pozières Ridge, including Mouquet Farm, was a part of the 1 July objective.

French and General Rawlinson's Army, made little progress. The exception was the 4th Australian Division, who secured and retained a toehold in Mouquet (or 'Moo-Cow') Farm, while the rest of the attacking troops fell back to their start lines. As the Australians had been fighting continuously since 20 July, suffering heavy casualties, the Canadians, along with 11th Division, including 5/Dorsets replaced them.

5th (Service) Battalion, The Dorset Regiment

In common with the other West Country service battalions, 5/Dorsets had been formed around a small cadre of regular soldiers, supplemented by special reservists and old soldiers coming out of retirement, along with Kitchener volunteers. From Grantham the 11th Division moved to the Surrey Heaths, where on 30 June 1915 it was mobilized to join the Middle East Expeditionary Force at Gallipoli. On 6 August, 5/Dorsets took part in the Suvla landing and received their first hostile fire and battle casualties.

After a chaotic landing, the advancing unsupported West Countrymen seized Hill 28, a mile and a half inland, and then captured Chocolate Hill. The Dorsets had done all that had been asked of them, but overall it had been an unsatisfactory and disappointing day for the 11th Division. Despite further

Lieutenant Colonel Hannay, commanding officer of 5/Dorsets.

limited advances, the Turks contained the British in their beachhead. In the trenches above Suvla Bay, the Dorsets endured both extremes of heat and cold, a high incidence of disease and the ever present danger of death. Those who experienced both theatres commented that 'Suvla was every bit as bad as a stretch in the trenches during the Somme'.

The Dorsets, along with the rest of 11th Division, left Gallipoli after four and a half months on 16 December 1915, returning to Alexandria. After a period manning defences in the Suez Canal Zone, 'perpetually digging in the sand', 5/Dorsets left Egypt and on 8 July reached Marseilles.

After only two days in the 11th Division's concentration area, 5/Dorsets, complete with tropical khaki drill uniforms, moved forward to the Third Army front south of Arras. The Battalion's historian wrote:

...the Germans were trying to hold their lines with reduced garrison and were not disposed to stir up trouble. The 5th Dorset therefore served their apprenticeship to Western Front trench warfare in a quiet quarter.

In comparison with Gallipoli, the Dorsets reported that the enemy artillery and machine guns were more active, but there was less sniping and patrolling. During this period, a significant number of experienced officers, NCOs and men returned to the Battalion, having recovered from sickness and wounds. Those returning included the much respected Commanding Officer, Lieutenant Colonel Hannay. 5/Dorsets numbered forty-three officers and 861 men including a draft of forty men from 9/Hampshires (Cyclists). The Battalion remained with the Third Army until September brought a move towards the Somme battle area. 5/Dorsets reached Bouzincourt on 7 September.

Mouquet Farm – the Battle of Flers – Courcelette

The tenuous toehold on Mouquet Farm and the surrounding trenches, that had been gained by the Australians was all but lost to a determined and well-coordinated German counter-attack on 8 September. In the following days although the Reserve Army ordered II Corps to reduce the tempo of its operations so as to conserve resources, low level, 'Glory Hole' type fighting around the Mouquet Farm strong point and Constance Trench continued unabated.

On 8 September, 11th Division relieved 25th Division in the trenches facing the Wunderwerk[2] (32 Brigade) and Constance Trench (33 Brigade). 34 Brigade (5/Dorsets) were in reserve. During this period, the West Countrymen became familiar with the hard grind of providing work parties on the Western Front, but to break up the drudgery they spent a turn learning the new tactics on the Division's training area. However, on 14 September:

> ... the 32nd Brigade stormed the Wunderwerk after desperate fighting, the 33rd at the same time gaining ground up Constance and Danube Trenches. The 34th Brigade stood by in readiness to reinforce but was not required. [3]

By the middle of September, the preliminary fighting to gain position on the right flank of the Fourth Army around Leuze Wood and Ginchy was complete. Consequently, Field Marshal Haig was able to launch his new offensive, the Battle of Flers-Courcelette, supported, for the first time, by tanks. General Gough's Reserve Army was to play a subsidiary role on the left flank. The Canadian Corps was to attack north-east towards Courcelette, with 2nd Canadian Division, who were allocated seven of the new tanks, while 3rd Canadian Division and 11th Division were

> ...to seize any opportunity to gain ground, particularly south of Thiepval, into which gas cylinders would be projected, whilst the 49th Division discharged smoke as though to screen an advance.[4]

For the time being, the Reserve Army's main effort had been transferred away from Mouquet Farm and Thiepval.

Relegated to a subsidiary task on the offensive's left flank, 8 Canadian Brigade occupied the entire 3rd Canadian Division's frontage, opposite Mouquet Farm. 7 Canadian Brigade was in reserve. The limited mission assigned to 8 Brigade was to 'secure its portion of the objective in order to protect the left of the main attack'. 34 Brigade was to support the Canadians if required.

Across the Somme, the battle began at 06.20 hours on 15 September 1916. The offensive gained ground with the help of the few tanks that remained mechanically operational long enough to get into action, but overall 'it fell short of expectations'. However, as General Gough wrote:

> About fifty tanks were now available, and the majority of these were employed under the Fourth Army, seven only being allotted to the Reserve Army. Of these numbers, a total of seventeen Tanks never reached their starting points, but six went on with the Canadians – starting half an hour after the infantry. Many were ditched or knocked out by shellfire, but those that were able to reach the German points of resistance had an immediate and decisive effect on the enemy, who in most cases ran away. They fully proved their value and effectiveness in assisting the infantry, though, being a new weapon, it was only natural that many defects were revealed ... Perhaps it was a pity to use them on the 15th September when decisive results were not possible and were not being sought. Coming as a complete surprise and employed on a much broader front, in far greater numbers, they might

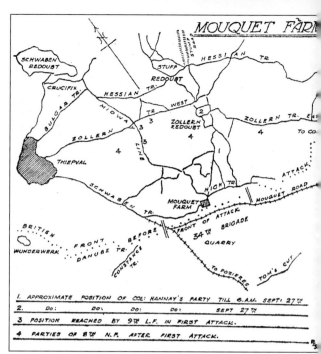

have materially assisted in bringing about a great decision.

In the Mouquet Farm area, the official historian recorded that 2/Canadian Mounted Regiment (CMR) launched a series of raids on the German positions. In one of these raids, 'covered by a smoke barrage, put down by the 5th Battalion of the Special Brigade, 5/CMR raided Mouquet Farm and accounted for about fifty Germans'. Although it was not expected that the raiders would hold the farm, the Canadians' took and held important posts and trenches south of the farm.

Meanwhile, the Dorsets, still in reserve, stood in the village streets of Bouzincourt to see the first tanks moving up to the front. The battalion's war diary for the day simply reads 'Bouzincourt. Standing by to reinforce. Ultimately not required.'⁵ The West Countrymen

A sketch map of the Dorsets' operations at Mouquet Farm, taken from the regimental history.

spent the day in the village, at thirty minutes notice to move, being subjected to occasional bombardment by heavy guns.

The following evening, with fighting now focused in a north-easterly direction, 34 Brigade was brought into the line. The Brigade's war diary recorded:

16 Sep. 5/Dorset and 9/Lancashire Fusiliers left Bouzincourt at 7.30 p.m. to relieve two battalions of 8th Canadian Brigade and took over trenches in line R.28.d57 through Mouquet Farm to R33a7754. On this night, the 8th Canadian Brigade reported taking Mouquet Farm. At daybreak we found the situation was not as stated by them but the line runs through the farm - relief completed, without any casualties at

A Mark 1 tank photographed broken down on the Somme front in September 1916.

A view from the area of Mouquet Farm back towards Pozières, showing the desolate battlefields.

6.30 a.m.[6]

The two battalions took over about 800 yards of line, with gaps of about 200 yards between the neighbouring brigades to the left and right. A and C Companies were in the front line, with D in support and B in reserve. The trenches they took over from the Canadians were shallow, being

> *...in places not much more than shell holes joined together. The line ran roughly along the Mouquet Road, passed through Mouquet Farm and linked up with the 33rd Brigade's right in Constance Trench. An abandoned tank a little way behind our front line, and quite close to Battalion Headquarters, was a feature of interest and attracted much shellfire, which was very inconvenient to the Battalion staff.*

II/212 Reserve Regiment of 45th Reserve Division now held Mouquet Farm, or as the British referred to it 'Mucky Farm'. According to the Dorsets, 'the Farm consisted of three groups of ruins, one behind the British front line, another in No Man's Land, and the third, despite assertions of the Canadians, very definitely still in German hands'. The complicating factor was that, as before 1 July, it had been a major German Headquarters location, there was a considerable network of dugouts below ground. 34 Brigade's war diary records that, 'A deep dugout was known to be under the ruin about 40 yards in front of our line'. The Dorsets' Intelligence Section discovered more information from Corps Headquarters, and recorded that the '... enormous dugout under Mouquet Farm is said to provide accommodation for two complete battalions,

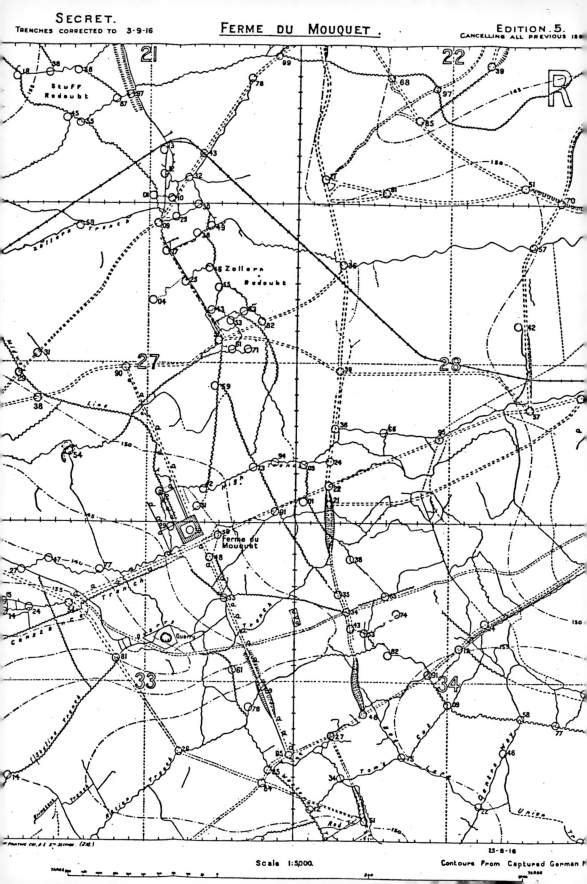

Ferme du Mouquet

Scale 1:5000

25-8-16

Contours from Captured German M

and is even now apparently quite full of Germans[7]'. With the underground complex still in their hands, the Germans made use of connecting tunnels and numerous exits and 'had the unpleasant habit of emerging in the rear of our line, until we posted men in readiness near exits to shoot them directly they emerged'. Over the following days, as further exits were identified, the Dorsets' bombers worked their way forward from shell hole to shell hole and blew in entrances with improvised charges. This kept the German subterranean activities in check and did much to assist with the farm's eventual capture.

The following day, 17 September, the author of the Brigade war diary recorded:

8th Northumberland Fusiliers and 11th Manchester Regt in Brigade Reserve. Fine weather. The Brigade front of about 800 yards held by a single battalion [5/Dorset]. B [Battalion] HQ is near the Pozières Cemetery and there is only one communication trench up to the quarry about 400 yards in rear of the front line. Just beyond the quarry is a support line with communicating trenches from each end to the front line. The 9th Canadian Brigade was on our right and the 33rd Brigade on our left.

The Dorsets' two main enemies during their time at Mouquet Farm were snipers and the weather. The Adjutant recorded in the war diary that the ruins in No Man's Land and behind the German lines were a 'stronghold for German snipers'. However, both plans, to raid the ruins to deal with the snipers, and the relief by 9 Canadian Brigade, were cancelled 'owing to the bad state of trenches from rain'. It is hardly surprising, even allowing for the understatement typical of war diaries, that the Adjutant went on to write, 'Conditions very trying. 2/Lt Prescott and 2/Lt Gomez casualties from shell shock'. Survivors recorded that 'The German guns blazed away freely: they were expecting a fresh attack and did not spare ammunition in trying to impede preparations for it.' With such a volume of fire, in such miserable and dangerous conditions, it is unsurprising that shell shock casualties were occurring. It is also revealing that shell shocked officers were now being openly recorded, whereas before the Somme, such mental conditions amongst officers were very seldom mentioned.

34 Brigade's war diary for the following two days reads:

18 Sep. Wet day 5/Dorset and 9/Lanc Fus holding trenches but latter relieved by a battalion of 9th Canadian Brigade. Dorsets patrol took 4 prisoners all belonging to 212 IR and Lancashire Fusiliers one belonging to 213 IR

19 Sep. Wet day that delayed ops. 5/Dorset Regt were relieved by 11/Manchester Regiment during night 19/20 September. Prisoners belonging to 169 and 126 IR.

The relief was complete by 02.10 hours, and having lost fifty-three men, killed, wounded and missing, the West Countrymen, now fully initiated in the awfulness of warfare on the Western Front, marched from the communication trenches to billets in Albert. The following day, 5/Dorsets moved to Englenelmer and as recorded in the war diary were on '22 September. Cleaning and training. 23 September. Training.' 'Rest' was not a word much used on the Somme in September 1916.

The Battle of Thiepval Ridge

The West Countrymen were not out of the line for long. On 25 September, the battalion moved up to shelter in captured German dugouts in Ovillers. Here they received orders. 5/Dorsets were to take part in a major Reserve Army offensive, with four divisions attacking on a 5,000 yard frontage. The aim was to complete the capture of the main ridge that had been started during the Battle of Flers – Courcelette. Objectives included the Thiepval Heights (18th Division), Mouquet Farm and, on the ridge beyond the farm, the German fortresses of Zollern and Stuff Redoubts (11th Division). II Canadian Corps were to continue to develop operations in the Courcelette area.

On 26 September, 34 Brigade of 11th Division was to attack the Mouquet Farm sector, 33 Brigade to attack on the left, and 32 Brigade was to be in reserve. The 34th's two assault battalions (8/Northumberland Fusiliers – right, 9/Lancashire Fusiliers – left), supported by tanks, were to form up and attack astride Mouquet Farm. The farm, as indicated by the following paragraph, was if necessary to be bypassed by the assault troops. 'OC 9 Lancs Fus will detail a party to block the northern exits from Mouquet Farm [dugouts], provided the place is not in our hands on the day of the attack.' 5/Dorsets were to be the Brigade supports. Their orders were:

5th Dorset Regiment will assemble in Reserve Trench and Ration Trench and push forward to Front Trenches as soon as these become vacated, and follow closely behind the assaulting battalions in artillery formation.

The Dorsets were to maintain position 500 yards behind the assault battalions. 11/Manchesters were Brigade reserve.

The first objective lay along a line that included High Trench and took the attackers as far as the southern edge of Zollern Redoubt. The second objective was the capture of Zollern Redoubt, and the third was Stuff Redoubt. It will be recalled that on the surface, these redoubts were a maze of shell-churned trenches, concrete machine-gun posts and barbed wire, while below ground there were deep, safe dugouts. Identifying objectives in the desolate battlefield was, however, a problem. A new paragraph started appearing in the orders format typically used by brigades and battalions. In the Dorsets' case, it read:

Officers and NCOs detailed to take part in the assault must study the ground beforehand to impress landmarks on their memory. Compass bearings will be taken beforehand.

Zero Hour for the attack on 26 September was 12.35 hours. A bombardment was maintained throughout the morning, designed to maintain a semblance of 'normality'. However, as Zero Hour approached, the artillery shelled the objectives, while 34 Trench Mortar Battery engaged the line of High Trench and Mouquet Farm for four minutes before creeping forward to Zollern Redoubt.

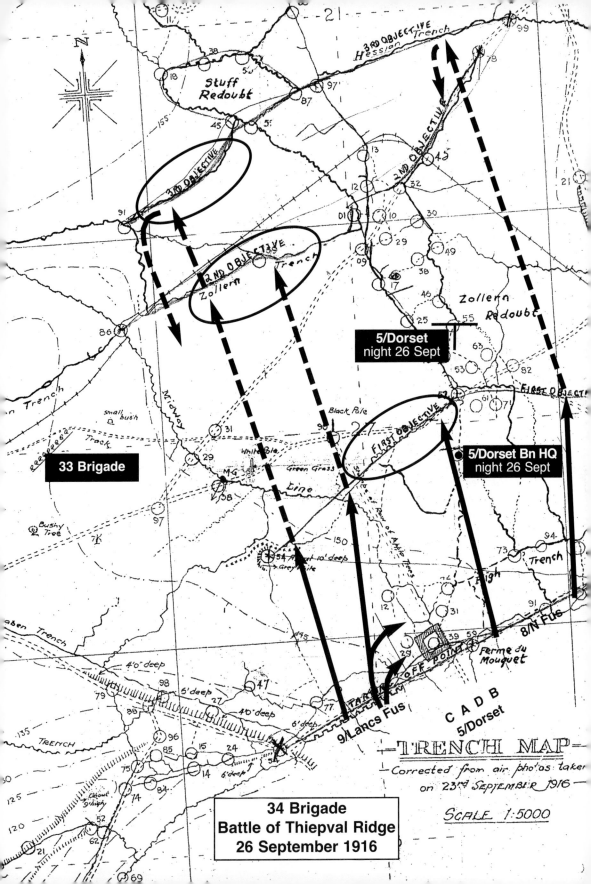

34 Brigade
Battle of Thiepval Ridge
26 September 1916

Following behind the barrage, the assault troops made good progress, and Brigadier Wright, Commander 34 Brigade, noted: '12.50 p.m. 1st Objective was reported to have been gained with apparently slight casualties,' despite having a sharp fight. However, the supporting tanks, initially accompanying the Lancashire Fusiliers did not fare so well. In his after action report, the Brigadier wrote:

> To assist this operation of clearing the Farm, the two tanks allocated to the Brigade were to pass the Farm on their way to Zollern Redoubt. 1.30 p.m. They both drove into a deep hole and remained stuck there for the next three days. Had the tanks been able to push on to Zollern Redoubt they would have been invaluable.

It was incidents such as these, where 'penny packets' of tanks failed to provide the promised support, that did so much to undermine confidence and enthusiasm in the revolutionary armoured fighting vehicle. However, despite its uncertain start, the tank became the predominant land-weapon system of the twentieth century.

Despite the short lived support of the tanks on 26 September, the leading battalions avoided the worst of the German response to the attack. However, as Lieutenant Colonel Hannay recorded in his war diary, the battalion advanced in line of companies, from right to left B, D, A and C:

> ...battalion started off well. From information received, the Battalion suffered heavily from enemy's barrage before reaching the 1st Objective and also suffered heavily from bombs, machine guns and snipers from Germans who were still in Mouquet Farm. Could not get any messages back. All coy commanders and coy Sergeant Majors knocked out early in the advance. Casualties amongst NCOs were heavy.

With senior commanders waiting in their headquarters and with heavy casualties among junior commanders, it was very much a soldier's battle. By mid-afternoon, there was little information to be had, and at 15.30 hours, Brigadier Wright ordered commanding officers and his staff officers forward to find out what was happening. As Colonel Hannay was setting off, Lieutenant King, who had been commanding D Company, was brought back by battalion stretcher bearers, via Battalion Headquarters, and 'passed on important information':

> It seemed that Germans were still resisting in parts of the first objective and as 34 Brigade had a very wide frontage [1,200 yards] its heavy losses caused the survivors to seem very thinly spread over the ground. The leading battalions had gone on ahead, so the 5th, instead of starting at once to consolidate, had to fight hard to complete the capture of High Trench, and the whole carefully arranged programme went completely to pieces.

Following the two Fusiliers' battalions were the rapidly thinning ranks of 5/Dorsets. When High Trench was cleared, two young Dorset officers, Second Lieutenants Franklin and Vale, led their companies forward to Zollern Redoubt, upon which, despite heavy enemy fire, the Fusilier battalions were advancing.

Clearing the surface defences, the three battalions, now badly mixed but few in number, moved on to their final objective at Stuff Redoubt. At 18.25 hours, reports reached Brigade Headquarters '... that the final objective had been taken and was corroborated by two wounded men from 9th Lancashire Fusiliers stating they had come from Stuff Redoubt'. However, so few men had reached the enemy position that flanking observers doubted that it had been taken. Aircraft flying overhead were expected to see the swarming ant-like British infantry on Stuff Redoubt 'signalling to them by waving their trench helmets' but they could distinguish little movement below them. Fighting in the shell-blasted mud of the Thiepval Ridge reduced men, their clothes and equipment to the colour of the surrounding ground, while fear of attracting enemy snipers or artillery deterred soldiers from making the exaggerated movements necessary to attract the attention of a speeding aircraft. The situation forward of Zollern Redoubt remained unclear.

The Fall of Mouquet Farm

Earlier, despite the best efforts of the Lancashire Fusiliers to contain the enemy in the dugouts below, Mouquet Farm, operations throughout the afternoon were hampered by machine-gun and rifle fire directed at the bypassing attackers. The last remnants of II/212 Regiment sheltered from British artillery and mortar fire in the dugouts below the wrecked farm, only to appear when an opportunity presented itself.

A tank crossing a wrecked trench during an attack in September 1916.

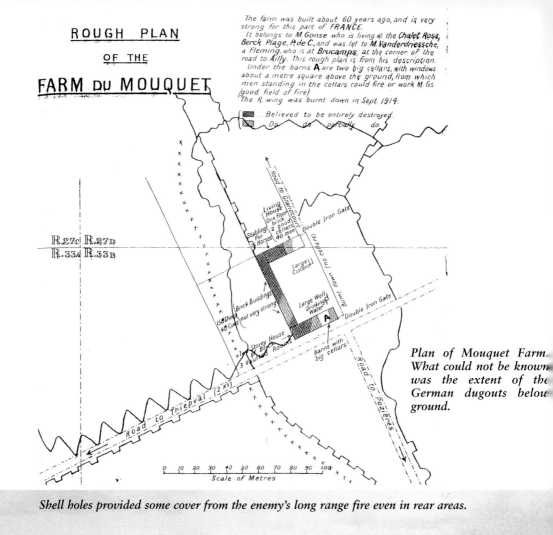

ROUGH PLAN OF THE FARM DU MOUQUET

Plan of Mouquet Farm. What could not be known was the extent of the German dugouts below ground.

Shell holes provided some cover from the enemy's long range fire even in rear areas.

As an experienced former senior NCO, now commissioned Temporary Second Lieutenant Dancer was in charge of a company-sized detachment of Dorsets at Mouquet Farm. Having relieved a party from 9/Lancashire Fusiliers who had been guarding the northern exits of the German dugouts, and having posted his platoon, Dancer ordered his men to throw bombs down the steps. Having secured the exits and dominated the area above ground, he co-opted a passing party of six pioneers from 6/East Yorkshire Regiment to help. Also coopted were the dismounted crew of tank 542 (one of the bogged tanks) and an officer, a sergeant and six men from the Manchesters. With all exits either blocked by riflemen or covered by the two tank machine-guns, smoke and tear-gas grenades carried by the Manchesters' section, were distributed and thrown down the dugout exits. The grenades' fumes eventually built up a sufficiently concentrated cloud below ground to drive out the last defenders at 18.00 hours. The Germans were either shot or, if their intentions to surrender were obvious enough, taken prisoner. Among the collected prisoners, Lieutenant Dancer counted one officer and other ranks, along with three machine guns and two flame throwers. The prisoners were marched back to the Brigade Collecting Point at Crucifix Corner under escort of the Yorkshire Pioneers. Second Lieutenant Dancer received the Military Cross for his action in taking the lead during the battle and finally taking Mouquet Farm.

In his report on operations, Brigadier Wright said, no doubt with a view to preserving harmony within his brigade, 'The actual taking of the Farm cannot be claimed by any one unit as 5th Dorset Regiment, 11th Manchester, 6th East Yorkshire Pioneers and Tank No. 542 were all represented'.

Zollern Redoubt

By early evening on 26 September, 5/Dorsets were spread out between Mouquet Farm, High Trench and the southern edge of Zollern Redoubt. Ahead of the main body of the Dorsets, Zollern Trench was partly held by isolated detachments of Lancashire Fusiliers, but it was apparent that even though the Northumberland Fusiliers had also penetrated Zollern Redoubt's wire, they certainly did not hold it. As dusk approached, at 20.00 hours, the Dorsets' war diarist recorded:

> Telephone message from GOC 34th Brigade to CO to move up Battalion HQ, collect the Battalion in front, consolidate 2nd Objective with two companies and move two companies up to 3rd Objective. Attempted to move at once but unable to reach the Quarry owing to machine gun and sniper fire...

However, by 22.30 hours the enemy's artillery fire was slackening. The diarist continued:

> HQ Coy carried up water for men in front. Waited a short time in Quarry for barrage to abate. Moved on to High Trench. Found Manchesters working on communication trench, East Yorks working on High Trench and RE on communication trench forward.

Lieutenant Colonel Hannay found Second Lieutenants Nash and Vale with

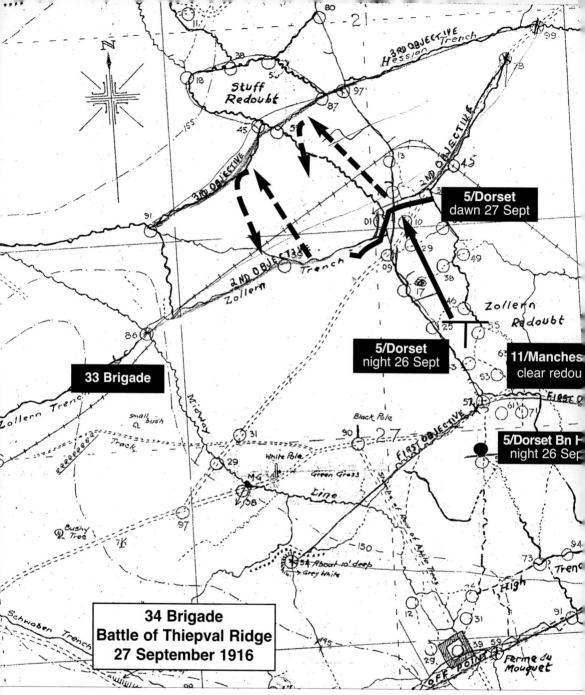

5/Dorset
dawn 27 Sept

5/Dorset
night 26 Sept

33 Brigade

11/Manches
clear redou

5/Dorset Bn H
night 26 Sep

34 Brigade
Battle of Thiepval Ridge
27 September 1916

about fifty men, established a new Battalion HQ south of the redoubt and led his small party of Dorsets to Zollern Redoubt's northern edge. During their advance, by killing Germans or driving them underground, the Dorsets cleared the surface of the redoubt. However, progress was checked by the enemy, who at 02.00 hours were:

> ...*sending up a lot of flares 100 yards to our front. Consolidated by*

digging a T trench. Decided to send out bombing party but no bombs available. Sent out party to reconnoitre. They were driven back by machine gun fire.

A 'T trench' was the basis of an improvised strong point. Economical in time and effort, it provided a firing line and depth fire positions, giving all round defence and mutual support. The regimental historian recorded that:

In consolidating this position, CSM Riddle did excellent work and Private Beaupre, the Commanding Officer's orderly, was indefatigable in collecting scattered men and bringing them back to the Battalion.

Overnight, the Adjutant, in common with other officers of the Brigade, had done much work locating isolated detachments and stragglers in the Mouquet Farm area. The Dorsets were therefore available to carry out Brigadier Wright's new orders. 5/Dorsets were to consolidate the northern edge of Zollern Redoubt and produce a coherent front, while 11/Manchesters cleared surviving groups of Germans out of the redoubt behind them. Second Lieutenant Nash was sent forward with his 'company' of just twenty men to help 9/Lancashire Fusiliers in Stuff Redoubt; where, according to the battalion war diary they '...had to withdraw from heavy machine gun and sniper fire'. Lieutenant Nash and his men started to construct defences in the trenches beyond the northern edge of Zollern Redoubt.

Lieutenant Colonel Hannay.

Further confirmation came, if needed, that Stuff Redoubt was not in British hands, when at 08.25 hours an: 'Aeroplane report received [indicated] that neither Germans nor our men could be seen in Stuff Redoubt'. Although 9/Lancashire Fusiliers had earlier reached Stuff Redoubt and Hessian Trench, they were insufficiently strong to overcome the German defenders, who emerged from their underground lairs to deal with them. The losses of 34 Brigade were too heavy for the battalions to resume the attack, so they consolidated along the line of Zollern Trench West, Zollern Redoubt and Zollern Trench East. Lieutenant Colonel Hannay wrote:

Enemy shelling became heavier and continued throughout the day. Enemy were also very active with snipers and machine guns, which made it very difficult to get up ammunition, bombs and rations.

CSM Riddle and Private Beaupre distinguished themselves again by keeping together and guiding the carrying parties forward from Pozières across a mile of shell-torn wilderness to Zollern Redoubt. Meanwhile, it is recorded that despite the shell and machine-gun fire, Private Fowler continued to stand up signalling with his flags. All three were awarded the Distinguished Conduct Medal for their exemplary conduct. The battalion's chaplain, the Reverend Barry, like so many of his fellow padres, earned in equal measure the affection and respect of the West Countrymen, by moving from shell hole to shell hole, searching for wounded. He bound up their wounds, comforted them and directed the stretcher-bearers. The German shelling was very heavy, and it was a marvel that this errand of mercy did not cost him his life.

With news of successful advances against the fortress village of Thiepval to his left, Lieutenant General Sir C.L. Woollcombe, commanding 11th Division,

Private Fowler DCM.

was not prepared to let matters rest without Stuff Redoubt being in his hands. The Dorsets recorded in their war diary that they

> received orders to attack Hessian Trench with the Manchesters attacking Stuff Redoubt on our left. This order was afterwards cancelled.
>
> Continued to consolidate under enemy shellfire throughout the night.

Brigadier Wright knew how badly depleted the Dorsets were, and represented this to the General. They were given a supporting but no less dangerous task, while two battalions of 32 Brigade were brought up to conduct the attack. The fresh battalions, starting from positions behind 34 Brigade, got off to a good start:

> The West Yorks reached Zollern Trench [the front line] with scarcely a casualty, but not being quite up to time, the barrage was ahead of them and lifted from Stuff Redoubt as they reached Zollern Trench, and so made it impossible for them to advance any further.
>
> The artillery, however, saw this and put another barrage on this line and after some eight minutes the infantry on their own initiative went forward: the guns stopped and the infantry took the position and got a footing into Stuff Redoubt. Large quantities of bombs were now needed and were supplied by parties of 5th Dorsets.

Throughout the afternoon, the West Countrymen carried forward ammunition and bombs to resupply 32 Brigade, and were put to work digging the communication trench back to Schwaben Trench. In this unglamorous role, 5 Dorsets undoubtedly contributed to the success of the clearance of Stuff Redoubt and helped the West Yorks hold their gains.

At 16.50 hours, a runner who had spent several hours lost in the wilderness between the levelled remains of Pozières and Mouquet Farm, arrived at Lieutenant Colonel Hannay's headquarters. He carried a message that 32 Brigade were to relieve 34 Brigade. Minutes later, almost on the runner's heels, the relieving force arrived, although, the relief was not completed for some time. 'The ground was so much ploughed up that it was hard to locate one's self or

The battlefield was devoid of landmarks and the only cover in the featureless landscape were shell holes.

anyone else in the wilderness of shell holes and almost obliterated trenches.' Colonel Hannay summoned men up from the transport lines to help evacuate the wounded; after a weary trudge, the remnants of the Dorsets were at Ovillers by 20.00 hours and were digging shell scrapes. In these 'shallow grave-like holes, the shocked infantrymen, their minds blanked by tiredness fell into a fitful sleep as the rain started to fall.' Initial casualty estimates, based on a sad roll call, were entered in that evening's war diary. Four hundred and ten men, nearly half the battalion, were killed, wounded or missing.

The following day, Lieutenant Colonel Hannay sent Second Lieutenants Fenton and Baker forward with forty men to search for, and bring in, the wounded. About thirty men who had become separated were returned unwounded but losses still totalled 382 men, of whom 260 were wounded and fifty-nine missing. Many of the bodies of these men were subsequently recovered from Stuff Redoubt, where they had become isolated and killed. Others numbered among the missing would have fallen wounded into shell holes, where dying, they were buried by the ebb and flow of battle, a few more were blasted by shellfire into unrecognizable fragments. Another West Country battalion had been sucked into the 'mincing machine' of the Somme and in a matter of days, spat out as a shattered remnant.

Execution

There is, another element to the Mouquet Farm tragedy however, that was to culminate in the court-martial and execution of two Dorset Regiment soldiers[8]. Now that the Dorsets were out of the line 'resting', they were detailed to provide carrying parties in support of the brigades at the front. Lieutenant Trotter's platoon of twenty-five men had been tasked to assist the Royal Engineers, as a part of the consolidation process, by bringing up stores. Having reached the battle area, they were to assist in building strong points at Mouquet Farm and Zollern Redoubt. Privates William Anderson and John Lewis, Londoners, were present at a roll call on 28 September, but were found to be missing the following day and were listed as such in the battalion's returns. It appears that they were not suspected of absence without leave or desertion, but were thought to be amongst those whose bodies were lost on the battlefield.

Anderson reached England, where he was arrested at Barking in January 1917, while Lewis was caught in Boulogne. 'Unconvincing pretence at a loss of memory and a frequently changing and inconsistent explanation' eventually condemned the two men to the hands of a courts martial. Anderson faced the firing squad on 31 March 1917, while, after a retrial, Lewis was executed the following month on 19 April. By this time both battalions had left the Somme.

Given the very high casualties and increasingly frightful conditions on the battlefield, it is a wonder that many more soldiers did not desert their posts. However, in speculating about the motivation and discipline that kept the vast majority of men fighting and fatalistically returning to battle, it is difficult to reconcile this factor with the human instinct for survival. Knowing that there was often an almost 50% chance of being killed or wounded in an attack along

SCHEDULE.

Date March 9th. 1917. No.

Name of Alleged Offender (a)	Offence charged	Plea	Finding, and if Convicted, Sentence (b)	How dealt with by Confirming Officer
Not more than six names to be entered on one form. 9828 Private W.ANDERSON. 5th. S. Battn. Dorset Regiment.	(1) "Absence without leave" (from 28/9/16 till 13/10/16)	Guilty	Guilty	Reserved S.H.Pedley Brig Genl 10.3.17
	(ii) When on active Service "Desertion."	Not guilty	Guilty Death	Confirmed D.Haig F.M. 27 March 17
No.15094. Private J. LEWIS. 5th. S. Battalion Dorset Regiment.	When on active service "Desertion."	Not guilty	Guilty Death	Reserved S.H.Pedley Brig Genl 10.3.17

(a) If the name of the person charged is unknown, he may be described as unknown, with such addition as will identify him.

(b) Recommendation to mercy to be inserted in this column.

S.H.Pedley   Brigadier General,

Convening Officer.

Commanding 34th. Infantry Brigade.

President.

The courts martial paper for Anderson and Lewis, confirming the death sentence for Private Anderson.

with the threat of being abandoned in No Man's Land, these, by modern standards, were remarkable men. Perhaps it was the social attitudes of the day, or military disciple, underpinned by the death sentence. However, with so many men coming and going, a battalion's hard core of habitual survivors did much to pass on a battalion's tradition, standards and ethos, which contributed to identity and success in battle. This was particularly marked in regular battalions, whose resilience was generally higher than that found in service battalions. However, the descriptions of the battlefield from soldiers returning from the front had prepared Private Harry Webb, who was shortly to take part in his first battle with the Dorsets, to expect the worst. 'They simply said it's hell on earth and you've got to make the best of it. There's no getting away from it.'

Approximately 31 of the 306 men executed during the Great War committed offences on the Somme in 1916. Not all were for offences such as cowardice and desertion, included murder as their offences and striking a superior. Only three men were actually executed in the immediate Somme area. To the 31 executions directly related to the Somme must be added those men who were executed, who had fought in the battle; and subsequently committed military offences resulting from service during the Somme. All three members of the Devonshire Regiment and the Dorset Regiment who were executed during the Great War were connected with the Battle of the Somme in 1916.

1   *The Fifth Army*, General Sir Hubert Gough, Hodder and Stoughton, London, 1931.
2   The German name for this redoubt was Wuntwerk, after *Oberst* Wunt, the commander of the regiment that built it, and corrupted by the British into the 'Wonder Work'.
3   *History of the Fifth Battalion, The Dorsetshire Regiment 1914 - 1919*, C.T. Atkinson, Dorchester, 1932.
4   *Official History. France and Flanders 1916* Volume 2.
5   5/Dorset war diary. PRO WO 95/1820.
6   34 Brigade war diary. PRO WO 95/1818.
7   The underground workings were so extensive that after the wars the farm had to be rebuilt on firm ground south of its original position.
8   *Blindfold and Alone*, Corns and Hughes-Wilson, Cassells & Co, London 2001.

Chapter 16

Morval

The Somme was the muddy grave of the German field army and the death of the belief in the infallibility of the High Command.

GERMAN OFFICIAL HISTORY

At exactly the same time that 5/Dorsets were fighting at Mouquet Farm (Battle of Thiepval Ridge), 1/Devons had returned with 5th Division to join the Fourth Army, in what afterwards became known as the Battle of Morval. These twin battles were a continuation of the renewed offensive that Field Marshal Haig had launched on 15 September 1916.

1/Devons had left the devastated Leuze Wood on 6 September but remained in trenches near Angle Wood as part of a composite brigade until 14 September, when the Battalion was finally relieved. They marched back for a very short but well-earned rest in Ville-sur-Ancre, where the West Countrymen remained, taking in replacements, until 18 September. Before dawn on that day, in pouring rain, the Battalion paraded and began the march to the front, via an assembly area at Briqueterie. The war diary recorded, 'after tea, Battalion paraded at 7.15 p.m. and moved forward and relieved the 8th Battalion, Bedfordshire Regt in old German trenches'. These trenches were now well to the rear, and in recognition of the extended period that the Devons had spent in the line, as well as the fact that they numbered just 400 men, the Battalion remained there until 24 September, as the 5th Division's reserve.

The Morval battlefield.

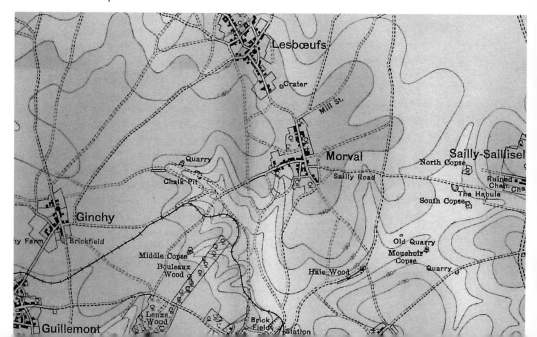

A platoon of tanks photographed in the rear area being prepared for battle.

In the words of the divisional historian, 'For a week no move was made, but plans were prepared and arrangements made for a resumption of the offensive'[1]. It was these arrangements that brought the Devons back to the front to take part in an attack. Throughout the history of warfare, time and again, commanders call on successful units to spearhead their attacks. While honoured by the recognition of their success at Leuze Wood, it was with foreboding that the West Countrymen marched forward from their bivouacs in Oxford Copse on the evening of 24 September, with the noise of the Division's preliminary bombardment growing as they neared the front. The line that the Devons returned to had moved forward by a mile since they captured Leuze Wood and was now on the slope below the Morval /Lesboeufs Ridge. Here they relieved 1/Royal West Kents.

The 5th Division deployed for the attack, with 95 Brigade on the right, 15 Brigade to the left and 13 Brigade in reserve. The divisional objective was Morval, which was protected by the trenches of the third German defensive position. These trenches barely existed on 1 July, but while the British had been fighting their way forward, the Germans had been working hard to improve their rear defensive lines. However, despite the new enemy line being backed by the fortified village of Morval, it was again far less strong than the first position that had taken such a heavy toll on the British on the first day of the battle. As elsewhere on the frontage to be attacked on 25 September, tanks were allocated to the 5th Division. Brigadier Hussey, the Division's Commander Royal Artillery, wrote that this

> ... *was the first occasion on which the Division was allotted tanks to co-operate with the infantry. Knowing the uncertainties of these first experimental land-ships, it was wisely decided that they should only be used to support the infantry, the attack being planned without absolute reliance on their assistance. Well it was so, for of the three tanks allotted, one failed to start, the second proceeded some distance*

but 'bellied' in the mud in the vicinity of our jumping off line by the sunken road...

The Devons, who had arrived in the front line at 00.15 hours, recorded in their war diary that 'during the morning the enemy artillery were quiet'[2]. As the time for the attack approached, a message was received from Commander XIV Corps. It read:

Special wishes of good luck to the 5th Division, who have already won highest honours on the Somme. Relief soon as possible faithfully promised.

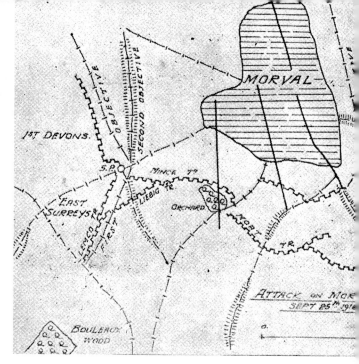

A sketch map from the regimental history, showing the salient points of the battlefield.

At 12.30 hours, a five-minute bombardment 'burst into a continuous roar of barrage fire' all along the front from Thiepval to Combles. At 12.35 hours, the infantry advanced. The Devons' first objective was the enemy front line, Bovril Trench, which was only a short distance across No Man's Land. With their remaining tank, 5th Division started well. 15 Brigade on the left made a speedy advance towards Morval, keeping up with the barrage. However, 95 Brigade, the East Surreys in particular, suffered heavily from enfilading machine-gun fire from the left and made slower progress. The Commanding Officer recorded the Devons' immediate problems:

Owing to the wire being insufficiently cut, No. 4 Company eased off to the left, leaving a small portion of the trench on the right up to the cross roads, still occupied by the enemy. Nos. 1 and 2 Companies immediately followed Nos. 3 and 4 Companies to the 1st objective. No. 1 Company proceeded to bomb the portion of the trench (which the enemy held) and captured it by 12.57 p.m.

With the remaining Germans bombed out of the traverses and dugouts in Bovril Trench, the Devons joined up with the East Surreys, who were making slow progress fighting their way up Leipzig Trench. 1/Devons' next objective was the line of the Sunken Road running north from the crossroads. Numbers 3 and 4 Companies resumed the advance across several hundred yards of open ground, but casualties were heavy and all of Number 3 Company's officers were hit. Lieutenant Ross had been wounded, 'but after having his wound dressed, insisted on returning to the fight and was killed leading the attack'.[3] Captain Halle brought up Number 2 Company and despite the fact that 'the Germans were full of fight and resisted stubbornly, neither Devons nor East Surreys were

254

to be denied and the objective was secured, with many prisoners being taken'.

With the Sunken Road taken at 13.45 hours, the final slope up to the ruins of Morval lay in front of the Devons. However, enemy fire prevented an immediate advance and the battalion needed to reorganize. With the Colonel up with the forward troops, the Adjutant and the Battalion's signallers would pay out telephone line and move on to Bovril Trench in time to record that the next advance began at 14.30 hours.

'Nos. 1 and 4 Companies advanced up Mince Trench to the crest of the Hill but could get no further. They at once made some strong points and consolidated the position.'

The West Countrymen had fought well. Attacking with captured German stick grenades and their bayonets, they drove the enemy back, taking numerous wounded Germans prisoner. The single remaining tank supported the Devons,

> *...providing considerable assistance ... in dealing with a system of stubbornly held trenches. Though the other tanks may have failed, their crews did not, and, dismounting their machine guns, they proceeded with the infantry in their attack.*

With 'their tank' firing into the trench ahead of them, 1/Devons' leading companies bombed along Mince Trench, across the upper reaches of the Valle de Morval to the area of a small wood known as 'The Orchard'.

A French airman observing the battle from above wrote:

> *A great calm falls on the battlefield. The blue coats [the French] have established themselves between Rancourt and Fregicourt, while more to the north, between Bouleaux Wood and Lesboeufs, a great line of khaki, harder to see, threatens the village of Morval. Large shells here and there tear up the ground. Looking from here one would say that after the hard*

Supporting infantry of 5th Division moving across No Man's Land during the Battle of Morval.

struggles of the day the men had reached the limit of their endurance. The fight is without doubt finished for the day. Here and there an exhausted soldier is waiting for darkness, to build up a small heap of earth to protect himself.[4]

From their advanced position, the Devons were able to give suppressive fire that enabled 12/Gloucesters on the left to join them on the ridge. Under cover of the Devons' fire, 1/East Surreys, 'meeting no resistance,'[5] moved up Leipzig Trench. Morval could now be attacked, and Major General Stephens moved battalions of 13 and 15 Brigade, 2/KOSB and 1/Cheshires, in from the flanks. Supported by heavy artillery, by the lighter guns of the divisional artillery and by both 95 Brigade's trench-mortar and machine-gun companies, the assault battalions swept into the piles of shattered brick and splintered wood that was the remains of Morval. Having cleared the German defenders from the village's cellars and dugouts, 15 Brigade pushed out into the open country to the east of the village. Meanwhile, as usual, the enemy's heavy artillery hit back, and caused casualties among the heavily laden men who were moving up to secure the gains.

The French aviator continued his eyewitness account of the 5th Division's successful attack:

But suddenly, just before 6 o'clock, the British artillery opens a tornado of fire on the German lines. The enemy, unable to discover the threatened point for this new attack, places a barrage at random behind the British lines.

The rain of shells has continued for half an hour, when suddenly, without anything to warn the enemy of a change in the situation, the khaki line swarms forward as one man. Just as it reaches the curtain of fire, the

The ruins of Morval after the battle.

Following the Battle of Morval, German prisoners of the 239 Reserve Infantry Regiment helped to evacuate the wounded.

Infantry digging in, in this case, by connecting up a series of shell holes.

latter, as if actuated by a single mind, moves forward in bounds, clears the village, and establishes itself some hundred yards beyond it, forming a barrier under cover of which the assaulting wave advances. A few German signals of distress [flares], a few bursting grenades around the dugouts, an attempt at defence rapidly overwhelmed, and the khaki line, having gained almost a kilometre of ground, reforms beyond the objective.

The 5th Division had taken all its objectives, remarkably, according to the planned schedule. So shattered were the defenders of the German 239 Reserve Regiment that, contrary to their normal practice, no counter-attacks were launched against Morval. As the Devons, now in reserve, repaired the trenches in the failing daylight, there came a congratulatory message from Major General Stephens: 'Hearty thanks and sincere congratulations to you. A very fine achievement splendidly executed.' As darkness fell at the end of another long day in action, along with the quartermaster's ration parties came a draft of fifty men from the Infantry Base Depot at Etaples, making good the Battalion's losses.

1   *The Fifth Division in the Great War,* Hussey and Inman, London, 1921.
2   1/Devon war diary. PRO WO/95/1579.
3   *The Devonshire Regiment 1914 - 1918,* C.T. Atkinson, Exeter, 1926.
4   Quoted in *Fifth Division in the Great War.*
5   *History of the East Surrey Regiment,* Vol 2, Pearse and Sloman, London 1923.

Chapter 17

Le Transloy

Infantry, sometimes wet to the skin and almost exhausted before zero hour, were often condemned to struggle painfully forward through the mud under fire against objectives vaguely defined and difficult of recognition.
OFFICIAL HISTORY

As the autumn weather continued to deteriorate, 2/Devons returned to the Somme. They had been in action on the first day of the battle with the 8th Division at Ovillers Boisselle and had suffered heavily. On the night of 1 July, the shattered West Country battalion left the Somme and marched north to join the First Army in the Bethune/Cuinchy sector of the Loos Salient. However, this sector was not as quiet as many had hoped. Both sides were busy mining, bombarding and raiding, which all added to 'a certain liveliness'. 2/Devons remained below strength, with 100 men from the Regiment's training reserve battalion arriving later in July, to start replacing some of the 450 casualties suffered in the attack. Meanwhile, a number of lightly wounded men returned to duty, but it was not until August and September that large drafts of 138 and 150 men arrived and the Battalion returned to its proper strength. With four battalions of the Devonshire Regiment taking their turn to fight on the Somme, priority for replacements had to be given to those who were about to return to the fray. The Adjutant, Captain Tillett, wrote:

> With the Somme Battle still continuing, the arrival of reinforcements to bring the companies up to strength, even though they were barely trained, was a sure sign to many of the more experienced men who recognized that our second turn was not to be long in coming.[1]

In Field Marshal Haig's report to the War Committee at the end of September, he estimated that the German employed some seventy divisions on the Somme, that they had suffered 370,000 casualties, and that the German position on the Somme was weak. Although British casualties were broadly similar, Captain Atkinson justified the continuation of the battle:

> Still, to relax the pressure meant throwing away the fruits of the earlier struggles. If allowed to settle down on the line to which they had been forced back, the Germans would be able to turn their still incomplete rearward defences into positions as formidable as those which the Allies had faced on July 1st, and the work would have to begin afresh.[2]

Consequently, Field Marshal Haig ordered a series of attacks for the middle of October. The Fourth Army objective was the village of Le Transloy. As the Fourth Army achieved 'meagre results' on 18 October, however, Haig ordered a

259

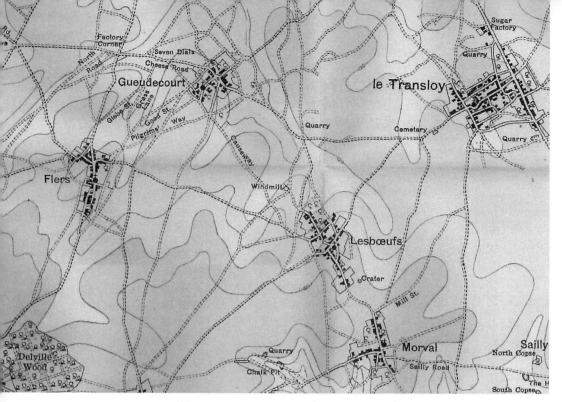

An extract from the official history showing the Le Transloy battlefield.

preliminary and limited attack towards Le Transloy for 23 October, which, 'weather permitting', was to be followed by an Anglo-French attack on the village itself, on 26 October. The attack was to be mounted by fresh troops, including the 8th Division. Consequently, it was to be the British Army's right flank, where the other West Country battalions had been fighting, at Guillemont, Ginchy, Leuze Wood and Morval, that 2/Devons were to return to. The division's historian wrote:

> *It had been to assist in the movement against le Transloy line that the 8th Division had been brought back to the Somme, but the weather had definitely turned. The 19th October, when the Division went forward from reserve positions in and about Bernafay and Trones Woods to relieve two brigades ... in the line, was a day of dismal and incessant rain. The tracks were for the most part impractical and the roads were deep in liquid mud and crowded with traffic.[3]*

In the trenches and dugouts, even in the reserve positions occupied by 23 Brigade, conditions were worse. The rainstorms of late August and early September had produced difficult and unpleasant conditions for the soldiers. However, the sustained rain of October, and active operations, accompanied by continuous artillery fire ploughing the ground, steadily reduced it to mud, and the trenches to little more than stagnant ditches. In many cases, the two sides were reduced to holding defences that were little more than a line of 'shell-hole positions' that were sometimes connected up by shallow, unrevetted, crawl

WONDER WHEN THE
'KIN' TIDE GOES OUT TED.

trenches. Landmarks on the battlefield were now even fewer and 'objectives could not always be identified from ground level'.[4] Villages could barely be identified; in the worst case, reputedly, shell-ground brickdust staining the chalk mud was the only indication of the presence of buildings, and in some cases, a forlorn sign marked the levelled ruins.

Maps were thereby rendered of no great assistance even in daylight; by night they were worse than useless. ...numerous tracks ploughed up in the mud; woods discovered themselves only, as a rule, when one stumbled among their mangled stumps. Add mazes of disused flooded trenches, stretches of old tangled barbed wire, desultory but persistent shelling, and over all, the inky blackness of a cloud-laden winter sky - small wonder it was that the unfortunate guide should fail to find a village that had no existence in actual fact.[5]

With a lack of landmarks 'it is no matter for surprise or censure that the British artillery sometimes fired short or placed its barrages too far ahead'. The artillery's accuracy was not helped by guns sinking into the mire as they fired, and by using barrels worn out by months in action, which increased margins of error. With awful weather and artillery difficulties '... the strain on troops,

A scene all too typical of the latter stages of the Somme; a sea of mud, with flooded shell craters and the shattered remains of a wood.

transport and staff was multiplied indefinitely, and it became a marvel that any pressure could be maintained on the enemy'. In the rear area, the poor state of the previously fought-over ground and the lack of intact buildings meant that reserve troops could do little more than shelter under muddy tarpaulins in shallow dugouts. Here, amidst the surrounding desolation, there was no comfort.

The Preliminary Attack

All three of 8th Division's brigades were in the line, preparing to attack enemy positions in front of the village of le Transloy on 23 October 1916. The divisional historian explained that 'the tactical objective of the XIV Corps, therefore, was to advance the Corps front to within assaulting distance of le Transloy'. However, the Devons were divisional reserve, and had the unenviable task of repeatedly labouring forward through the mud, supplementing the horses of the Royal Artillery, or dragging the guns into position by hand and carrying forward ammunition. The hours of exhausting, unglamorous and often dangerous labour involved in stocking the gun positions with shells for each attack is mentioned in war diaries but virtually always ignored by regimental

Fatigue parties were issued with mud scoops in a vain attempt to clear trenches of liquid mud.

historians. Despite the mule trains and light railways to bring up stores, the repeated work parties weighed heavily on the memories of the ordinary infantry soldier:

> It was one task of labouring after another. A night carrying up food and water to the front line, trudging back with the dawn behind us, a short sleep - all too short, before parading for work with the pioneers making a road. Another short rest before going up to dig a communication trench after dark. Men took on the hue of the ground, being wet, caked in mud from head to foot for days on end and we were tired, oh so tired. At the time it seemed like a never-ending purgatory![6]

On 23 October the battlefield was shrouded by a persistent autumn fog which caused Zero Hour to be delayed from 11.30 hours until 14.30. 2/Devons 'furnished a carrying party which worked under cover of the fog'.[7] On the Division's long front of over 2,000 yards, 24 Brigade had the strictly limited objective on the left flank of broadening a distinct salient to the east of Gueudecourt around Mild Trench. This was successfully achieved. In the centre, 25 Brigade had less success against the alert Bavarian infantry, as they were unable to keep up with the barrage. However, the leading infantry of 23 Brigade made good progress and captured Zenith Trench, and occupied positions, including Orion Trench, several hundred yards further on. Here they were able to repulse two weak German counter-attacks delivered later in the afternoon. However, the Germans were reluctant to concede the loss of Zenith Trench and counter attacked vigorously just before dark. They retook Orion Trench but failed to retake Zenith. The British had pushed the line forward towards Le Transloy, with most of the first objective being taken and held by the forward battalions.

Throughout 23 October, the Devons had remained inactive as brigade reserve. Captain Tillett recorded in the Battalion war diary:

> The CO returned from advanced Brigade HQ about 7 p.m. About 11 p.m. orders were received that the Battalion was to move at once to Needle Trench and that Battalion HQ were to be established at the German Dump, which was Advanced Brigade HQ. Some difficulty was found in getting the Battalion into this trench as the ground was wet and sodden and it was an extremely dark night.
>
> When it was light a considerable number of wounded were discovered near HQ which it

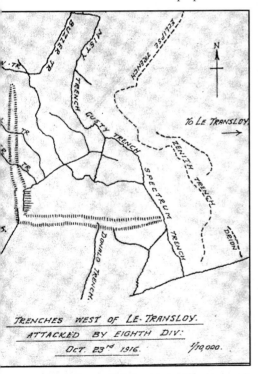

A sketch map of the Devons' regimental history showing the main features of the Le Transloy battlefield.

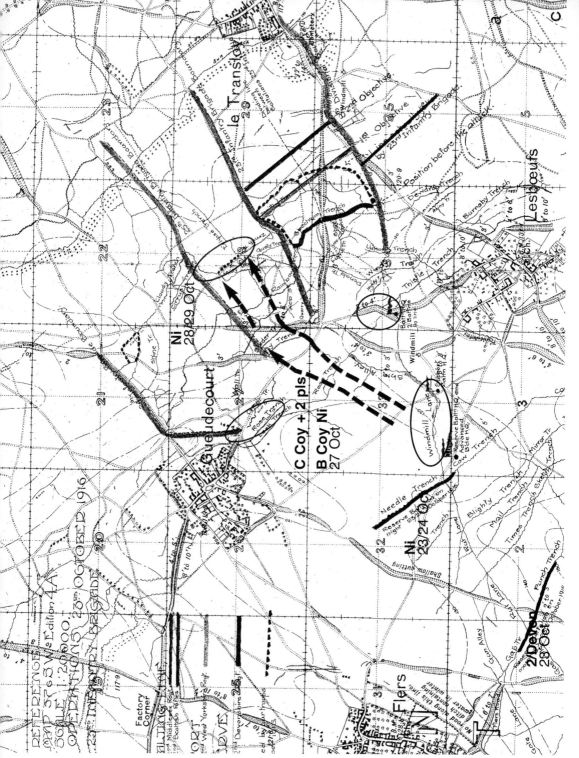

A map from 23 Brigade's war diary, annotated to show 2/Devons, part in the battle.

264

*had been impossible to move further in owing to the state of the ground
and lack of stretcher bearers.*

On 24 October, as the Brigade's supports in Needle Trench, the 2/Devons '...
assisted as far as possible in getting these men away'. In the support trenches
there was no respite from the fatigue parties. It is recorded in the war diary that
on 'the night of 24/25, A Company was employed carrying wounded and B and
D Companies carried stores from Brigade HQ to the battalions in the line'.

For 1/Devon, the constant labouring, danger and appalling ground
conditions were too much to endure. Private Lawrence, who was to be the third
and final West Countryman to be executed by a firing squad, began his slide to
the death penalty by 'going absent' on the Somme in the autumn of 1916. On
this first occasion, he was tried by a Field General Court Martial and awarded
forty days Field Punishment Number 1.[8] This thoroughly unpleasant
punishment was considered a relatively light sentence. However, as a serial
deserter, after four more absences/desertions the courts' patience was at an end,
and he was sentenced to death in 1917. The Commanding Officer wrote on the
court martial papers 'This man has been a constant source of annoyance and is
absolutely untrustworthy ... he is sullen and inclined to be insolent'.[9]

Holding the Line

On 26 October, 2/Devons were placed at the disposal of 25 Brigade who were
to attack the portion of Zenith Trench still held by the Bavarians. Captain Tillett
wrote:

> *The attack was to be carried out as soon as possible after the necessary
> arrangements had been made, as the weather offered a reasonable
> prospect of success.*

As the afternoon progressed, the rain fell 'without a break and prosecution of
the attack was for the moment out of the question'. The Battalion reverted to 23
Brigade's command, and was 'under orders to be prepared to deliver a counter
attack if required to do so at a moment's notice'. Overnight, the West
Countrymen furnished further carrying parties. However, unknown to the
British, the conditions were also telling on the enemy, and 19 Reserve Division
was replaced by the Bavarian *Ersatz* Division.

On 26 October, 2/Devons were again under the command of 25 Brigade. This
time the attachment was for five days, and they were promptly required to
provide yet more carrying parties! The following day, 25 Brigade issued a
warning order for an attack by 2/Devons and 1/Sherwood Foresters on 28
October. Captain Tillett recorded in the war diary:

> *The CO accompanied by the Adjutant, company commanders and
> company sergeant majors visited the trenches the Battalion would
> occupy prior to the attack. It was found that owing to the bad
> conditions of the trenches and the bad weather, also the fact that there
> was no Battalion HQ and that sufficient stores had not been taken
> down, the attack for the moment was not feasible.*

Consequently, the battalion was to remain in reserve, with yet another entry

265

recording that they 'furnished carrying parties'. However, during the night of 27 October:

> C Company and two Platoons of B Company relieved the 2nd Royal Berkshire Regiment in Larkhill and Spider Trenches during the night.
>
> These platoons came under fairly heavy shell fire during the relief.

Casualties in moving over the top to the front line, due to the communication trenches being 'non-existent', were relatively light, as enemy shells plunged into the deep mud, which absorbed much of the explosion. Three men were killed and six wounded. In the conditions, documents were taken off the dead soldiers and their bodies left on the battlefield to join the mounting number of missing. As recorded in the war diary:

> It was decided that the attack would be carried out at 3 p.m. on the 29th October 1916, and that the 1st Sherwood Foresters who were to take part in the attack would not do so, the whole attack to be carried out by the 2nd Devon Regiment. The attack was to be carried out as follows:
>
> A, D and half B Company were to attack the hostile trenches from the front; 1/2 B Company under Capt Archer posted on the left of the 23rd Infantry Brigade was to attack the enemy from the rear. C Company was to be held in reserve. Battalion HQ to be established in the front line.

On the evening of 28 October, the Devons moved forward at 21.00 hours and relieved 1/Sherwood Foresters in the front line Misty Trench. The war diary continued:

> Owing to the guides supplied by 1st Sherwood Foresters not being able to lead the Companies into the positions they were to occupy, it was discovered that D Company, C Company and two platoons of B Company and two platoons of A Company only were in position at 4.50 a.m. on the 29th. All these troops were greatly fatigued owing to the fact that they had been marching in waterlogged trenches since 9 p.m. 28th instant.

It had taken the West Countrymen almost eight hours to cover a distance of less than a mile. Leading the battalion in single file, the guides got lost in the dark featureless wilderness, and men lost boots and putties in the mud. Extricating men from the clutches of the mire took time, and contributed to the breaking of the column, and four platoons from B and A Companies becoming lost. With the bulk of the Battalion occupying the front line (Misty Trench), the Devons found themselves standing up to their waists in liquid mud, with only a sodden great coat and waterproof cape for protection. However, 'most of us were sufficiently thankful to have emerged at all from the enveloping terror of that wilderness of trackless mud'.

Captain Tillett wrote in the war diary for 29 October:

> The artillery on both sides were very active. The enemy directed most of his energy in shelling the support line. Only a few shells burst near our front line. It rained at intervals during the day and the trenches soon became very bad. The Brigadier 25th Infantry Brigade sent the

Brigade Major to see the CO at 9 a.m. to ascertain if the CO still considered it inadvisable to carry out the attack, informing him at the same time that it would not be possible to carry out the attack on the next day as the Division was being relieved [by 17th Division]. The CO informed the Brigadier that the missing platoons were still absent and that the remainder of the men were too fatigued and that under the circumstances it was out of the question to carry out the attack.

At 11 a.m. the missing four platoons were in position but in a very exhausted condition.

So bad were conditions that a pair of the Devons' rear link signallers, who took cover from enemy fire in a shell hole near Brigade Headquarters, became stuck, and it took an hour's digging to get them out again. Apocryphal stories from this period abound. One of the most common is of units being relieved in the line, signing over men stuck in the mud to a new battalion, only to find them still there when they returned to the front. As with all good tales, there is evidence that it was based on a degree of fact.

Lieutenant Burke's Patrol

Conditions in the front line were appalling, so much so that the West Countrymen's main enemies were the mud, water and battlefield wreckage, rather than the Germans. Even so, Lieutenant Colonel Sunderland was determined to dominate the enemy, and sent patrols out into No Man's Land. Lieutenant Burke led one of these patrols. It had become apparent to the Devons that a new German division had occupied the trenches opposite, and the intelligence officer needed to identify them. Therefore, his mission was to snatch a prisoner for identification from the enemy front line. Tracking German divisions around the front was important in order to predict the enemy's future intentions, particularly where they were concentrating prior to an offensive. Lieutenant Burke explained[10]:

Lieutenant Burke.

We left our line and went out into No Man's Land after dark and moved carefully forward in what passed for a silence on the battlefield; only the occasional shell, minewerfer or burst of machine gun fire. There was plenty of cover for us to use in the form of flooded shell holes. We reached the enemy wire, but at the point where we were told that the artillery had cut the wire, there was no gap. We moved to left and right but could not find a way through. Either the report was in error or the Germans had also seen the gap and been out to block it.

I chose my spot and, kneeling down, had started to cut my way through the wire, when up went the enemy [Very] lights and they opened fire. As taught, I froze but the strands of wire closed around me and I was caught. The enemy fire was wild and inaccurate but bullets were ricocheting off the wire and the stanchions around me.

When the firing died down, I found that the barbs had snagged my uniform and I was alone in the enemy wire. The men had withdrawn.

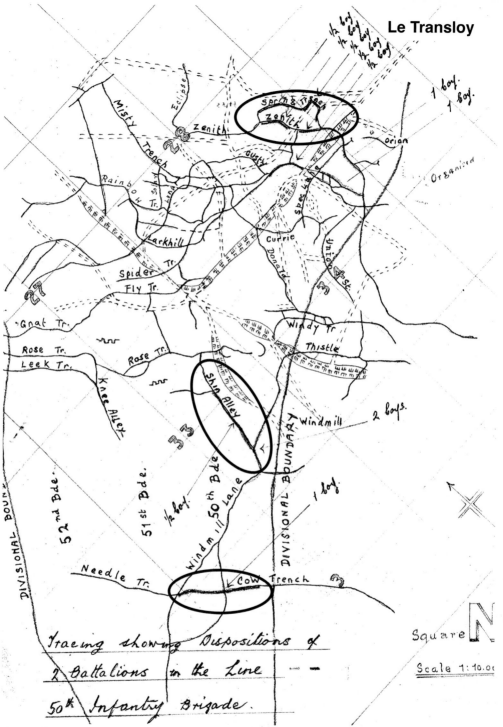

A map from 50 Brigade's war diary showing the position of its two forward battalions, including 6/Dorsets. Most of the trenches shown on this map were in reality badly shelled or collapsed due to the wet conditions. The Dorsets' positions are circled.

When it was eventually quiet, I disentangled my clothing from the wire and I made my way back to our line. The Company were surprised to see me. The men had reported that they had left me killed in the enemy wire.

Relief by 17th Division

On 30 October, it continued to rain throughout the day, adding to the West Countrymen's misery in the trenches. One officer commented, 'The prospect of relief in the line was only marginally better than the prospect of spending six hours struggling back four miles through the mud'. Due to the difficulties of extracting men from the muddy trenches during this phase of the battle, the relief would take place during the nights of 29-30 and 30-31 October. Even then, the 8th Division's artillery would remain in action. The incoming division, 17th Northern, was predictably late, and at 05.30 hours, when the relief should have been completed, only the leading platoons of 10/Sherwood Foresters had arrived. Eventually, however, the West Countrymen were able to get away. The war diary recorded:

> *Owing to the communication trenches being impassable the last company did not leave the trenches until 7.30 a.m. on the 30th. A Company and two platoons of B Company came out over the top in broad daylight,*
>
> *The Battalion arrived at C Camp [between Trones and Bernafay Woods] in a muddy and exhausted condition. Tea was issued to the troops and rifles, equipment, etc. cleaned. At 2 p.m. the Battalion fell in and marched to Mansel Camp [near Mametz] and again came under the orders of the 23rd Brigade.*

With the incoming 17th Division were 6/Dorsets returning for their third 'stint' on the Somme. Since their last tour of duty in the trenches near Longuval during early August, the Battalion had been in the relatively quiet Gommecourt area under command of the Third Army. 6/Dorsets' march to the trenches before Le Transloy took five hours, and once off the duckboard tracks, it was a case of:

> *Slushing through mud, in many places over the knee and sometimes waist deep, the men trudging along, carrying bags of rations, ammunition and Lewis guns. The Battalion was hopelessly muddled up, first a C Company man, then a D Company man, then a West Yorks, then a South African; so on all night. Such guides as there were soon became lost, and the Huns seemed to know there was a relief in progress, and shelled the roads of approach vigorously. Daylight showed a pool of bloody water in front of the entrance to the Headquarters' dugout.[11]*

A Private soldier from 6/Dorsets, Harry Webb, explained that:

> *The guide who had gone up during the day laid white tape stuck into the mud and wherever that tape went it led to the front line. But before we got there the Germans had shelled the area pretty heavy and blown the tapes all to blazes. You couldn't find the ends and unless there was a blown down building or something you didn't know where you*

were. If we were lucky, the outgoing battalion sent out a runner to meet us in the communication trenches.[12]

With the protracted relief of 8th Division, it was not possible to renew the attack on Zenith Trench and Le Transloy. In fact, commanders were beginning to think that it was impossible to take the village from the current position, and that it would most easily be taken by the French from the south. The French agreed, provided the British maintained pressure by limited attacks, while they attacked north from Sailly Saillesel. 17th Division's limited objective was to be the portion of Zenith Trench that 1/Devons were to have taken opposite Misty and Gusty Trenches. This objective, along with Spring Trench, was taken by a company from the Border Regiment and was subsequently held by 6/Dorsets.

For the Dorsets, this tour in the front line was to be relatively short, as, 'four days in all were found to be long enough for endurance, and companies interchanged at half-time between front and rear'. Another commentator recorded that 'hot drinks depended on a supply of Tommy Cookers', as carrying up hot food from the area several miles to the rear was out of the question. Private Webb described the feeding arrangements:

Rations were bully beef, biscuits and jam, which got wearisome and we often threw it away but when the ration parties couldn't get up we

A hand drawn map showing 6/Dorsets' positions during their time at the front before Le Transloy.

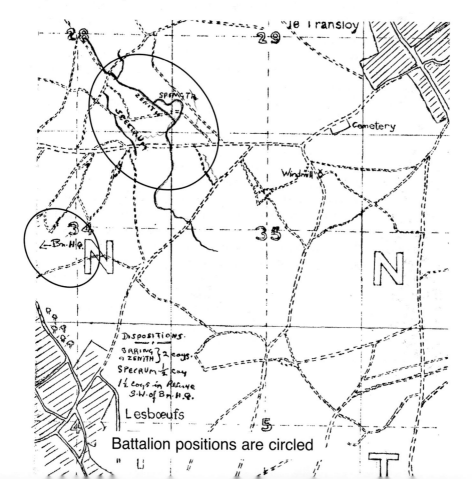

Battalion positions are circled

went out in to No Man's Land to get it back again. The biscuits were big and square like dog biscuits and we used to crack them up with an entrenching tool handle to get them small enough to eat. Bread was very rarely to be had. Occasionally, instead of the more plentiful bully beef, we got Macaunachy; a tinned ration of sliced potatoes, vegetables and a piece of fat pork. Amidst the mud and water, drinking water was scarce. We were only allowed a water bottle a day. When we could, we shaved in cold water from shell holes and ate when we were hungry.

We had a Corporal who had done the impossible and could make tea when no one else could. He used to collect water from all six of us into a canteen. We had this ration of tea and sugar mixed which used to come up. We used a small tin with rifle cleaning tow which we would light and dissolve the candle. It would burn without smoke, as smoke was a fatal thing for us, as the Germans would shell us to hell if they saw it. Once the water was boiled we put in the ration instant tea mix. At Le Transloy we couldn't light a fire in the trench.

On one occasion, as recorded in the war diary, pack mules brought the tinned rations further forward than ever before, and the Germans so concerned with their own survival, ignored them. Most welcome of all rations was the nightly rum ration. The earthenware jars, which along with everything else had to be carried up from the rear, were marked with the initials 'SRD' (Special Rations Department) which, according to the front line soldiers, translated as 'Seldom Reaches Destination'.

The Germans were also suffering, as witnessed by the number of enemy soldiers taking the extreme and dangerous step of coming across No Man's Land to surrender. Captain O'Hanlon wrote:

One fell into Zenith Trench. He was remarkably clean, 'a good catholic and the father of many children' – one of the sort Colonel Campbell of the Bayonet School said should be killed at once. One of the men gave him a cigarette saying: 'Hullo Alleyman; compris Verdun'. Another German came into D Company's Lewis gun post, narrowly escaping being shot or bayoneted.

The fact that these men survived the nervous sentry's tendency at night to shoot first and worry later reveals that the defenders thought there was a much-reduced probability of German attack in the prevailing conditions. However, a ration party of Dorsets had a lucky escape in No Man's Land, when 'one party inadvertently made for the German line after delivering the goods; it came back two battalions further down the front, where it had been watched with interest as a raiding party'.

During their four days in the line, the Battalion's sick rate was high, with trench foot being a particular problem. The cause was hours spent standing in cold water, with virtually no opportunity to carry out well-established preventive procedures. In the flooded trenches, it was not possible to remove sodden boots, or to dry and restore circulation to chilled feet. These measures, combined with greasing feet and fresh socks, normally prevented the progressive blackening of the foot as trench foot set in. Men became unable to walk, and in the worst cases were crippled for life. The Dorsets recorded that the condition was particularly prevalent amongst a detail of battle casualty replacements that had been trained in Ireland as cyclists, who were 'altogether unfit for the rigours of the Somme'. The number of sick for November totalled 146, against 14 killed and 52 wounded. When it came time for the 17th Division to be relieved by the Guards Division, so numerous were the cases of trench foot that the Guardsmen, helped by the exhausted West Countrymen, 'carried the worst cases to the road, without murmur'.

Casualties were relatively light, despite the fact that the Germans had far more artillery ammunition available, now that Verdun was all but over. Shells were described as '... falling with a plop and throwing up a geyser of mud' that absorbed the shell splinters. Air-burst (shrapnel) shells, however, remained effective.

It was becoming obvious that continuing the battle in the current conditions was becoming impossible. The opportunity to mount major offensive operations against the Germans on the Fourth Army's front had all but passed. However, before winter finally brought an end to the Battle of the Somme, Field Marshal Haig wanted one more attack.

PREVENTION OF "FROST-BITE" OR "CHILLED FEET."

1. All Officers and Non-commissioned Officers should make themselves acquainted with the following facts, in order that an effective system for the prevention of this serious ailment may be established and understood by all units which have to occupy trenches in cold or wet weather. It has been shown that when troops newly exposed to these conditions have not followed the precautions observed by more experienced and seasoned units, disastrous consequences have followed. It is, therefore, necessary to explain what has been the result of the best experience so far.

Main Principles.

2. The main principles to be observed are :—

(a) To put as few men as possible in trenches that are wet.

(b) To keep them there for only short periods without relief (not exceeding 12 hours, if practicable).

(c) To give them special treatment both before and after their tour of duty.

(d) To keep boots always well oiled or greased, and to avoid tight boots or putties which interfere with free circulation of the blood.

(B 3425) Wt. w. 11735—1550 1,500M 2/15 H & S P.15/63

---

1   Extract from a post-war letter to the author of the regimental history. RHQ D and D archive.
2   *The Devonshire Regiment 1914 - 1919*, C.T. Atkinson, Exeter, 1926.
3   *The Eighth Division in War, 1914 - 1918*, Boraston and Bax, London, 1926.
4   *Official History. France and Flanders 1916* Vol 2.
5   2Lt McConville 2/W. Yorks, also in 23 Brigade with 2/Devons. Quoted in the divisional history.
6   Lieutenant Burke notes. RHQ D and D archive.
7   2/Devons war diary. PRO WO 95/1712.
8   Field punishment consisted of serving a court's sentence supervised by the regimental provo staff with the soldiers unit in either the front line or rear area. The soldier would conduct hard labour, with little rest or food.
9   *Blindfold and Alone*, Corns & Hughes-Wilson, Cassells & Co. London, 2001.
10 IWM Sound Archive.
11 *A Plain History of the Sixth (Service) Battalion, The Dorsetshire Regiment 1914 - 1919*, Captain O'Hanlon, Dorchester, 1932.
12 Keep Military Museum Dorchester archive.

Chapter 18

Battle of the Ancre

In a conversation with General Gough during early November 1916, Field Marshal Haig's Chief of Staff, General Kiggell, reflected that 'the heavy losses entailed by the fighting on the Somme were making their effects felt at home, and sorrow, suffering and anxiety were undoubtedly weakening the resolution of some people'.[1] However, the official historian records that Haig planned to attack in General Gough's Fifth Army area:

> He said that a success was much wanted, as it would have favourable repercussions upon the Russian and Rumanian fronts, and create a heartening effect at home: yet he did not desire to risk too much.

Despite these words highlighting political requirements at home and abroad, there is an abiding suspicion that military vanity underpinned the Battle of the Ancre. The by-now notorious villages of Serre and Beaumont Hamel, where

Regimental transport horses up to their hocks in liquid Somme mud during late October 1916.

attacks had failed so disastrously on 1 July, could not be left in enemy hands. The resulting aim was a 'limited operation' designed to reduce the head of what was now a pronounced German salient between the Albert-Bapaume Road and Serre.

After the rain of late October had caused operations to bog down before Le Transloy, eight days of dry weather had allowed the ground to dry out somewhat. These conditions presented Haig with an opportunity to mount his final attack of the battle. Even though the Germans still held the approximate line of their original 1 July front in the Beaumont Hamel / Serre area, after nineteen weeks of battle, the German Army was worn down; but the British had improved their tactical position by considerably reducing the width of No Man's Land at key points.

On the other side of the strip of wrecked countryside that marked the battle area, German commanders no longer feared a serious problem developing on the Somme. Despite the marginal improvements, the weather could only deteriorate, and, in addition, the situation at Verdun had been stabilized. German commanders recognized however, that the British had now driven them back into a salient astride the River Ancre. They had successfully held the old Serre/Beaumont Hamel line but had lost much of the Thiepval and the Pozières Ridges, including Mouquet Farm, to the Allies, thus producing a vulnerable salient. As with all salients, the Germans found their positions swept by shellfire from guns on three sides, and some commanders suggested a withdrawal to a line between Serre and Grandcourt. Ludendorf supported the proposed 'evacuation of the salient between St Pierre Division and Beaumont Hamel'.[2] However, General Below believed that doing so would give up important high ground, along with its valuable observation posts, which had given the Germans a significant tactical advantage throughout the summer and autumn fighting. Instead of withdrawing, the Germans reinforced the Beaumont Hamel area in anticipation of a British attack.

The Opening Moves

Although described as 'limited', a considerable number of British troops were to be committed to battle. The attack was to be on a frontage of almost nine miles, astride the flooded valley of the River Ancre, involving troops from two army corps, with nine divisions in the line. 1/Dorsets along with the rest of 32nd (New Army) Division were to be V Corps Reserve, located in forward concentration areas. The Dorsets were just three miles behind the front at Mailly Mallet, to the rear of, (from left to right), 3rd Division (Serre), 2nd Division (Redan Ridge), 51st Highland Division (Beaumont Hamel) and 63rd Royal Naval Division (Beaucourt), ready to exploit success. At the same time, II Corps was to attack east of the Ancre.

It was General Gough who agonized about the risk of mounting the attack, as Haig delegated the decision to him. However, they both agreed that Zero Hour should be 05.45 hours, or thirty minutes before sunrise on 13 November. On the morning of the attack, the Battle of the Ancre opened amidst a dense white fog. General Gough wrote:

> By 8.50 a.m. the II Corps had gained all its objectives and captured
> over 1,000 prisoners. North of the Ancre, the Naval Division and the
> 51st Division carried all before them[3]. ... The 3rd Division, however,
> which was faced with a veritable quagmire in its front, was repulsed,
> but only because the men were unable to keep close to the barrage -
> this in spite of the fact that they were only required to advance at the
> rate of 200 yards a minute. Mud was on this occasion, as on many
> others, our greatest difficulty and our most unconquerable enemy.

2nd Division had some success fighting towards the crest of Redan Ridge, and
a few individuals from 3rd Division, despite the mud, managed to reach their
objectives towards Serre. However, they were too few, and their rifles were
useless, being choked with mud. They were eventually pushed back by the
Germans, who similarly laboured through the mud to counter-attack.
Nevertheless, to the north of the Ancre, the main prize of the day, the fortified
ruins of Beaumont Hamel, was firmly in the hands of the 51st Highland
Division. A German regimental history recorded that 'the men could scarcely
believe in the loss of Beaumont Hamel, which they had held for so long'. To the
east of the Ancre, II Corps pushed on over the Thiepval Heights towards
Grandcourt, but 39th Division failed to reach its final objective.

As the front moved forward, General Gough moved up to the line and
spotted the cavalrymen of the Life Guards and Blues, labouring as pioneers

A layered map showing the Serre battlefield of November 1916.

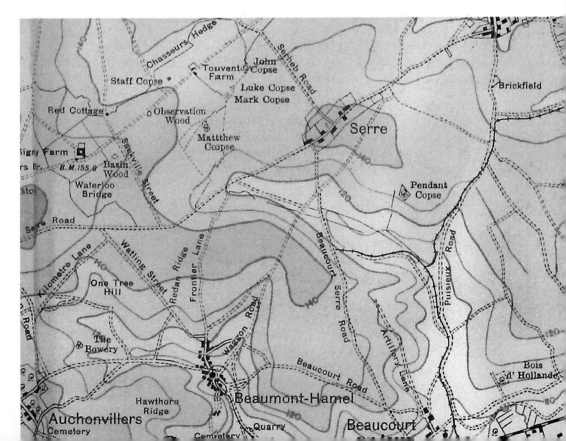

under command of his cousin. They were using the village's bricks and rubble to make a rudimentary road forward across the shell-churned strip of No Man's Land. 'I chaffed him about the work I found him engaged on - very different from doing a Royal escort or guard in London, but at the moment a good deal more useful.' More than useful, it was essential so that fresh troops, trench stores, ammunition and most importantly the Royal Artillery's field guns could get forward to consolidate positions before the Germans could mount a significant counter-attack.

The British attack had been the limited success that General Gough had planned and expected, but above all the talisman of Beaumont Hamel had been taken. The enemy had been pushed back a thousand yards in the centre, and no less than 6,300 Germans had been taken prisoner. However, the enemy were, as usual, quick to seal off the threat. In this context, it is recorded in the Official History that:

> Immediate steps were taken by the enemy to reinforce the sorely tried troops, which had been driven from the front system north of the Ancre. Units of the 223rd Division not yet in the line were brought up ... The remnants of the 55th Reserve Regiment retired ... The Beaucourt Road was a crater field and the ruins of the neighbouring villages were in flames; in view of the uncertain situation no counter attack could be contemplated.

In addition, German formations rushed from other parts of the First Army front to seal off the British attack, from as far afield as the rear area at Cambrai.

During the attack, the 32nd Division was not called on, and 1/Dorsets remained in the badly shelled billets of Mailly-Maillet. V Corps continued the

A 60-pounder gun being manhandled through the mud prior to the attack.

attack on 14 November, but an impetus to drive back the reinforced Germans could not be developed and further gains were minimal over the following days. By 16 November, 2nd Division, had suffered 3,000 casualties and 'having fought itself to a standstill' started being replaced by Major General Rycroft's 32nd Division. First to the front was the Dorsets' Brigade. It is recorded that

> At dawn on the 16th November the 14th Brigade (Brigadier General Compton) had taken over the northern defensive flank where there was considerable doubt as to the exact situation of the front line.

The Dorsets were located on the northern end of Redan Ridge, in the labyrinth of smashed trenches of the Germans' forward trench system that had defied the British on 1 July. Despite the damage on the semi-frozen surface, the West Countrymen 'were able to locate and bring into use some remarkably well made German dugouts that had survived four months of shellfire'. Once 97 Brigade had joined 14 Brigade in the line, '32nd Division then held the front from Leave Avenue as far as the Quadrilateral at the western end of the defensive flank'.

During 17 November, air reconnaissance reported that some of the German trenches were abandoned ,and as a result, Commander V Corps was ordered by General Gough to push forward patrols under cover of darkness and if possible occupy these trenches. However, when these orders reached the front, problems in execution were apparent. Major General Rycroft recorded in a personal note, which he, unusually, included in the divisional war diary:

> I was asked to capture Munich trench and Frankfort Trenches before daybreak tomorrow including a position in front of 51st Division. I pointed out that this would be a practical impossibility as the line had not been properly reconnoitred or forming up places marked out, so the Corps Commander agreed to the attack being carried out about dawn on 18th November when II Corps is also attacking south of the Ancre.

Meanwhile, ground patrol reports quickly refuted those of the RFC. '...Germans working on the wire in front of their line, [was] sufficient indication that the trenches - now a maze of shell-craters and half frozen mounds of earth - were still occupied.' Orders for a new limited advance to seize the German front line system were being prepared. However, there were no longer any grand intentions to break through to objectives in the depths of the enemy position.

Orders for the Attack

V Corps was to attack with two divisions; 32nd left and 37th right. According to the 32nd's operation order[4], which was issued at 15.45 hours on 17 November 1916: 'The objective of the V Corps is to establish a line on the spur West of *Bois d'Holand* and to drive the enemy off the spur south of Ten Tree Alley'. However, as the operation order goes on to say, it was not entirely clear where the Germans were: 'The enemy is believed to be occupying Munich Trench and Frankfort Trench and the trench running east and west just north of Glory Lane...' Major General Rycroft's intent was:

> to capture and hold Munich trench and Frankfort from Leave Avenue to Lager Alley and at the same time to advance his left Northwards

towards Ten Tree Alley.

97 Brigade were to attack on the Division's right flank and 14 Brigade on the left, in a northerly direction towards Serre. 32nd Division's attack was to be lavishly supported by the guns of no less than five divisions of artillery, as well as the heavier guns of the corps artillery, which together would concentrate on the enemy trench lines. Meanwhile, the brigade trench mortar companies were to heavily bombard the forward German strong points.

Brigadier Comptons orders[5] for 14 Brigade allocated the role of delivering the assault to 2/Manchesters and 15/HLI, with 1/Dorsets as supports in the area astride Frontier Lane, among the old German 1 July frontline trenches.[6] 5/Royal Scots were to be the brigade reserve in 'readiness in the trenches about Ellis Square'. 14 Brigade's objective was the seizure of an un-named line of trenches between Lager Alley and Ten Tree Alley, which would require the assault troops to advance about 500 yards. From here, the battalions were to push forward outpost patrols by about 150 yards. It was explicitly intended not to take Ten Tree Alley or the prized ruins of Serre that lay temptingly beyond. Serre had been attacked disastrously by the Pals' battalions of 31th Division on 1 July, and was a tempting target for infantry commanders.

The Brigade Operation Order also contained the increasingly complex procedures for aircraft identification of ground troops:

> *The contact plane of 15th Squadron RFC will co-operate in the attack* [It will be marked with] *distinguishing marks – black bands under each wing with black streamers in continuation of the bands.*
>
> *At Zero* [plus] *40* [i.e. dawn], *the advanced infantry will show their positions by lighting three green flares successively at the same spot, under orders from platoon commanders. Flares will be lit subsequently by the advanced infantry whenever called for by the plane by means of light signals or succession of short blasts on the klaxon. Green flares only will be used...*

The timely issue of orders has been an important principal of battle procedure throughout the ages; and in this case, 32nd Division came in for criticism. 14 Brigade's orders were finally issued at 23.30 hours, just six hours and forty minutes before Zero Hour. This gave little time for messengers to deliver the orders and for battalion headquarters to digest them and conduct essential commanders' and guides' reconnaissance. Orders to junior officers and NCOs would have been very brief, and those to the ordinary soldier, necessarily perfunctory, as the companies had to move to their assault positions.

The Final Attack

During the night of 17-18 November, the weather window finally broke and the first snow of winter fell on the uplands of the Somme. The official historian described the conditions

> *at 6.10 a.m. on 18 November the assault was delivered in whirling sleet which afterwards changed to rain. More abominable conditions for active warfare can not be imagined: the infantry, dark figures only visible for a*

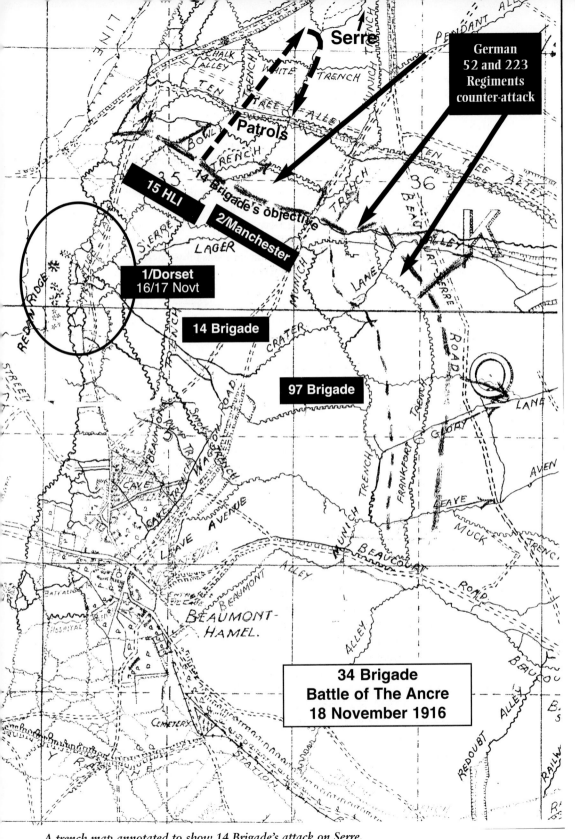

A trench map annotated to show 14 Brigade's attack on Serre.

short distance against the white ground, groped their way forward as best they could through half-frozen mud that was soon dissolved into chalky slime. Little wonder that direction was often lost and with it, the precious barrage, whilst the objectives, mantled in snow, were hard indeed to identify. Observation from the air was impossible; ground observers could see little or nothing, so that the batteries, in almost as bad a plight as the infantry, were, for the most part, reduced to firing their prearranged programme, regardless of the fortunes of the advance. To the sheer determination, self sacrifice and physical endurance of the troops must be attributed such measure of success as was won.

Despite the bad weather, the British artillery was well registered on the enemy positions, and when the barrage opened at 06.10 hours, shells fell accurately on the enemy trenches. The initial 'intense bombardment' lasted for just four minutes. As the labouring artillerymen fired their last shells, the HLI and the Manchesters both left their trenches, attacking with three companies forward and one in support. Advancing on a frontage of 900 yards, they made some progress. However, after a matter of 250 yards, they were held up by machine-gun fire. To make matters worse, the hitherto accurate artillery support was replaced by a creeping barrage, which was placed too far in depth, leaving the enemy machine gunners largely untouched. Communications back to the British guns broke down, as heavy German shellfire cut the inadequately buried telephone cables and, consequently, the barrage could not be adjusted.

Casualties amongst the forward battalions mounted, and it was not long before the Dorsets were called forward from Lager Alley, to which they had moved once it had been vacated by the HLI and Manchesters. Individual companies were sent forward to reinforce the assault battalions, while Battalion Headquarters remained in dugouts at the junction of Lager Alley and Serre Trench. The battalion historian wrote:

At 8.45 a.m., A Company [three platoons] was sent to support the 15th Highland Light Infantry, on the left; at 9.45 a.m. B Company was sent to the 2nd Manchester, and they called for a second company, D, at 10.15 a.m.

The ground conditions were appalling, as the snow and crust of ice broke under foot the battlefield reverted to mud. Once committed to battle, troops quickly lost all contact with their headquarters, and in the case of 2/Manchesters, three platoons pressed on beyond their first objective to Ten Tree Alley. These platoons were never seen again.

The attack had not been well prepared. Proven necessities, such as white canvas tapes for the assault troops to follow to their start line, and for orientation as they entered No Man's Land, could not be laid in the time available. In addition, the German defenders were alert, reinforced, and ready to meet the advancing British. The lightly held front line was taken but, as ever, German officers and NCOs had planned counter-attacks in detail. Consequently, 14 Brigade's infantry, who had arrived in the enemy trenches in small groups, were driven back before they could properly consolidate their gains.

German records show that two reserve battalions from 52nd and 223rd Regiments mounted the counter-attacks across the open ground from the direction of Pendant Copse to the south-east of the ruins of Serre. The 66th Regiment records that the 'British were driven out of Serre', so it seems likely that at least small groups of Manchesters along with B Company 1/Dorsets had exceeded their orders and reached the rubble of the infamous village. The Germans eventually rounded up seventy Britons as prisoners, along with four machine guns. These guns were almost certainly Lewis guns belonging to the infantry battalions, as the Machine Gun Company's Vickers were all accounted for.

Those infantrymen not captured in Serre were driven back by the Germans. British sappers, pioneers and machine gunners, who were moving up to help consolidate the gains, met the remains of the assault infantry heading back towards their startlines. The Dorsets' historian wrote 'At mid-day, with the exception of the left of the 14th Brigade, the attacking troops were back in their old front line'. On the left, 15/HLI, supported by A Company 1/Dorsets, held some enemy trenches. However, B and D Companies of 1/Dorsets, under the redoubtable and inspiring leadership of Captain Kestell-Cornish, were left holding the majority of the old British front line. With the thaw that now set in, the temporarily firm trenches started to collapse, and much work was required to maintain anything more than 'an ill-defined ditch'.

Casualties from the attack had at first seemed to be exceptionally heavy. However, the total had been inflated by the fact that dispersed and isolated assault troops tended to hold their gains until hunger or loneliness drove them back. Some were holding positions amongst the enemy for several days. An entry in the divisional war diary on 21 November records that a

Captain Robin Kestell-Cornish.

> Company Sergeant Major and a private 11/Border reached our lines in early morning and reported that there are over 100 offrs and Ors holding out in dugouts in Frankfort Trench including 1 offr and 30 OR wounded.

The Dorsets held the front line until 23 November, when the slowing tempo of the battle was immediately apparent. But now, with the weather rapidly deteriorating, the prospect of gaining further advantage receded. Sergeant Major Shephard (see Chapter 6) now commissioned as a Temporary Second Lieutenant with 5/Dorsets, was nearby. He met his old friend, the Officers' Mess Sergeant of his beloved 1st Battalion, and heard how the First had performed during the Battle of the Ancre.

> The 1st Bn attacked at Beaumont Hamel and did good work. They had heavy casualties. Captain Carew, the Doctor (Captain Clarke) amongst the killed. They withdrew last night to Mailly Maillet, only a short distance from here. They lost a lot of men from exposure and some who got stuck in the mud and could not be rescued.

So ended the 1916 Battle of the Somme for the ordinary West Country soldier.

Before concluding, it is worth remembering that Clausewitz wrote: 'the political object, being the original motive, must be an essential factor in the product'.[7] In this case, the object of the Battle of the Ancre was to boost morale at home and to ensure control in the Empire. In that context, General Gough wrote of the battle:

> The Fifth Army received a telegram from the Commander-in-Chief congratulating us on the great results obtained:- 'Under such difficulties of ground, the achievement is all the greater, the accuracy and rapidity of the artillery fire and the full advantage taken of it by the infantry were admirable'.

> Remembering Kiggell's words, I knew that Sir Douglas Haig's Message was no formal courtesy, but a deeply felt congratulation.

The End of the Battle of the Somme

The West Country regiments of Devon and Dorset had been involved in the battle from first to last. On 19 November,[8] orders were issued for the armies on the Somme to go into 'winter quarters and training, and for the organization of a strong defensive line behind our newly won positions'. The tempo of battle continued to ebb away over a period of weeks and, by the end of the month, the front was 'thinly held'. However, the bickering with the enemy typical of a British held front continued, and conditions in the trenches gradually improved, as the labours of the infantry outpaced that of the slackening enemy artillery fire. Even so, the West Country battalions had to endure a second and even harder winter on the uplands of Picardy. On the British side of the line, what had been a quiet sector, with intact villages and comfortable billets close behind the lines, was replaced by a desolate wilderness of overlapping shell craters. The sanctuary of villages and woods had all been swept away, and miles of brick, duckboard and light railway track wound through the craterfields to the new front line. It was a grim winter.

In February 1917, the Germans withdrew to the strongly built Hindenburg Line, ten miles to the east, in order to shorten their line. As spring approached, the troops marched to a new focus of battle. First to Vimy Ridge, then to Arras and, in high summer, north to the Ypres Salient, which burst into life during the successful Battle of Messines Ridge, and then on to the protracted battle of attrition fought at Passchendaele.

In 1917, the British Army was certainly wiser, and the painfully learned lessons of the Somme had led to development in battle tactics. In the run up to 1 July, the British had virtually ignored both field security and surprise. In contrast, the most successful attacks of 1917 relied heavily on surprise and its close ally, deception, to ensure success. Artillery fire was henceforth better coordinated, and further developments, such as protective box barrages and more sophisticated creeping barrages, helped to ensure success. Infantry tactics progressed, from men moving forward in rigid waves at a steady pace, to advances screened by smaller well supported groups of infantry in looser formations, designed to identify and overcome enemy strong points.

Despite these and other tactical and technological developments, the unbroken line of trenches running from Switzerland to the North Sea, with its belts of barbed wire, artillery and machine guns, along with mud, were not to be overcome in 1917. The battles of attrition set in, but the collapse of Russia and the arrival of the Americans in force offered new opportunities to both the Germans and the Allies. In the German offensives of 1918, the full horror of battle again swept across the uplands of Picardy, forcing the British from their hard won gains of 1916; but that is another story.

The Cost

Much time and effort has been spent calculating relative casualty rates suffered by the Allies and the Germans during the four-and-a-half months of the Somme, and statements, estimates and counter claims abound. The figures quoted in the Official History are between 660,000 to 680,000 German and 630,000 British and French casualties. However, the number of casualties suffered by the seven West Country battalions in action on the Somme is almost impossible to calculate. Some war diaries and casualty returns were written immediately after

Leather jerkins were issued to the troops as winter set in.

the battle, before some of the lost, marooned and very lightly wounded men returned. Other diaries were neatly typed during periods out of the line, up to three weeks after the event, when losses were more certain. The figures quoted in the Regimental histories in some cases have little provenance and are difficult to reconcile. Very rough figures, of 1,500 killed, 3,000 wounded and almost 1,000 men missing, give an indication of the order of magnitude of the losses suffered by the West Country Regiments during the Battle of the Somme.

Lieutenant Charles Douie, in writing a passage about his platoon, provides an epitaph for all those who fought with the West Country Regiments on the Somme:

The hand of death lay heavy on that company. To my certain knowledge fourteen, nearly one half gave their lives, and of the remainder I do not know the fate of several. The conditions under which the war was carried on decreed that those fourteen numbered most of the best loved, the gallant and single-hearted. They sleep, many of them, on the uplands of Picardy. They asked for no reward, no sunlit fields of heaven. They played a man's part, and held their heads high, till Death came in a roaring whirlwind and one more little hour was played. Yet perhaps, as they sleep, they hear a voice across the ages 'Well done.'

'Semper Fidelis'
Who's Afeared?'

1 Kiggell, quoted in *The Fifth Army*, General Sir Hubert Gough, Hodder and Stoughton, 1931.
2 *Official History. France and Flanders* 1916. Vol II.
3 In the south and north respectively of the present day Newfoundland Memorial Park.
4 32nd Division Operation Order No. 65 dated 17 November 1916, PRO WO 95/2368.
5 14 Brigade Operation Order No. 88 dated 17 November 1916, PRO 95/2390.
6 Trenches in the area attacked by 4th Division on 1 July, 1916.
7 Carl von Clausewitz, *Von Kreig. On the Nature of War,* Book One, Berlin, 1832.
8 There is a popular view that the Battle ended on 14 November with the capture of Beaumont Hamel. This is incorrect. It officially ended on 18 November 1916.

INDEX

BRITISH ARMY

First Army, 84, 259

3rd Army, 23, 49, 58, 234, 269

4th Army(Gen. Rawlinson's), 25, 51-2, 56-60, 63-4, 69, 76, 84, 86, 102, 116, 137, 142, 173-4,189; 205, 211, 231-2, 235, 252, 259, 272, Plan, 151-6

5th Reserve Army (Gen. Gough's) 58-9, 92, 102, 156, 203, 231, 234-5, 273, 282

Kitchener Army ('K1', K2, K3), 17,

'New Army' 18, 23, 34, 51, 58-9, 62, 86, 105, 113, 128, 130, 158; K1 formations, 17, 19,

II Corps, 234, 274-5, 277

III Corps, 69-71, 74, 76, 151, 154, 156, 174, 208

V Corps Reserve, 274, 276-7

X Corps, 90-2

XII Corps, 156

XIII Corps, 116, 132, 137, 151, 154, 156, 174, 215

XIV Corps, 206, 254, 262

XV Corps, 105, 107, 116, 122, 132, 137, 141, 145-6, 151, 154, 156, 168, 173-4, 208

Guards Division, 272

2nd Division, 274-5, 277

3rd Division, 21, 156, 161, 167, 170, 274-5

4th Division, 66

5th (Regular)Division, 21, 23, 25, 27-8, 30-4, 49-50, 173-4, 176, 186, 189, 196-7, 205-6, 208, 214, 218, 252-6, 258

7th Regular (Northern), Division, 49, 60 105, 107, 110, 113, 116-17, 131-2,134, 140-2, 152, 154, 156, 159, 166-8, 171- 4, 186, 206, 215, 221, 224, 230

8th Division, 15, 21, 50-1, 54, 62, 69-85, 94, 101, 137, 259-63, 269

9th (Scottish) Division, 156, 173

11th (Northern) Division, 19, 233, 235, 240

12th Eastern Division, 84, 86-7

14th Division, 216

16th (Irish) Division, 214

17th (Northern) Division, 20, 107, 109, 111-12, 140, 142, 144-5, 149, 195-6, 199, 267, 269-70, 272;

18th Division, 156, 240

19th Division, 71

20th (Light) Division, 206, 208, 210-11, 213, 218

21st Division, 107, 109-11, 116, 118, 132, 140, 145, 149, 156, 168

23rd Division, 276

24th Division, 227

25th Division, 234,

31st Division, 278

32nd (New Army) Division, 34-5, 51-2, 67, 91-2, 98, 101, 274, 276-8

33rd Division, 168, 174, 178m, 185

34th (New Army) Division, 51, 71-3, 85

35th (Bantam) Division, 206

36th (Ulster) Division, 90

37th Division, 277

38th Welsh Division, 147-8, 159

39th Division, 275

43rd Wessex Division, 15

48th Division, 87, 232

49th (West Riding) Division, 91-2, 104 (note), 235,

51st Highland Division, 274-5, 277

Devonshire Regiment, 6-13, 173, 195, 251

Dorsetshire Regiment, 6-13, 251

Gloucester Regiment, 174-5

West Country Regiments, (Devons & Dorsets), 6-13, 21, 282;

13 Brigade, 186, 189, 208, 210, 253, 256,

14 Brigade, 26, 34-5, 52, 91, 93-4, 98, 100, 102, 104, 277-8, 280-1

15 Brigade, 34, 210, 212-13, 253-4, 256

20 Brigade, 50, 53, 113, 117-21, 127-8, 141, 152, 156, 158-62, 165-7, 172, 174, 176-9, 182-8, 216-17, 221, 223-5, 226

22 Infantry Brigade, 117, 121, 133, 141, 158-9, 166-7, 216-7, 224

23 Infantry Brigade, 71-3, 81, 85, 263-5

24 Brigade, 263

25 Brigade, 71-2, 77, 81, 263, 266

32 Brigade, 234-5, 240, 248

33 Brigade, 234-5, 237, 239-40

34 Brigade, 234-6, 240, 242, 245, 247-8

41 Brigade, 201

50 Brigade, 105, 107, 110-12, 117, 140, 142, 144-5, 148, 196, 199, 201

51 Brigade, 112, 140, 143, 145, 148, 196, 201

52 Brigade, 196,

63 Brigade, 107

64 Brigade, 107

70 (New Army)Brigade, 71-3

91 Brigade, 117-18, 158, 168, 172, 216,

95 Brigade, 173, 189, 208, 210-11, 214, 253-4, 256

96 Brigade, 44, 52, 91, 93

97 Brigade, 52, 91, 93, 178

110 Brigade, 156

113 Brigade, 144, 147-9

Devon & Cornwall Brigade, 15

South African Brigade, 173, 269

Special Brigade, 66, 236; 5th Battalion, 236

Service Battalions, 15

3rd Special Reserve battalions, 13, 15, 194

reservists, 13

West Country Territorial Force, 15

Infantry Battalions:

Bedfords, 26

8th Bedford, 252

2nd Borders, 113,118, 123-4, 131, 158-62, 164-6, 174, 220-1, 228 270,

11th (Lonsdale) Borders, 96-97, 99, 281

1st Cheshires, 26, 102, 1049(n),195, 256

1st Devon, 10, 12-14, 15-16, 21, 23, 26-30, 33-4, 49, 51, 65, 173, 189, 194-6, 205-6, 208, 210-15, 223, 252-8, 270; 1 & 2 Companies, 193

2nd Devon, 15, 21, 50-1, 54, 62-4, 69-71, 73-7, 84-7, 89, 101, 113, 137, 259-69

A Company, 73, 265-6, 269; B Co, 73, 79, 265-6, 269; C Co 73, 75, 78-9, 81, 266; D Co, 73, 75, 78-9, 81, 265-6

3rd Devons, 159

4th, 5th, 6th Devon, 15; 7th Devons (Cyclist) Battalion, 15,

8th (Service) Devons, 15-18, 21, 49-50, 52-3, 59, 105, 113, 118-21, 124-36, 141-2, 151-2, 154, 158-67, 171-8, 180-6, 206, 215, 221-2, 230; Bombing Platoon, 161,

A Company, 126, 161-2, 164, 177, 182, 186, 222

B Company, 124, 129, 161; 165, 221-2, 225-6

C Company, 128-9, 161, 164; 167, 177, 182, 186, 222, 225-6

D Company, 125, 127-8, 130, 161-2, 164, 222, 226

9th (Service)Devons, 17-18, 21, 50, 53-4, 59, 113-14, 118-24, 126, 128, 130-6, 142, 156, 158-60, 167-8, 171, 173-6, 178-82, 187, 206, 215, 217-225, 227-230; A Company, 49; No. 1 Company, 114, 118, 122-4, 176, 178-82, 187

No. 2 Company, 118, 123-4

No. 3 Company, 118, 123-4, 224

No. 4 Company, 118, 123-4, 126, 224

1st Dorset, 9, 13, 19, 21, 23, 26-7, 30-4, 44, 48, 50, 59, 65-6, 86-7, 89-104, 137, 202, 274, 276, 278;

A Company, 35-7, 41, 93, 96, 281

B Company, 33, 37-9, 42-3, 93, 96-8, 100-1, 280-1

C Company, 44-6, 92-3, 95, 99,

D Company, 44-6, 93, 280-1
2nd Dorset, 15; 3rd Dorset, 19
5th Dorsets, 16, 18-19, 231, 233-42, 245-9, 252, 281
6th Dorsets (Service) Battalion, 18-21, 105, 108-112, 138, 140, 142-9, 195-202, 268-71
A Company, 147-8,
B Company, 144,
C Company, 147-8
D Company, 19-20, 143, 271,
1st Duke of Cornwall's Light Infantry (DCLI), 189-90, 195, 208, 210
1st East Surreys, 189, 195, 207-08, 211-12, 254, 256,
6th East Yorks pioneers, 245
7th East Yorks, 108, 110-12, 144,
9th Essex (12th Division), 86
12th Gloucesters, 208, 210, 256,
2nd Gordon Highlanders, 113, 118, 125, 127, 130-1, 134, 158-9, 167-8, 174-5, 178-81, 183-4, 186-8, 221, 223-8
7th Green Howards, 108-9, 111, 145; A Company, 109-11
1st Hampshire, 195
9th Hampshire (Cyclists), 234
15th Highland Light Infantry (HLI), (Glasgow Tramways), 34, 52, 94, 100-3, 278, 280-1
17th HLI (Glasgow Commercials), 94, 97, 101
2nd King's Own Scottish Borders (KOSB), 208, 256
King's Own Yorkshire Light Infantry (KOYLI), 93
Kitchener Battalions, 34; Kitchener's volunteers, 16-17, 34, 58, 233
Lancashire Fusiliers, 97
9th Lancashire Fusiliers, 236, 239-40, 242-3, 245, 247
15th Lancashire Fusiliers (1st Salford Pals), 44
16th Lancashire Fusiliers, 87
19th Lancashire Fusiliers,(3rd Salford Pals),34, 44, 52, 97-9, 102
7th Lincolns, 140-1, 201
2nd Manchesters, 34, 37-8, 52, 98, 102-3, 135, 216, 278, 280-1
11th Manchesters, 239-40, 245, 247-8
21st Manchesters, 221
22nd Manchesters, 228
24/Pioneer Manchesters, 161
2nd Middlesex, 63, 73, 78, 184
8th Northumberland Fusiliers, 239-40, 245
9th Northumberland Fusiliers, 196
Queens, 168-70; 2/Queens, 222

2nd Royal Berkshires, 77, 266
10th Royal Inniskilling Fusiliers, 46
2nd Scottish Rifles, 73, 84,
5th Royal Scots, 278
2nd South Staffords, 118, 134, 140-1, 168-170
Sherwood Foresters, 141;
1st Sherwood Foresters, 265,
10 Sherwood Foresters, 269
2nd R Irish Regiments (RIR), 159, 166-7
7th Royal Irish Fusiliers, 214, 216
Warwicks, 221
2nd Warwicks, 166
Royal Warwicks, 127-8
14th Warwicks, 186
15th Warwicks, 195
1st Royal Welch Fusiliers(RWF), 133, 174, 183, 186-7, 216,
2nd Royal Welch Fusiliers, 185
14th (Royal?)Welch (38th Division), 142
15th Royal Welch Fusiliers 144-5, 148
Welshmen of 113 Brigade, 148
Royal West Kents, 186, 212; 1st Royal West Kents, 253
2nd West Yorks, 73, 81
10th West Yorks, 107-12, 199
12th West Yorks, 156,161, 164
West Yorks, 248
95th Field Company 161
1st Wilts, 104
Artillery, 85, Royal Artillery, 154, 262;
Royal Field Artillery, 113, 132;
Brigade Trench Mortar Batteries, 278
Brigade Machine Gun Companies, 61
23 Brigade's Machine Gun Company, 74, 141, 161, 281
15 Brigade Trench Mortar Battery, 210
20 Trench Mortar Battery, 121
23 Trench Mortar Battery 77
34 Trench Mortar Company, 240
Cavalry Divisions, 59, 92, 154, 156, 159, 167; 1st, 156; 2nd Indian, 156, 158, (Secunderabad Brigade), 168-73, 175; 3rd Indian,156
7th Dragoon Guards, 168, 170; Decan Horse, 168
Life Guards, & Blues, 275
Royal Army Medical Corps (RAMC), 82, 87, 100, 283
Royal Artillery, 276
Royal Engineers, (RE), 21, 28-30, 39, 43; 50, 53, 74, 118, 160, 245, 249
Royal Flying Corps, (RFC), 61, 154; 15th Squadron, 278
Royal Horse Artillery, F & T Batteries, 162; T Battery, 228
Royal Navy, 8-9; 63rd Royal Naval Division,   274-5

Abbeville, 195
Albert, 37-8, 43, 71, 168, 174
Albert-Bapaume Road, 22, 35, 37-8, 90, 105, 132, 137, 151, 205, 231, 274
Algeo, Capt, 41, 46-9, 92
Allenby, Gen. Sir Edmund, 58
Ancre River, 25, 35, 44, 67, 92, 105, 156, Battle of, 273-82;
Andrews, Capt, 78
Archer, Capt, 266
Armin, Gen. Sixt von, 152, 167
Arras, 23, 34, 59, 66, 194, 234,
Asquith, H.H., Prime Minister, 15, 57
Atkinson, Capt C.T., 21(n), 167, 259
Australia & New Zealand Army Corps (ANZAC), 203; Australian Divisions, 232-4
Authuille, 44, 46, 67, 94-5, 98, 100-1
Barber, Lieut, 108, 110, 112, 201;
Bauer, Sgt Maj, 81-2
Bazentin Ridge, 107, Battle of, 151-172; area, 152, 155; Wood, 158, 162, 164-5,, 173, 179
Bazentin-le-Grand, Wood, 158, 164, 171, 176, 179; village, 168
Bazentin-le-Petit, Klein Bazentin, 133, 158, 164-8; Wood, 156
Beaumont Hamel, 89, 273-6, 281
Beaupre, Pte, DCM, 247
Bellwood, Capt., 161
Below, Gen. Fritz von, 137, 152, 157, 274,
Bernafy Wood, 217, 260, 269
Black Road, 177-9, 182, 185
Blackhorse Bridge, 46, 67-8, 92, 100-1;
Blakeway, 2nd Lieut, 41, 44
Bois Francais, 26-8, 116-17
la Boiselle, 34-40, 42, 50-1, 69-73, 76, 79, 85-6, 110, 137, 259
British Expeditionary Force (BEF), 59, 203
Burke, Lieut, 267
Butcher, Lieut., 96-8, 103
Campbell, Maj Gen, 107, 110
Canadian Army, 233, 235-6, 239
Carden, Maj, 16
Carnoy, 23, 26, 28, 116
Carrington, C.E., 87, 88(n)
Cary, 2nd Lieut., 178-9
casualties, 60, 173, 230, 249;
XV Corps, 132; 2nd Division, 277; 8th Division, 80-88;5th Division, 195; 7th Division, 215; 17th Division, 197; 21st Division, 109-11; 20 Brigade,182-4; 34 Brigade, 242, 247; 50 Brigade, 140; 1/Devons, 173, 195, 214, 254; 2/Devons, 85, 259, 266; 8/Devons, 128-9, 132, 160, 162-8, 177, 182, 186, 222, 226; 9/Devons, 122, 142, 159, 171, 172(n), 174, 212, 218, 220, 228-9;

1/Dorsets, 27, 40, 43-49, 93-104;
5/Dorsets, 233, 249, 242;
6/Dorsets, 20-1, 142, 148-9, 196, 199,
272; 12/Gloucesters, 210; 2/KOSB, 208;
2/RWF, 185-6; South Staffords, 170;
commanders, 125, 149, 219-20, 242;
officers, 59, 124-6, 228, 239, 254;
cavalry, 171, 175; shell-shock, 239;
working parties, 54; at Ancre, 280-1;
at Fricourt,110-11; at Morval, 256;
Australian, 233; German, 149, 151, 181,
259; German & Allies, 283-4
Caterpillar Valley, 117, 158, 171, 175;
Caterpillar Wood, 158-60, 167, 171, 174
Clarke, Lieut, 41, 148
Clay, L/Sgt MM, 127,136n
Compton, Brig. Gen., 277-8
Courcelette, 92, 240; see Battle of Flers-
Courcelette
Crosse, Rev. E.C., 136, 181, 185
'Crucifix Corner', 176, 178, 183, 245
Cummings, Pte. DCM, 144
D'Albertanson, Lieut. MC, 144-5, 198
Dancer, 2nd Lt., MC, 245
Danger Spot, see Rose Valley
Davidson, Lieut, MC, 148
Davies, Col, CB DSO, 18
Dawes, Maj., 160-2, 167, 176-8, 182, 185
'Death Valley', 171, 175
deception, 42, 85, 155-6
Delville Wood, 156, 159, 172-4, 181, 189,
192-3, 196-7, 201, 203, 214, 217, 221-
9, 232
desertion, 249-51, 265
Deverell, Brig., 113-114, 118, 124-5, 158,
174,
Devon Trench, 206-7, 210
Devonshire Cemetery, 136
Dorset Trench, 201
Douie, Lieut Charles, 6, 35-7, 40, 42-4,
55(n), 66-68, 89, 92-3, 284
Duff, Lieut, MC, 52, 129-30, 184-5
Ennos, L/Cpl., MM, 148
Fabeck, Major von, 90
Falfemont Farm, 208, 211-13, 219
Falkenhayn, Gen. E. von, 150, 174, 203
Fife, Col, 109-10
Flatiron Trench/Copse,158, 161-2, 171
Flers, 221; Battle of Flers-Courcelette, 234-
5, 240
Forrester, L/Cpl.MM, (cited for VC), 180-1
Foss, Maj. C.C., 227
Fowler, Pte, DCM, 247
Franklin, CSM, 149; 2nd Lt., 242
French, France, 8-9, 15
French Army, 57-9, 116, 137, 154, 156,
161, 206, 208, 223, 232, 255, 260; 4th

Army, 58; 6th Army, 57; 22nd Division,
23; 127 Regiment, 208; trenches, 23, 26-7
Fricourt, 26, 28, 44, 49-50, 52, 105, 107-
11, 115-18, 121, 132, 137, 196; Salient,
113; Wood, 140-1, 143, Farm, 141
Garlowitz, General von, 189
gas, 33, 44, 55, 64-6, 196, 235; tear-gas,
245
German army, 9, Formations: 1st Army,
174; 2nd Army, 152; II Corps, 237; IV
Corps, 152; 3rd Guards Division, 152 (=
3rd Prussian Guard, 87) Prussian Guard,
50, 98, 104n.; 7th Division, 152, 167;
8th Division, 174; 19th Reserve Division,
replaced by Bavarian Ersatz Division,
265; 26th Reserve Division, 44, 69, 89
28th Reserve Division, 43, 106, 115,
140; 45th Reserve Division, 237; 56th
Division, 217; 66th Regiment, 281;
111th Division, 208, 212,
183rd Division, 152, 167; 223rd
Division, 276; 1/Lehr Regiment, 149; 9th
Grenadier Regiment, 143
23 Regiment, 115; 35 Fusilier Regiment,
217, 228; 52 Regiment, 281;
55 Landwehr (Reserve) Regiment, 106,
115, 276; 66th Regiment, 281
72 Regiment, 174; 73 Fusilier Regiment,
208, 210-12; 88 Regiment, 217, 219, 221;
99th Regiment, 50, 90; 109 Regiment,
115, 128, 130, 133; 110 Regiment, 71;
111 (Reserve) Regiment, 106, 140; 118
Regiment, 217; 164; Regiment, 208, 210;
180th Regiment, 69, 77-81, 85; 3rd Co,
97; 212 Reserve Regiment, 237, 243
223 Regiment, 281; 239 Reserve
Regiment, 258; German Imperial Fleet,
9; Germany, 8-9; infantry, 23-5, 31;
Bavarian infantry, 263, 265;
intelligence, 85-6;
Ginchey, 49*text, Ginchy, 174, 206, 208,
210-11, 215-30, 232, 235, 260
Glasgow, Brig., 108, 111, 140,
Glory Hole, 35-7, 39-40, 42, 234,
Goddard, L/Cpl, 184 (commended)
Goodwillie, Sgt, 49 (photo)
Gordon, Col, 126, 130
Gordon-Lennox, Brigadier Lord, 210
Gough, General, 231-2, 235, 273-7, 282
Grant, Lieut Col, 16
Graves, Capt. Robert, 115, 186
Green, 2nd Lieut., 179-80, 184
Green, Brig., 221, 224, 228
Green, Major, 219, 222, 228
Gregory, Brig., 168
Grubb, RSM, 18 (offered a commission)
Guillemont, 203-206, 208-210, 212, 214-

15, 219, 260, Road, 227-8
Haig, Field Marshall, 44, 57-8, 86,102,
137, 152-4, 161, 172, 205-6, 211, 214,
231, 252, 259, 272-4, 282
Halle, Capt., 254
Hammerhead Sap, 46-8; Hammerhead, 158
Hannay, Major C.C. 18, Lieut-Col., 234,
242, 245, 247-9
Harris, Pte MM, 145
Hearse, Lieut, 124 (Adjt, 9/Devons),
Capt. (9/Devons), 228
Heyward, Capt., 177
Hicks, Pte, (MM citation: 150n)147,
Hidden Wood, 116, 118, 128-9
High Wood, 156, 159, 166-7, 201, 205-6,
208, attack on, 168-88, 232
'Hill 60', 21, 23, 27, 33, 64,
Hindenberg Fort /Redoubt /Strasse, 94, 97,
102
Hodge, Sgt. Maj., 95
Hodgson, Lieut. William Noel, MC, 114-
15, 118-19, 127
Hole, Capt., 226
Horne, Lieut-Gen. H. S., 105, 112, 140,
150, 156
Hudson, Maj Gen, 81
Hughes-Onslow, 142 (photo), 147-9
Hughes-Wilson, Col. John, 7
Hussey, Brig., 253
Ireland, 21; Irish, 51
James, Lieut Col, 124-5, 127-30, 224-5
Jardine, Brigadier, 94
Joffre, Field Marshall, 57, 150
Johnson, Maj, 111, 144
Joseph, 2nd Lieut, 164, 167
Junger, Leutnant Ernst, 66
Kavanagh, Major-General, 31
Kerr, Drum Major, 95
Kestell-Cornish, Capt., 281
Kiggell, General, 273, 282
King, Lieut., 242
Kipling, Rudyard,115
Kitchener, Field Marshall Lord, 15, 18;
volunteers, 16; labouring, 53-4
Kury, Grenadier, 122, 125-6
Lancaster, Capt., 96-7
Leipzig Redoubt, 35, 67, 89, 97-8; Fort,
101-2; Salient, 71, 90-1, 94, 97-8, 232;
Trench, 254, 256
Leuze Wood, 156, 203, 206, 208, 211-14,
223, 232, 235, 252-3, 260
Lewis guns, 41, 52, 62, 99, 144, 162, 164,
176, 179-82 (photo, 180), 185, 193,
269, 271, 281
Lewis, Lieut., 162
Lock, Lt., MC, 225-6
Longueval, 151, 170-5, 189-91, 194-5,

198, 201; Alley, 219, 222, /Ginchy
    Road, 225
Loos, 21, 23, 30, 50, 65, 114, 259
Macmullen, Sgt Maj 'Mac', 20
Mahaffy, Capt, 124
Mailly Mallet, 274, 276, 281
Mallins, Geoffrey, 134
Mametz, 49, 55, 105, 107-8, 110; 113-18,
    122-4, 126-132, 134, 158-9, 173, 217,
    231, 269; Wood, 137, 144, 146-9, 151-
    2; area, 152, 155-6, 159, 161, 165,
    168, 175
Mansel-Carey, Lieut, 54;
Mansel Copse, 54, 113-14, 116, 118, 120-
    1, 124-6, 128-9, 135-6; Mansel Camp,
    269
Mansel-Pleydell, Lieut., 41, 47, 92
Martin, Capt Duncan, 114, 118, 122, 128
Mash Valley, 35, 43, 71-3, 75, 85, 87
Matthews, Pte, (cited), 199
Meault, 108-9, 111, 140,
Melhuish, Sgt Major DCM, 130, 135, 177,
Millencourt, 35, 41-2, 84
Mills, CSM, 99
Mills bomb /hand grenade(Number 5
    Grenade), 52 (photo), 114, 120
Montauban, 155-6, 162, 168, 173, 217, 219,
    221, 223
Morgan, Pte. MM,198-9
Morrison, Capt., 229
Morval, 252-8, 260; Morval-Lesboeufs
Ridge, 253
Mouquet Farm (German Farm), 52, 68, 91,
    231-40, 252, 274;
New Trench, 75-8, 82, 121, 148,
Oatley, Pte., 174-5, 179-82
O'Hanlon, Capt Geoffrey, MC, 111-12,
    147, 150(n), 271
Orchard Trench, 118, 130, 141, 197-9
Ovillers, 35, 43, 51, 54, 63, 94, 113, 137,
    156, 231-2, 240, 249, 259; attack on,
    69-88

Oxley, Maj., 224
Pilcher, Maj Gen, 105, 140, 150
Pilsen Lane Trench, 222, 226
Pont Street, 190, 197, 199, 201
Porter Trench, 217-20, 224, 227
Potter, Sgt DCM, cited for VC, 164, 180-1
Pozieres Ridge, 25, 59, 69, 73, 89, 151,
    171, 174, 231, 274, 205, 232, 248,
    cemetery, 239
Plowman, Lieut. Max, 199
Price-Davies, Brig, 144
Prince Ruprecht, 217*text has 2 Ps
Quadrangle area, 143-7, 151
Quadrilateral, 277
Ransom, Capt, 9, 11; Lieut.Col., 21(n), 66
Rawlinson, General, 51, 58 (photo), 59,
    76, 116, 137, 151-4, 205-6, 232
Riddle, CSM, DCM, 247
Robertson, General, 196
Rose Valley (Danger Spot)113-16, 118,
    122-130, 135
Rowley, Lieut. Col. DSO, 19, 199,
Russia, 9, 273, 283; Russian saps, 54, 76,
    98
Rycroft, Maj Gen, 91, 277
Sassoon, 2nd Lieut. Siegfried, 115, 133-4,
    186
Saville, Lieut, 128, 164, 177, 184-5
Scheytt, Unteroffizier Paul, 116, 121, 133
Schlieffen, Alfred von, 8; Plan, 9, 21, 203
Scotland, 21; Scottish, 51, 176, 201
Serre, 44, 201-2, 273-5, 278, Trench, 280
Seymour, Lt-Col, 224, 228
Shephard, Sgt-Maj Ernest, 6, 26, 28-30, 33,
    37-40,   43, 47, 52, 92-4, 96-104, 281
Shrine, 114, 122-8
Shute, Maj, 27, 36, 41-2, 44, 46, 49, 92,
    97-8
the Snout, 154, 158-62, 164
Stephens, Maj., 256, 258
Storey, Lieut Col, 114, 118, 124, 126, 130
Stout Trench, 217-20, 224, 227-8

Stuff Redoubt, 240-1, 243, 247, 249
Sunderland, Lieut Col, 73, 79-80, 267
Switch Line / Trench, 171-2, 174-5, 178,
    180, 189
Thiepval, 34-5, 44-6, 48, 50, 89-91, 102,
    232, 235, 247, 274-5, Battle of Thiepval
    Ridge, 240-3, 252
Thwaytes, Maj, 100
Tillett, Lieut., 80; Capt, 259, 263, 265-7
le Transloy, 6, 133, 259-72, 274
Tregelles, Capt, 124
Trones Wood, 151, 156, 260, 269
Tucker, Sgt., MM,125-6
Turnbull, Sgt., VC, 97
Tuson, Brig Gen, 73
Usna Redoubt / Hill, 38, 43, 75
Vallee St Martin, see Rose Valley
Veale, Pte. T. VC, 173, 184-5
Verdun, 34, 40, 44, 58, 174, 203, 217,
    272, 274
Wales, 20-21
War Office, 30
Ward, Maj. C. H. Dudley, 21(n)
Watts, Maj Gen, 113, 158, 171-2, 221, 224
Webb, 2/Lt, 96, 103
Webb, Pte. Harry, 269-71
Westropp, 2nd Lieut., 190, 192-4
Wood Lane, 177-8, 197-8
Wood Post, 94-5, 100
Wood Trench, 144-9; Wood Support, 147
Wollocombe, 2nd Lieut Frank, 49-50, 53,
    134, 215, 229, 247
'Wonder Work' (Wundtwerk), 90-1, 94,
    102; 'Wunderwerk', 234-5
Wright, Brig., 242, 245, 247-8
Y Sap Raid, 41-44
Ypres, 21 Ypres Salient, 21, 23, 64, 152,
    282
Zenith Trench,, 263, 265, 270-1
Zollern Redoubt / Trench, 240-9
ZZ Trench, 218-23, 225-6, 228